Jacobean City Comedy

Jacobean City Comedy

A Study of Satiric Plays by Jonson, Marston
and Middleton

Brian Gibbons

HARVARD UNIVERSITY PRESS
Cambridge, Massachusetts 1968

© Brian Gibbons 1968

Printed in Great Britain

To My Mother and Father

Contents

List of Illustrations

Preface

In this book I am concerned with a kind of drama in which three major Elizabethan dramatists — Ben Jonson, John Marston, and Thomas Middleton — excelled. T. S. Eliot wrote that Ben Jonson was the legitimate heir of Christopher Marlowe, and in Jacobean City Comedy we find many traces of that heritage. Eliot wrote that this kind of drama 'is not to be circumscribed by a reference to "comedy" or "farce" . . . but it is something which distinguishes Barabas from Shylock, Epicure Mammon from Falstaff, Faustus from — if you will — Macbeth'. I have tried in the course of a close study of the plays to define this complex and un-Shakespearean kind of drama and to account for my admiration — born in the theatre — of Marston and Middleton, who seem still undervalued and relatively neglected, and of the still too rarely performed plays of Jonson. This, then, is a critical study, though I have tried to keep alert to the distance between the Blackfriars Theatre in James's reign and any modern company, and between Thomas Middleton and Bertolt Brecht. I begin with a study of aspects of the social, economic and political background in Jacobean England which are related to the plays, in order to establish how far the satire penetrated the 'time's deformities' and how far the plays reveal a social turbulence which was finally to erupt into Civil War. The main part of the book traces the chronological development of City Comedy from Jonson's early

Comical Satyres, through the early plays of Marston and Middleton to The Dutch Courtezan, A Trick to Catch the Old One and The Alchemist, and finally to the climax in Jonson's masterpieces Bartholomew Fair and The Devil Is An Ass.

I have tried to acknowledge my significant debts to previous scholars by appending a Select Bibliography of works from which I have profited, and of course by giving footnotes in the text. I am particularly grateful to Mr Christopher Morris of Kings College Cambridge, for advice on a historical bibliography at an early stage in my work, and to Professor M. C. Bradbrook I am more grateful than I can say for the advice and constructive criticism so generously given throughout my work on City Comedy. I am further grateful to Professor Nicholas Brooke for criticism which modified my view of the relation between plays and historical background, and to Professor L. C. Knights for criticism and suggestions, as well as for critical guidance in appreciation of Jonson.

While preparing this book I have enjoyed the company of my colleagues at the University of York. To them, especially Mr Bernard Harris, I am indebted directly and obliquely.

I am grateful to the Phaidon Press for permission to quote from Art and Illusion and Meditations on a Hobby Horse by E. H. Gombrich, and to Mr M. B. Yeats and Macmillan & Co. Ltd, for permission to quote from 'Meditations in Time of Civil War' by W. B. Yeats. The illustrations are reproduced by courtesy of Professor Allardyce Nicoll, The British Museum and Dr T. W. Craik, and The Guildhall Museum, London.

BRIAN GIBBONS
The University of York
March 1967

Why? though I seeme of a prodigious wast,
   I am not so voluminous, and vast,
      But there are lines, wherewith I might b(e) 'embrac'd.

'Tis true, as my wombe swells, so my backe stoupes,
   And the whole lumpe growes round, deform'd, and droupes,
But yet the Tun at *Heidelberg* had houpes.

BEN JONSON's *Answer to Burlase*

1 City Comedy as a Genre

Our *Scene* is *London*, 'cause we would make knowne,
No countries mirth is better then our owne.
No clime breeds better matter, for your whore,
Bawd, squire, imposter, many persons more,
Whose manners, now call'd humors, feed the stage:
And which have still beene subject, for the rage
Or spleene of *comick*-writers.

THE AUDIENCE AT the first performance of *The Alchemist* in 1610 probably did not need this reminder. The first decade of the Jacobean Age had witnessed a sudden profusion of comedies satirising city life, and among such plays were the major comedies of Ben Jonson, John Marston and Thomas Middleton, as well as the bulk of the repertoires at Blackfriars and Paul's. These playwrights had selfconsciously, sometimes aggressively, forged the new form, City Comedy, and the mood of their plays was notably hostile to the earlier tradition of non-satiric, Popular, often sentimental London comedies such as Thomas Dekker's *The Shoemakers' Holiday*.

In this study I hope to show how City Comedy may be seen as a distinct dramatic *genre* with a recognisable form and conventions of theme, setting and characterisation. A fresh approach is gained by emphasising each play's relationship to the common form of the *genre*, and this may add to our knowledge of the development of drama in the Jacobean Age. My primary purpose is to offer a fresh critical appreciation of the major comedies of Jonson, Marston and Middleton; but City Comedy as a *genre* has not been explored or documented before, and this too seems to me worthwhile.

To approach these plays in the perspective of the developing *genre* involves a fresh critical appraisal, in the first place, since the plays of Jonson and Middleton have long been admired for their realism.

But in what sense can we use the term realism in relation to Jacobean
City Comedy, and how far is it important to an appreciation of the
plays? The art of Middleton and Jonson is highly mannered, and
shaped by particular dramatic conventions. Surely we cannot read
or watch the plays and talk of their 'photographic' realism, even
though we may perhaps criticise them for lacking any theme,
purpose or form, merely presenting comic incident in familiar
settings. This was in fact T. S. Eliot's criticism of Middleton's
comedies, whereas Jonson has been so admired for the satiric account
of Jacobean life in his comedies that, it has been suggested, we
should take them as reliable documentary evidence of the actual
historical situation; so the historian Unwin declared that 'a study
of the leading characters of *The Devil Is An Ass* . . . would be by far
the best introduction to the economic history of the period'.[1]

Yet of course the realism of Jonson is not the realism of Zola or
of Henry Mayhew in *London Labour and the London Poor*; it differs also

---

[1] Quoted in L. C. Knights, *Drama and Society in the Age of Jonson*, new ed.
(London 1962) p. 178. The primary importance of *genre* and style in
shaping artistic representation of reality is discussed most pertinently by
E. H. Gombrich in 'Truth and Stereotype', (chapter II of *Art and Illusion*
London 1962) where admirably clear examples of the power of the schema,
in artistic creation, support the famous remark of Wölfflin that all pictures
owe more to other pictures than they do to nature. The artist must always
catch a motif within the network of a schematic form; Gombrich uses the
example of two virtually identical engravings done by a Dutchman in 1598
and an Italian in 1601, the first representing a giant whale washed up on
the Dutch coast, the second claiming to represent another whale washed
up near Ancona, and 'drawn accurately from nature' according to the
artist. Gombrich writes (pp. 69–70) 'the claim would be more trustworthy
if there did not exist the earlier print recording a similar 'scoop' from the
Dutch coast in 1598. But surely the Dutch artists of the late sixteenth
century, those masters of realism, would be able to portray a whale? Not
quite, it seems, for the creature looks suspiciously as if it had ears, and
whales with ears, I am assured on higher authority, do not exist. The
draughtsman probably mistook one of the whale's flippers for an ear and
therefore placed it far too close to the eye.' Both artists were misled by the
familiar schema of the typical head, for to draw an unfamiliar sight is more
difficult than is generally realised; hence the Italian's dependence on the
Dutch: his whale, too, has ears. On this point see also my note to Visscher's
View of London.

from the subjective realism of James Joyce. The critic George Lukács, discussing the modern novel in The Meaning of Contemporary Realism, distinguishes between what he calls 'critical realism' and 'modernism'; between for example Thomas Mann's The Magic Mountain and Joyce's Ulysses.

As the comparison implies, the critical realist writer is primarily concerned to shape character and incident in order to bring alive the underlying social and moral issues through the specific and local experience. The dynamic of his art springs directly from the creative dialectic implicit in his criticism of life.

I hope to show that the dramatists of Jacobean City Comedy articulated a radical critique of their Age. They dramatised conflicting forces in the confused development from the England of Elizabeth towards the Civil War. But there is a distinction between dramatising conflicting forces and merely reflecting manners. When Middleton presents a situation of a merchant ambitious to become a country gentleman, on the level of comedy of manners this is completely conventional; what makes it serious and meaningful is that the conventions also have metaphoric richness, the merchant embodies forces of appetite and materialism which Middleton represents as dominant in Jacobean society, related to a correspondingly spreading interest in scientific method and the scepticism implicit in that method. The realism of the significant plays, I would argue, is essentially in transforming typical elements of city life into meaningful patterns, expressing consciously satiric criticism but also suggesting deeper sources of conflict and change.

Jacobean City Comedy, then, is purposefully selective in its choice of themes and responses, and so I have begun by comparing — in my second and third chapters — the account of society we find in the plays with wider and more objective evidence about society in Jacobean England, interpreted in the discipline of modern historical scholarship. This is in order to sharpen our alertness to the critical element in the realism of City Comedy, and to concentrate our interest on the imaginative and dramatic achievement — at its best, in plays such as The Malcontent and The Alchemist, a great achievement — which draws on the form and conventions of the genre City Comedy. If I seem to attend too closely, in the major part of the book, to dramatic form, convention, and art, that is because the best plays often seem to rival actuality; we do well to accord an artist respect, in the first place, for his art.

B

Jonson was certainly insistent about his own stature and achievement as an artist, and awarded himself the 'Chaire of wit', scorning
wolvish envy and asses' detraction, in his two odes to himself. A
more acute critical insight is to be found in his reply to Burlase, who
had written of the impossibility of conveying in a portrait the unique
living quality of Jonson the man. Jonson compares himself to a gargantuan barrel of wine:

> Why? though I seeme of a prodigious wast,
> I am not so voluminous, and vast,
> But there are lines, wherewith I might b(e) embrac'd.
>
> 'Tis true, as my wombe swells, so my back stoupes,
> And the whole lumpe growes round, deform'd, and droupes,
> But yet the Tun at Heidelberg had houpes.

Jonson's 'mountain belly' and great thirst were famous, but the
image is more than visually apt and witty — it is suggestive. For it
reveals Jonson's own sense that his strong appetites, his creative yet
potentially anarchic comic imagination were in tension with his
classicist's discipline and shaping intelligence. The critic might do
well to follow this suggestion and attend to the inner spirit of the
comedies as it expresses itself through the form.

The approach to Jonson's plays is the key to the approach to City
Comedy as a whole, for Jonson fathered the genre, powerfully shaped
its growth and crowned its maturity with two great plays,
Bartholomew Fair in 1614 and The Devil Is An Ass in 1616. I have traced
the chronological development of the genre to show how the playwrights — Jonson, Marston, Middleton and others — learned from
each other's plays as they appeared, modifying, reshaping or copying
the form, its conventions and themes, and how the great plays of the
genre, in their turn, drew on the riches stored in the convention.
The process is a complex and delicate one, partly intuitive, partly
deliberate and conscious, as is implied by Jonson's remark that
right imitation is 'to draw forth out of the best, and choisest flowers,
with the Bee, and turne all into Honey'.[2] It has proved necessary to
follow out this process in some detail, and I have risked the fault
of neglecting certain aspects of individual plays, in the hope of
achieving a corresponding virtue of clarification and freshness of

---

[2] Jonson Discoveries, 2476–78 ed. Herford & Simpson (Oxford 1925–52)
I have used this edition throughout the book.

approach. In writing about drama the critic can in any case only hope to offer an approach towards a fuller appreciation in the theatre; he will always over-simplify; for the depth and texture of that collaborative creation of actor and spectator result from the interplay of many effects, some evanescent — changing shades and tones of colour, light and sound — some continuous — rhythms of movement, situation and language. The feelings and resonances set up there cannot be detached from the space of time during which the actors perform, the lights burn, and we participate. It would require a critical method with 'a point as subtle as Arachne's broken woof' to analyse the experience completely. On the other hand this is no warrant for wanton clumsiness of response to the problem of writing about drama. If the critic cannot be comprehensive, he can seek for the most sympathetic approach to an understanding of the kind of dramatic experience which mature Jacobean City Comedy, in the hands of Middleton and Jonson, offers. It may be illuminating to approach the plays from our own experience in the theatre of the modern playwright, Bertolt Brecht. We may then become freshly aware, in plays like *Michaelmas Term* and *The Devil Is An Ass*, of a sinewy dramatic energy and a closely intelligent dialectic which corresponds to our experience of Brecht.

To connect Brecht with the Jacobeans is not of course wholly arbitrary, for not only did Brecht admire the plays of Marlowe enough to adapt *Edward II* early on in his career, but his experiments with Epic Theatre derive in part from his admiration for Elizabethan drama and its popular theatre. Brecht perceived that to bring life into the twentieth century European theatre he would have to change the audiences first. Their expectations were formed by what is typified either in the opera of Wagner or the 'well made' play.

Elizabethan dramatic form, on the other hand, grew partly out of the medieval didactic drama, while Elizabethan audiences were accustomed to stand for an hour or more to listen to public presentation of didactic argument in sermon and in homily. The form of drama designed to express argument and illustrate it gives central prominence to the issues, not to the private emotional condition of characters. Equally, the emblematic appearance of characters, the clear presentation of issues through *tableaux* and dumb show, the articulation of contrasting scenes and the resoundingly didactic conclusions reinforced by *tableaux* (the marriage dance or its unexpected absence, as in *Love's Labour's Lost*, the burning villain in *The Jew of Malta*) — all these techniques the Elizabethans inherited from the earlier didactic tradition. They give structural coherence and strength, they are a rich source of dramatic vitality. The audience does not simply dream like Wagner's, it does not attend merely to indulge in wish-fulfilling fantasies; the dramatic method encourages a certain detachment, an awareness of ideas and attitudes as essential elements in the drama.

The plays of Marlowe are dramatically rich in conflicting ideas about morality and faith. It was both because of the centrality of the issues and because of this questioning of traditional beliefs that Marlowe excited Brecht, who once remarked that the modern theatre needs to be questioned 'not about whether it manages to interest the spectator in buying a ticket, i.e. in the theatre itself — but about whether it manages to interest him in the world.'[3] The tone of this might be called conservative yet revolutionary. Brecht went back to Luther's Bible to revitalise his style, and he went back to anti-naturalist theatre to revitalise his dramatic art. The flavour of paradox which is so strong in his life and art may remind us of Jonson, another ostentatiously conservative revolutionary. It is illuminating to reflect on the fact that the marvellous dramatic ebullience of Jonson's character Volpone is created out of the *conflicting* attitudes to appetite which generate the dynamic of the play. Similarly, in *Mr Puntila and his Servant Matti* the vitality and hilarious comedy arise from the conflicting principles of life within the breast of Brecht's hero: for when he is drunk his generous good nature expresses itself freely, and when he sobers up he recognises the necessity of being evil. Jonson, like Brecht after him, instinctively chose to dramatise the conflict and paradox at the centre of social and moral man, and this kind of drama also best achieved the revolutionary aim of interesting the audience in the *ideas* which, at the same time, were embodied in living character and motive. Such drama might be deeply serious yet hilariously funny; intellectually rich yet not schematic. Brecht remarked that it was necessary to have a sense of humour to understand Hegel's dialectics; the plays of Brecht and of Jonson express paradox and conflict in comedy, and demonstrate the comic spirit alive in paradox.

---

[3] *Brecht on Theatre*, trans. John Willett (London 1964) p. 161.

As Brecht's early years as a dramatist in Berlin coincided with a vigorous period of satiric cabaret and experiments in 'political theatre', so Jonson's early career as a dramatist coincided with the rise of Elizabethan satire, and Jonson completed the satiric play begun by Nashe (The Isle of Dogs) which embroiled him in trouble with the government. In fact Elizabethan verse satire provides the most powerful formative influence, and stimulus, for the genre City Comedy. Such dramatic precursors of City Comedy as The Three Ladies of London, in which the playwright Robert Wilson offers a survey of representative social types whose errors sap the common-wealth, owe much to the interwoven non-dramatic literary lineage of Satire and religious Complaint invective. These late Interlude-style plays, sometimes called 'Estates Moralities',[4] offer little beyond the basic form of a survey of social types. The dominant rich stimulus of Elizabethan satiric poetry on Jonson the dramatist is certainly clear. We might note, in the present context, that the satirist demands certain responses from his reader which correspond to the demands Jonson and Brecht made on their spectators. Brecht wished to recapture certain aspects of the Elizabethan theatre as he imagined it; an arena full of spectators out to enjoy themselves, having more in common with the knowledgeable audience at the circus or a boxing match than with the middle class, unspontaneous, apathetic faces at a 'well made' play. He condensed his requirements into the aphorism that he would like his audience to smoke cigars and cigarettes and never permit them to go out.[5] He wanted them to think critically, to observe acutely, yet to enjoy themselves. In a somewhat comparable way we find Jonson's persona in Every Man Out of His Humour offering his invitation:

> Let me be censur'd, by th'austerest brow,
> Where I want arte, or judgement, taxe me freely:
> (Induction 1. 60–61).

Jonson's intention is to encourage the spectators to find a certain serious enjoyment in this kind of response to a play. The comic character Carlo Buffone suggests a more boisterous, but no less

---

[4] See Alan Dessen, 'The Alchemist: Jonson's Estates Play' in Renaissance Drama VII (Evanston, III, 1964) an interesting and useful article.

[5] See P. Demetz's introduction to Brecht: Twentieth Century Views (Englewood Cliffs, N.J. 1962).

critical approach, in his ridicule of the author's pose: the poet, Buffone says, enjoys his drink

> when hee comes abroad (now and then) once in a fortnight, and makes a good meale among Players, where he has Caninum appetitum: mary, at home he keepes a good philosophicall diet, beanes and butter milke: an honest pure Rogue, hee will take you off three, foure, five of these, [brandishes his glass] one after another. . . . Gentles, all I can say for him, is, you are welcome.
>
> (335–340, 348–9).

It may be most useful at this point to look more closely at a particular play and recall the characteristic atmosphere and texture of City Comedy. The collaborative venture of Chapman, Marston and Jonson, Eastward Ho, performed in 1605, is highly suitable for this purpose since it not only satirises citizens, usurers and gallants, but it also incidentally parodies the genre's typical styles of comedy and language.

The action of Eastward Ho arises from the conflict of the industrious and idle apprentices of a London goldsmith. The industrious apprentice, fortified by and continually quoting Puritan precepts (the banality of which is not disguised) is commended by his master for his honest industry. The goldsmith tells him, with a mouthful of comically predictable clichés, that he expects to see him

> one o' the Monuments of our Citty, and reckon'd among her worthies, to be remembred the same day with the Lady Ramsey, and grave Gresham: (IV, ii. 70–72).

The other apprentice is dissolute and insubordinate, the conventional Interlude prodigal-gallant, complete with feather. He is warned equally predictably to

> thinke of huskes, for thy course is running directly to the prodigalls hogs trough, huskes, sirra.
>
> (I, i. 98–100).

His name is Quicksilver; we can be sure that he is due for gulling and ridicule before the play ends.

Corresponding to the two apprentices are the goldsmith's two daughters; one is humbly earnest and modest, the other vain, empty-headed and licentious. Her snobbish ambition is to 'bee Ladyfied forsooth: and be attir'd just to the Court-cut, and long

tayle'. She marries the absurdly foppish and typically destitute
knight Sir Petronell Flash; both of them are satirised for their
mannerisms and foolish obsessions with dress in a way reminiscent
of Jonson's early 'Comical Satyres' of 1599 and 1600 (Eastward Ho
was written in late 1604). Sir Petronell has lost his country estates
to usurers long ago, and he summarises the typical interests of the
gallant in Jacobean City Comedy with the lamenting survey

> Taverns growe dead; Ordinaries are blowne up; Playes are at a stand;
> Howses of Hospitallitie at a fall; not a Feather waving, nor a Spurre
> gingling any where . . . my creditors have laide to arrest me,
>
> (II, ii. 220–222, 259–260).

The play's setting in the city of London is accurately achieved with
many placing references to street and district names, to attract local
interest; for similar reasons, lawyers' and usurers' jargon is accurately reproduced.

Security the usurer's scheme to bring the gallant to his knees —
another conventional City Comedy element — is here unexpectedly
reversed, as part of the general parody, and the usurer is himself
gulled of his money and cuckolded; he actually acts as pandar to
his own wife when she is disguised! Quicksilver's speech to him
summarises relations between usurer and gallant in City Comedy:

> Come old Securitie, thou father of destruction: th'indented Sheepeskinne
> is burn'd wherein I was wrapt, and I am now loose, to get more
> children of perdition into thy usurous Bonds. Thou feed'st my Lecherie,
> and I thy Covetousnes: Thou art Pandar to me for my wench, and I
> to thee for thy coosenages: (II, ii.11–16).

Sir Petronell and the idle apprentice Quicksilver set out on a voyage
to make their fortunes in Virginia. We are offered a malign view of
the motives and 'adventurous' spirit of Elizabethan merchant
investors and colonisers: Virginia is a paradise of Mammon:

> I tell thee, Golde is more plentifull there then Copper is with us; and
> for as much redde Copper as I can bring, Ile have thrice the waight
> in Golde. Why man all their dripping Pans, and their Chamber pottes
> are pure Gold;
>
> (III, iii. 25–28).

The evocation of the new world is also an occasion for comment on
the political scene at home in James's London; for in Virginia 'you

shal live freely . . . without Sergeants, or Courtiers, or Lawyers, or Intelligencers, onely a few industrous Scots perhaps'. This hit at James and his favourites is followed by another, uttered this time in a mock Scots accent, when the two voyagers, still drunk from their farewell party, are washed up on the Isle of Dogs in the lower Thames (which they suppose to be France) and are greeted with the line

> I ken the man weel, hee's one of my thirty pound knights.

James's wrath descended on the three playwrights, and the play was banned; so Jonson repeated his achievement of 1597 in *The Isle of Dogs*.

The play's various episodes result in the undignified arrival in the Counter Prison of the two prodigals, the snobbish daughter and the usurer, who suffer the necessary ridicule and judgement. True to convention, the play ends on a cheerful note once folly and error are corrected. The goldsmith who has distributed credit and censure, as in the Morality Play and Interlude Presenter, emphasises the traditional nature of his *role*, and the play's form, by explaining to the audience the didactic meaning of the *exemplum* (as we now recognise the play to have been). The comic rhymes and thumping rhythm amusingly parody the old style (it is worth noting that in 1601 on the Blackfriars stage there had been a revival of *Liberality and Prodigality*), and the hollow *clichés* resound indeed:

> Now London, looke about,
> And in this morall, see thy Glasse runne out:
> Behold the carefull Father, thrifty Sonne . . .
> The Usurer punisht, and from Fall so steepe
> The Prodigall child reclaimd, and the lost Sheepe.
>   (V, v. 205–207, 209–210).

The hypocritical nature of Quicksilver's repentance, incidentally, is implied simply by the fact that he expresses it in Puritan jargon!

We might define the *genre* City Comedy, then, by the fact that the plays are all satiric and have urban settings, with characters and incident appropriate to such settings; they exclude material appropriate to romance, fairy tale, sentimental legend or patriotic chronicle. In fact the urban settings and characters derive partly from the tradition of popular prose narratives: Jest Books, Coney-Catching pamphlets and comic fantasies like Nashe's *Jack Wilton*. The form of the plays derives from the medieval Morality Play — more specifically, the Estates Morality — and the Tudor Interlude, and they contain trickery episodes, or 'lazzi', deriving from Italian Popular Comedy. The *genre* naturally has broad affinities with Elizabethan dramatic convention and language, though this is more evident in its good humoured comedies (*Bartholomew Fair* for example) than in its bitterly satiric works such as *Michaelmas Term* or in later masterpieces vitally related to City Comedy, *Women Beware Women* and *The Plain Dealer*. It was however in the years 1597 to 1616 that the *genre* grew to maturity and produced its masterpieces, and though subsequent plays in the Jacobean and Caroline period may fit the definition, they do not extend the range and development of the *genre*. It was vitally rooted in the first two decades of the century of revolution.

The growth of City Comedy in the early years from 1597 to 1601 was not of course as precise and smooth as the definition given above might suggest. Several other *kinds* or *genres* influenced its course, and of them verse satire and Coney-Catching pamphlets are among the most significant; it might be helpful to consider them briefly. The satiric form involved the poet in adopting a *persona* of disgust with social and moral corruption and folly. He might point out examples of these faults to an interlocutor, or directly to the reader, while surveying the social, urban scene. Satire of this kind, of course, can often include the traditional invective of the medieval Church against such general and unchanging evils as the depravity of women and the corrupt state of worldly ambitions and appetites. Horatian satire is essentially particular in its targets and precise in its focus, while Juvenilian satire has a harsher tone comparable to that of the Church's invective (often called Complaint[6] to distinguish it from Roman Satire). When a satirist like Marston turned from writing verse to drama he embodied the satiric *persona* in a dramatic character. Malevole in *The Malcontent* is the best known example. But before that play Jonson had dramatised not only the satiric *persona* but the whole form of Horatian satire, in which the satiric view takes us through a survey of folly and vice in recognisably familiar urban locations; in Jonson's *Every Man Out Of His Humour*, *Cynthia's Revels* and *Poetaster* the audience can recognise their own city of London in the detail

[6] See J. Peter, *Complaint and Satire in Early English Literature* (Oxford 1956).

and the styles of dialogue, and it was out of Jonson's experiments
in these plays, the 'Comicall Satyres', that the form of Jacobean
City Comedy evolved.

The writer of a Coney-Catching pamphlet[7] is no less eager to
adopt the *persona* of authoritative censurer though his concern is
restricted to the trickery of various kinds of urban thief. His literary
manner derives from popular Jest Book narrative prose. Complaint
and Homily, rather than Roman Satire, provide the source for the
moralising and invective, but the vigour, life and comedy of
certain pamphlets probably owe much to traditional 'bitter jesters'
who entertained at fairs, revels and on the stage. G. R. Hibbard has
noted[8] how Thomas Nashe, the most talented of the pamphleteers,
adopted a literary *persona* akin to that of the Vice of the medieval
drama, and points out that Nashe was familiar with the antics of
Tarlton, the most famous clown of his age; indeed Nashe's opponents often described him as a 'Tarltoniser', and we can see that
Nashe's prose is that of an instinctive dramatist. There are further
links between dramatists and pamphleteers, for, like the dramatists
of City Comedy, the pamphleteers Greene, Dekker and Rowlands
deliberately created a kind with form and conventions analogous to
drama. In a Coney-Catching pamphlet the author explains to the
reader what the tricksters do, and dramatically conceived episodes
provide illustrative *exempla*. Character and incident are conventional;
indeed the pamphleteers created the kind by absorbing material from
earlier, rather pedestrian writers such as Awdelay and Harman.
This material was mixed with Jest Book incident and atmosphere,
characters were created in the conventions of Popular dramatic
comedy, and much trouble was taken to give local colour by setting
episodes in particular streets and districts of London and assigning
familiar urban activities to characters. Significantly enough the most
convincing pamphlets are those shaped by the dramatist Greene,
who took his material at third or fourth hand. The Coney-Catching
pamphlet was a minor *genre* just preceding the beginnings of City
Comedy; it could not develop further without being absorbed into
drama, and this is what in fact happened.

We cannot see the rise of City Comedy in full perspective without
some consideration of the theatres and companies for which the

---

[7] See my Appendix A for a fuller study of Coney-Catching pamphlets.

[8] G. R. Hibbard, *Thomas Nashe* (London 1962), p. 24.

plays were written and on whose boards they were performed. This is the more important since in a well known study (*Shakespeare and The Rival Traditions*) Alfred Harbage underlined his preference for the 'Popular' style of the adult companies which he distinguished from the satiric 'Coterie' style of drama performed by the boy actors. The adult companies performed on open stages, with spectators in galleries and on the ground surrounding their scaffold. The boy actors by contrast performed in closed, smaller and more expensive playhouses: Paul's, Blackfriars and Whitefriars. There was probably some difference in acting styles between the boys at Blackfriars or Paul's and the men at the Globe in the early years from 1599 to 1602, where the term 'Coterie' usefully serves to distinguish between adult and boys' companies — though it should not carry any suggestion of deliberate exclusive 'in-group' intimacy or triviality or social snobbery. However from 1602 to 1608 the boys matured physically and professionally, and when Blackfriars was taken over by the King's Men in 1608 Paul's had already closed, and Whitefriars was never successful.

It is probably impossible to define the difference between Popular and Coterie styles, since the former was progressively influenced by experiments in the latter during the years 1600 to 1606. Certainly the repertories of the boys contain many plays marked by artifice and stylisation of form and subject, in contrast to the bustling activity and robust style of the adult repertoires. Jonson's *Cynthia's Revels*, written for boys in 1600/1601 has simplified, mannered characterisation, with much opportunity for parody acting — the boys were noted for this. There are opportunities, similarly, for declamation of set speeches, and the cast is large with no unduly taxing parts. However subsequent plays such as *Poetaster*, *The Malcontent*, *Michaelmas Term* and *The Dutch Courtezan* not only develop a much more flexible and varied dramatic style but contain parts to extend an experienced adult actor — Tucca, Malevole, Quomodo, Franceschina. When *The Malcontent* was transferred from the boys house to The Globe, where the King's Men performed it, it was modified only in the opening and closing Acts;[9] the essential

---

[9] I am indebted to Mr Bernard Harris, editor of *The Malcontent* for the New Mermaid Series (London 1967), who informs me that two extra scenes, I viii and V i, were added when the King's Men took the play over. These two scenes were written for Malevole and Passarello (I viii) and for Bilioso

structure, mood, stagecraft and acting roles remained in substance
unaltered. This rather undermines the clear distinctions drawn by
Alfred Harbage between Coterie and Popular drama. Harbage defined
Coterie theatre style as satiric intellectual and cruelly critical,
opposing and rivalling the adult Popular repertory's humane,
generous, sentimental and respectful character. Harbage's may indeed
be a valid account of Coterie style from 1599 to 1602, but we ought
to note that progressively after 1600 many of the plays performed
by the King's Men at The Globe shared the satiric and intellectually
questioning mood. Shakespeare himself not only glorified the
courage, brotherhood, strength and patriotism of men at war in
Henry V (1599); he also displayed war's brutal futility in the
nihilistic, diseased world of *Troilus and Cressida* (c. 1602). Both
plays were performed at the Globe by adult actors. In fact the King's
Men performed nearly every major play in the period irrespective
of its style. Even if a playwright was principally a Coterie writer,
like Marston, his best work seems to have been acted at the Globe.
Despite the fact that City Comedy originated at Blackfriars and Paul's,
nevertheless the King's Men performed *Volpone*, *The Alchemist* and *The
Devil Is An Ass*. City Comedy was never so tied to Coterie style that its
development had to cease when the zenith of Coterie popularity
passed in about 1606, and in fact the great triumphs of City Comedy
appeared after Blackfriars was taken over by the King's Men in
1608–9. The *genre* grew out of a process of creative imitation and
cross-fertilisation between playwrights competing both as individuals and as servants of rival companies, Coterie and Popular.
Both the untalented conventional writers and those with original
creative gifts profited from this situation. They learned from each
other, adapting, imitating and absorbing each other's original
achievements as they appeared. The *genre* grew as this process continued to produce fresh art; but it was an art essentially different

---

and Passarello (V i). Passarello is the only new role added for The Globe
performance, and Mr Harris notes that in V, i Bilioso is extended only to
help fill out what would otherwise have been a thin night for Passarello.
The other additions are as follows: (a) I, iii. 102–43; (b) I, iii. 149–66;
(c) I, iv. 43–88; (d) V, ii. 64–93; (e) V, iii. 10, 12–13, 21–33. It seems
probable these were written in to make up for the absence of songs which
the boys' company would have performed during the play.

from the genially sentimental romantic comedy of *The Shoemakers'
Holiday* or *George a Greene the Pinner of Wakefield* or *The Four Prentices of
London.*

It will be remembered that L. C. Knights emphasised in *Drama and
Society in the Age of Jonson* that the Age witnessed the 'taking shape' of
the 'capitalist system' which there destroyed a 'native tradition'
springing from an 'individual and social morality'. I would emphasise
rather that the playwrights contrasted the idealised Tudor philosophy
of the state, which owed much to Christian doctrine, with a stylised,
Complaint-derived account of the lamentable evils of 'nowadays'.
Of course the many economic abuses of the time have been documented, but in the light of recent re-assessments of the economic
and social history of the Age by the contributors to the 'Rise of the
Gentry' debate, and their critics, it seems worthwhile to emphasise
the continuity of the Elizabethan and Jacobean economic and
social situation, and to modify the view that the Age witnessed a
sudden change from the rural, stable, ancient 'organic society' (a
Marxist and a Christian ideal) to the urban swirl of competing
individuals in a New Capitalist State. There had in any case, after
all, been a steady and unchanging stream of invective from the
Church throughout the Middle Ages against the Rise of Capitalism,
New Men, Usury and Economic Individualism.

L. C. Knights did of course also note that the plays presented
criticism of society in which 'the diagnosis was moral rather than
economic', and further declared 'the reactions of a genuine poet to
his environment form a criticism of society at least as important as
the keenest analysis in economic terms'.[10] It is certainly not the aim
of this study to assert that there is no relation between the form and
mood of Jacobean City Comedy and the Jacobean moral and social
world; merely that the plays do not present in any useful sense 'a
keen analysis in economic terms' nor may they be rashly cited as
evidence of actual conditions at the time. What they present is a
keen analysis in moral terms first and last. Such a concern is clearly
less ephemeral and more profound than any economic analysis,
and accounts for the permanent value of the *genre* as dramatic art.

City Comedy playwrights were interested in moneylending in the

---

[10] L. C. Knights, op. cit. p. 148.

first place as a modern manifestation of the deadly sin of avarice. Of course in the Jacobean Age there was increasing popular recognition that money was a science to be feared for its power; this is probably to be related to the spread of scientific method in the preceding century and to its sensational impact on English popular imagination in the form of Niccoló Machiavelli.[11] The dramatists feared the scientific method because, essentially, 'the notions of right and wrong, justice and injustice, have there no place.'[12] The usurer is the villain in City Comedy because he symbolises forces of aggression, ruthless materialism, aspiration and anarchy in Jacobean society. The plays delineate the forces of human emotion which money unlooses, not the workings of money itself.

There are striking likenesses between the world brought alive in City Comedy and that formulated by Machiavelli in The Prince and by Hobbes in Leviathan. The plays measure this world against the ideally stable and morally coherent Christian Tudor model in, for example, Hooker's Ecclesiastical Polity. City Comedy shows that 'ample proposition' failing in the promised largeness, checked by the forces of appetite and aggression released by money. The plays articulate a conflict arising within the human microcosm but spreading through the body politic

> As knots, by the conflux of meeting sap,
> Infect the sound pine and divert his grain
> Tortive and errant from his course of growth.
>   (Troilus & Cressida I, iii. 7–9).

We may begin to gauge the turbulent force of this conflict by reflecting how much it is still shocking to meet the steely pragmatism of Machiavelli: 'one prince of the present time, whom it is not well to name, never preaches anything else but peace and good faith, and to both he is most hostile, and either, if he had kept it, would have deprived him of reputation and kingdom many a time' (The Prince, chapter 18) and the iron insistence of Hobbes in that moment when he kicks the Tudor carcase aside: 'To this war of every man, against every man, this also is consequent; that nothing can be unjust. The notions of right and wrong, justice and injustice have there no place. Where there is no common power, there is no law: where no

---

[11] See F. Raab, The English Face of Machiavelli (London 1964).
[12] Thomas Hobbes, Leviathan ed. M. Oakeshott (Oxford 1946), p. 83

law, no injustice. Force, and fraud, are in war the two cardinal virtues. Justice, and injustice are none of the faculties neither of the body nor the mind. . . . It is consequent also to the same condition, that there be no propriety, no dominion, no mine and thine distinct; but only that to be every man's, that he can get: and for so long, as he can keep it.' (*Leviathan*, chap. 13).

2 A Fountain Stirr'd

City Comedy in relation to the Social and Economic
Background

THE MOOD OF satiric pessimism registered in *Troilus and Cressida* is
representative. The dramatists were alarmed yet excited by the steely
lucidity of the sciences of power and of money, so self-sufficiently
exclusive of influence from morality or tradition. Expectation indeed
set all on hazard, and the words of Achilles find many explicit and
implicit echoes in Jacobean drama:

> My mind is troubled, like a fountain stirr'd;
> And I myself see not the bottom of it.
>
> (III, iii. 314–315)

It seemed that with luck the manipulator of money might get
literally limitless riches. Lord Burghley had faith in Sir Edward
Kelly's claim to the secret of transmuting base metal into gold, and
actually joined Leicester and others in financing one William
Medley, who set up a plant to transmute iron into copper in 1574.[1]
Like Sir Epicure Mammon in Jonson's *The Alchemist*, Burghley might
have been deluded in thinking alchemy possible, but he was right
in supposing that gold could bring him more wealth and experience
than his imagination could conceive. Almost twenty years before
The Alchemist Marlowe had created characters in the grip of voracious
appetites for riches and power. *Doctor Faustus* concerned a man's

---

[1] L. Stone, *The Crisis of the Aristocracy* 1558–1641 (Oxford 1965) p. 368.

aspiration for limitless knowledge and his use of an instrument of evil, Mephistophilis, to attain it. Jonson's Sir Epicure is partly a parody, partly a comic counterpart of Faustus. Marlowe's Jew of Malta is freed by his non-Christianity, indeed atheism, and his career of money-manipulator, from all moral sanction; his riches and his scientific policy gain him control of Malta — and, by implication, of society. Barabas the Jew is manifestly capable of sustained success in practical life; it is this which makes his career so disquieting. Nor is it ambition which causes his fall; on the contrary Barabas falls because he rejects the dominion which his empirical methods have brought within his reach. Barabas dies because he relaxes in a society composed of men driven by greed and fear, at war with one another. The Jew's rise and fall may be interpreted in the formulation of Hobbes; his career ceases in death as soon as he falters in his 'restless desire for power after power'.[2] Of course Marlowe's hero-villains are also shown to deserve death; it was still the Elizabethan Age.

Marlowe's hero-villains fall; but their vitality and the power of their appetites invigorate the plays and accord with our sense of the complexity of human nature and the ambivalence in our attitude to them and to similar motives within ourselves. The Jacobean playwrights are similarly ambiguous in their attitude to the money-lender and Machiavel, but nevertheless every usurer is cast as a rogue if not a villain, for above all the usurer is the aggressor in the urban civil war of appetites aroused by money. We constantly meet the implication of civil war in the dramatic imagery; so Middleton's usurer Quomodo typically remarks

There are means and ways enow to hook in gentry.

Resistance to such a state of affairs was instinctive to the Jacobeans, integral to their Christian upbringing and to the satiric-didactic tradition in which they wrote. If they acknowledged the exciting possibilities, the expanding world of power and wealth which the scientific method offered, yet their satiric approach focused on its damaging repercussions in individual lives. Jonson's *Every Man Out Of His Humour* memorably declared that a hostile and selective attitude marked his work; he showed

---

[2] Hobbes, *Leviathan*, Part I, chapter 11.

> the times deformitie
> Anatomiz'd in every nerve, and sinnew,
>
> (Induction 120–121)

There was from the outset no question of empirical, openminded, balanced observation.

Today not much stir would arise from the reiteration of Francis Bacon's observation 'that it is a vanity to conceive that there would be ordinary borrowing without profit; and it is impossible to conceive the number of inconveniences that will ensue, if borrowing be cramped. Therefore to speak of the abolishing of usury is idle . . . It appears by the balance of commodities and discommodities of usury, two things are to be reconciled. The one, that the tooth of usury be grinded, that it bite not too much; the other, that there be left open a means to invite moneyed men to lend to the merchants, for the continuing and quickening of trade.'[3] Here the clarity of the empiric approach reveals itself in the firm logical deductions from openminded observation of 'what men do, not what they ought to do'. Here is the method of thought which produced the discovery that the earth circled the sun and the blood circulated in the body. Of course Bacon is still discussing money in relation to human behaviour; others by this date were approaching the subject by treating money as a machine with its own discoverable laws of operation. They were all opposed utterly by the doctrine and preaching of the Church.

A steady stream of invective against riches and all their uses poured from the writers of Complaint throughout the Middle Ages. St Jerome, typically, wrote 'let him deny that avarice is idolatry who is prepared to describe the selling of Our Lord for thirty pieces of silver as a just act.'[4] In fact the Papacy itself exploited sophisticated and indeed criminal financial techniques for centuries, as Richard Ehrenburg's *Capital and Finance in the Age of the Renaissance* shows, but the doctrine remained unchanged. R. H. Tawney memorably wrote in *Religion and the Rise of Capitalism*[5] that 'the social doctrines advanced from the pulpit offered, in their traditional form, little guidance. Their practical ineffectiveness prepared the way for their theoretical

---

[3] Of *Usury* in *The Works of Francis Bacon* ed. Spedding Ellis and Heath (London 1861), Vol. VI, p. 475.

[4] Cit. Peter, *Complaint and Satire in Early English Literature*, p. 85.

[5] Penguin edition (1961), pp. 188–189.

abandonment. They were abandoned because, on the whole, they deserved to be abandoned. The social teaching of the Church had ceased to count, because the Church itself had ceased to think . . . in the age of Bacon and Descartes, bursting with clamorous interests and eager ideas, fruitful, above all, in the germs of economic speculation . . . the social theory of the Church of England turned its face from the practical world, to pore over doctrines which, had their original authors been as impervious to realities as their later exponents, would never have been formulated.' In Elizabethan and Jacobean outbursts against bloodsucking usury and the evils of making money beget money, we should beware of the anachronistic attitude and rhetorical artifice of Complaint tradition, and we should be alert to detect the dishonest mustering of argument by borrowers and spendthrifts in that great age of litigation. In fact powerful moneylenders such as Thomas Sutton preferred to prolong mortgages to the landed aristocracy at ten per cent rather than foreclose on property, if it was scattered and hard to administer, and he usually allowed three or four years renewal before he clamped down. Lawrence Stone tells us (in *The Crisis of the Aristocracy 1558–1641*) how Sutton had £45,000 out at interest when he died; earls would address him as 'my verrey lovinge frend'.[6] Though moneylenders may not have foreclosed as savagely as satirists suggest, they had a great deal of business with the aristocracy, many of whom found life at Court cripplingly expensive. Elizabeth's chief courtiers mostly died heavily in debt, Leicester owing £68,500 and Hatton some £64,700.[7] These figures give some idea of the scale of capital transactions involved, and in fact there is a contrast between the ignorance and anachronistic sincerity of those who wrote about the evils of money, and the advancing knowledge and skill of those who actually controlled and used money in large amounts, but rarely wrote about it at all. Hence we find neither Myddleton nor Cranfield troubling to write about money except to scribble in the margins of their account books, when profits were high, the pious exhortation 'Allmighty God be praised'.

Outbursts against usury in the sixteenth century resulted in part from the misunderstood phenomenon of the price rise. The period

---

[6] Stone, op. cit. p. 535.
[7] Ibid.

from 1500 to 1642 may be seen as a single phase dominated by the price rise. In the first forty years of the sixteenth century prices rose by half; by 1560 they had more than doubled; by 1600 they were five and a half times the level in 1500.[8] The cause of this phenomenon was ascribed at the time to the greed of unscrupulous individuals; an ascription which, being preserved in printed literature, dies hard. Inexperience with the phenomenon of a price rise in time of good harvests led to a search for scapegoats and reiteration of the old doctrine of just price. This declared that in time of plenty everything reverted to a price determined by natural law; money itself was thought to represent the intrinsic value of the metal it contained. Statutes against rigging markets and enclosures show the prevalence of the search for scapegoats, though in 1574 a Frenchman, Jean Bodin, produced a theory rejecting the just price. Bodin discovered that prices represent the relationship between the money available and the goods available. If goods become scarce while purchasing power remains constant, prices will rise. Similarly, if the supply of goods remains constant but supplies of money increase, the value of the money will drop and prices rise. Bodin argued that the vast increase in minted bullion (brought by Spain to Europe from America) was the cause of the price rise, and he was correct.[9]

European trade was sufficiently busy to ensure that a price rise in one place would soon have extensive effects. In England, where commercial life was dominated by the export trade in raw wool and cloth, a price rise would soon be sensed throughout all ranks of society, from the king who took customs revenues to the merchants, the producers — on the largest monastery ranches as well as the smallest pinfolds — down to the carriers and sailors. Henry VIII had a disastrous effect on prices between 1544 and 1551 when he debased the coinage, because newly minted shillings were treated as a quarter the value of old minted, the former containing twenty-five per cent silver, the latter ninety per cent; but even after the Duke of Northumberland restored the coinage in 1560 prices continued to climb, and the cause was the flood of coinage minted from Spanish silver mined in Peru.

The unabated violence of the price rise had a thoroughly disturbing effect on the social life of England throughout the period 1500 to

---

[8] G. R. Elton, *England Under the Tudors* (London 1962), pp. 224–225.
[9] *Ibid.* p. 226.

1642. On the land, the price rise turned what had once been a good income into a liability. Landlords became poorer, their tenants prospered in a rising market. For the landlord the choice was between raising rents or taking control personally to profit from the yield. The increase in the profitability of land gave added impetus to what became, as a result of Henry VIII's dissolution of the monasteries, the most fluid land market since the Norman Conquest.

Plainly this was to affect the situation of tenants. A widespread redistribution of property — monastic lands, crown lands, the land of nobility or gentry reorganising or disposing of their estates — obviously must have resulted in rent-raisings and evictions, especially in the case of tenants-at-will who had little legal standing. However, not all landlords were harsh, and many in the North preserved earlier conditions even at the cost of personal impoverishment. Where land was bought to make a quick profit obviously rents would be raised, enclosures ruthlessly carried out and evictions effected. However, most of the monastic lands actually went to landowners who merely added them directly to what they already had and farmed them as before. Rents rose in the second half of the sixteenth century but so did prices. Land sales and enclosures continued in the seventeenth century but the enclosure movement had a history stretching back before the Dissolution, on monastic lands as well as private,[10] while complaints about rent were traditional.

In place of the view presented in the literature of Complaint and Satire, then, we must substitute an account more complex and less Romantic. The picture of rapacious extortioners depopulating the countryside and impoverishing those who clung on — particularly the 'old' nobility and gentry who had given Christian hospitality, and their faithful tenants — is too bad to be true. It has been estimated that in a county where enclosures were made, not more than thirty per cent of arable land, or four per cent of all land, was affected in this period,[11] and squabbles would hardly have been confined to the pattern of very rich versus very poor, and city usrer versus old gentry, which is so familiar in verse and prose Complaint and dramatic plots. The inexorable shift to higher, more economic rents in the early seventeenth century undermined the loyalty of tenants on big estates, slowly but surely; for changing patterns of

[10] The foregoing derives from Elton, op. cit. pp. 224–238.
[11] Ibid. p. 232.

life drew the aristocracy and gentry increasingly to London, caused
their territorial possessions to shrink and their influence over tenants
to weaken. Ties of sentiment lasted in many cases for more than the
next two centuries, but political and religious issues became increasingly alive to tenants as the reign of James I continued.

The greatest landlord was in fact the monarch; though his income
was fixed, he also had the highest expenditure in the land, and therefore had most to lose by inflation. The Tudor governmental budget
was unfortunately based on this fixed income, from which all ordinary
expenses were supposed to be paid. How far this income had become inadequate by Elizabeth's reign is revealed by the fact that her
ordinary revenue stood at £200,000 per annum, yet it cost her
£126,000 to send men to the Netherlands in 1585.[12] As a result in the
six war parliaments between 1585 and 1601 she was forced to ask
for subsidies, but even with them, and higher income from raising
rent on crown lands, she was forced to find more capital by selling
off crown lands like her father before her. The significance of this
steady royal impoverishment during the price rise may be clearly
seen in the struggle between James I and parliament, and becomes
crucial in the struggle between Charles I and parliament. The House
of Commons was aware that the king's power and dominion contrasted with his progressive pauperisation; they appreciated the
connection between capital and power.

The more literal connection between capital and power in this
period manifests itself in the expanding raw material and manufacturing industries. The dissolution of the monasteries released
from ecclesiastical control large areas of coal and metal bearing
land. The growth of towns, especially London, created a big demand
for coal (though the immediate impetus behind the expansion of the
coal industry was the imminent exhaustion of the native timber
supply) and the expansion of the coal industry encouraged the
expansion of the salt, metal mining and metal working industries. In
both coal and salt industries heavy investment was necessary.
J. U. Nef in his study *The Rise of the British Coal Industry* tells us[13]
that 'there were probably not more than fifty men in Elizabethan
England with sufficient wealth to finance, single-handed, the largest
colliery of the day even had they been able to realise all their

---

[12] Ibid. p. 362.
[13] Vol. I, p. 378.

assets'. In his article 'Technology and Industry 1540–1640' published in the *Economic History Review* in 1934, Nef describes the striking rate and size of developments in technology; such new techniques backed by increased capital investment caused annual trade in waterborne coal alone to increase from 51,000 tons in 1541–1550 to 1,280,000 tons in 1690. In the Durham coalfields for example coal seams practically abandoned in the fifteen-fifties could be reached easily by the early Jacobean period with the use of new pumping equipment. Of course mining was a highly speculative venture. Workings failed, expenditure was heavy, it was hard to calculate the break-even point in a new working, harder still to guess how long it would be profitable. Capital clearly played a vital part in the development of the industry from 1500 onwards.

These facts are an essential balance to the view offered by satirists that industry was a stamping ground for immoral, voracious profiteers alone. So we read J. U. Nef's account of how 'the first shaft rarely struck coal. In sinking, the capitalist was guided in Elizabethan times "by the judgement of those that are skillful in choosing the ground for that purpose". Even in the most extensively exploited district the miners sank many useless shafts. Boring rods . . . were too crudely constructed to determine whether to mine at all.'[14] Adventurers had to be prepared to spend from £100 to £1,000 or more before reaching seams, and on the Northumberland coast every attempt before 1640 to start large scale mining failed completely. The demands on the determination, courage, intelligence and, notably, capital, of mining adventurers were clearly great. We may pursue this matter further by considering how the Sunderland salt pans were finally developed with success, in the face of typically severe sixteenth century industrial conditions.

One John Mount, backed by a group of influential Court officials who obtained an exclusive patent in 1566, undertook to buy out the small men and install a number of expensive iron pans, all to be operated as a unified enterprise. He failed for want of capital. During the fifteen-nineties groups of merchants from London, King's Lynn and the North took up the project. They installed up-to-date equipment in a nearby mine — including one machine costing £2,000 alone — and this mine supplied the salt pans with fuel. The capital

---

[14] Ibid. p. 353.

was raised through merchants and the Earl of Huntingdon, who
bought shares in the venture.[15] The good planning which ensured
control of fuel supplies at an economic cost, installation of good
equipment, and sufficient geographical proximity of the two
enterprises to allow co-ordination, resulted in success. Yet it is worth
noting that the venture was only possible because capital was available
and had been secured at the outset. It is doubtless true that the
history of Tudor and Stuart industry affords many cases of fraud, and
disastrous mismanagement of capital and labour. On the other hand
it is possible that such cases were in the minority, that many worked
intelligently and shrewdly. In the coal industry they certainly worked
profitably, for on the eve of the Civil War Britain was producing over
four times as much coal as the whole European continent.[16]

The importance of skilful handling of capital was manifest in
other mining industries — iron ore, zinc ore used in brass founding,
and alum used in cloth dyeing. The role of industry in the national
economy was of course still considerably less important than agri-
culture; but it was growing throughout the period. To trace the
development in processing iron ore is to see the progressive demands
for heavier investment, to become aware of the crucial function of
capital in sixteenth century England.

The earliest processing technique with iron ore was to produce
blooms of pig iron which were then hammered into the required
shapes. Blast furnaces were imported from Europe to produce cast
iron, but their fuel was wood, and no success attended the many
experiments in adapting the furnaces to coal. Yet the first iron cannon
was cast at Buxted in England in 1543, and by 1590 there were a
hundred forges and iron mills. Aristocrats were prominent investors
in new technological developments such as slitting mills and tinplate
mills; Bevis Bulmer patented a new iron cutting machine in 1588
and two years later the first slitting mill was brought over from
Liège. Earlier, in 1565, Sir Henry Sydney tried to manufacture steel
(as Lawrence Stone tells us in *The Crisis of the Aristocracy*). Sydney's
venture involved bringing fifty-five Flemish technicians to set up
forges in Sussex and Kent, supplied with ore brought by sea from
his own Glamorgan estates, financed by himself, his receiver general

---

[15] J. U. Nef, op. cit., Vol. I, pp. 175–6.

[16] See also Nef's article in E.H.R. 1934: 'Technology and Industry 1540–
1640'.

and (of course) a London merchant.[17] Ironically enough the effect of European wars stimulated the expansion of English metalworking industries so that British sailors began to complain about the efficiency of Spanish cannon, actually made in Britain and exported! Such technological developments required heavy capitalisation: the readiness to replace old fashioned plant and expand production implies the availability of money.

The long term importance, in the economic history of Britain, of investment in such industries, suggests that the attention given to the successes of Elizabethan privateers at sea may be misplaced. Drake's voyages were certainly sensational. Here is the description in Hakluyt[18] of Drake's capture of the treasure galleon *Cacafuego*: 'about sixe of the clocke we came to her and boorded her, and shotte at her three peeces of ordinance, and strake down her Misen, and being entered, we found in her great riches, as jewels and precious stones, thirteene chests full of royals of plate, foure score pound weight of golde, and six and twentie tunne of silver.' The ready glamour of Drake's prizes is a marked contrast to the grimy, slow and wet process of extracting wealth from Durham mines, or the obscure and diverse results of trading agreements and gradually expanding export markets. Yet S. T. Bindoff writes in *Tudor England* about Drake with notable objectivity. Bindoff declares roundly that 'it is impossible to regard the exploits of Drake and his fellow gangsters as anything but a curse on the economic life of the age. At a time when the country was short of capital for peaceful enterprise they diverted considerable quantities of capital to sterile or destructive ends. When international credit was making patient headway in the face of ignorant hostility they dealt its delicate mechanism wanton and damaging blows. They pandered to the fatal lure of gold and silver when economic thought was beginning to grow out of its agelong preoccupation with the precious metals.'[19]

The clarity of this argument picks out the important part played in economic life by the merchant. Of course to understand the term 'merchant' in its modern sense of intermediary between producer and retail distributor is to have little idea of the seventeenth century connotations of the term, when merchants were involved in the

---

[17] Stone, op. cit., pp. 346–352.
[18] *Everyman* edition (London 1962), Vol. VIII, p. 60.
[19] *Tudor England* (London 1950), p. 286.

whole chain of production and distribution processes, financing and accounting. An idea of the merchant's co-ordinating function in the cloth trade, and of the essential function of the capital he provided, can be gained from a petition made during the Jacobean period, and cited in Unwin's *Industrial Organisation in the Sixteenth and Seventeenth Centuries*.[20] The petitioner explains 'there is in England 39 English shires and of these but 12 that use any quantity of clothing and of these 12 but 5 that have any store of woolle of their owne breeding . . . the places of the growing and the places of the converting are as far distant as the scope of this kingdom will give leave. The woolles growing in the counties of Worcester Salopp and Stafford are spent partly in Worcester and a great part of them in the countries of Gloucester Devon and Kent and much of them in Southampton. The woolle of the counties of Lincoln Northampton Rutland Leicester Warwick Oxon and Buckingham are thus dispersed. One sort of it is carried into the North parts to Leeds Wakefield Halifax Ratsdale . . . some to the farthest parts of Essex and Suffolk. Some woolles growing in Norfolk are brought three score miles or more to London and from thence carried eight score miles and more into N. Wales and there draped into clothe and soe sent back againe and soulde in London . . . because in those places those sorts of woolle will be improved to the greatest advantage for the King and common-wealth.' This makes crystal clear the vital function of the middleman and financier. The merchant experienced in floating loans and with access to capital was a prominent figure in industrial development, as we saw in the history of the Sunderland salt pans; often the same merchant whose main income was from the production and distri-bution of cloth bought shares in privateering voyages now and again, jockeyed for rights of sale with other merchants when a spice laden carrack was brought captive up the Thames to London, acted as agent in London for foreign business interests, and might dabble in mortgages, land speculation or land-owning, or even invest in a blast furnace in the forest of Dean, when he was not combining governmental and private business on trips to Europe.[21] The activities

---

[20] (Oxford 1904), p. 188.

[21] See L. Stone, *An Elizabethan: Sir Horatio Pallavicino* (Oxford 1956), for a biography of a merchant with many strings to his bow — some crooked, notably; for a more disreputable case see A. F. Upton, *Sir Arthur Ingram 1565–1642* (Oxford 1961).

of such rich merchants included the provision of services now provided by banks (the term 'banker' was coined during the seventeenth
century) although the Jacobean and Caroline money market lacked
the resources demanded by government needs, that is to say, it was
too small and under-organised to provide large sums to be repaid at
low interest rates over long periods.[22]

When the Antwerp bourse was destroyed by the Spanish in 1576
Britain's chief trading outlet was closed. War with Spain closed
further outlets all down the west coast of Europe and trade stagnated.
Merchants knew of no other outlets until the maritime discoveries
of the preceding half-century were developed for trading purposes.
Capital was attracted to these by the potential for large profits, even
though the high risk resulted in many heavy losses. Yet Bindoff
observed that 'few investments have yielded such a stupendous
dividend as the £72,000 which floated the East India Company out
onto the stream of time.'[23] The recovery of trade in the peace which
followed the Spanish wars resulted in general prosperity on the eve
of the Civil War, with developing trading outlets in Russia, the
Levant and the Orient for staple products and for the swiftly
developing manufacturing industries. These achievements of merchants were accomplished despite the abuses of patent, the financial
and governmental incompetence of King James I and Charles I; little
is heard of these ventures of the merchants in City Comedy, except
as subjects for derision and censure. That may have been ultimately
just, but it may prove worthwhile to consider the merchants
objectively first.

R. H. Tawney wrote in *Religion and the Rise of Capitalism* that 'to a great
clothier, or to a capitalist like Pallavicino, Spinola or Thomas
Gresham who managed the Government business in Antwerp . . .
usurious interest appeared, not bad morals, but bad business.
Moving, as they did, in a world where loans were made, not to meet
the temporary difficulty of an unfortunate neighbour, but as profitable investment on the part of not too scrupulous businessmen,
who looked after themselves and expected others to do the same, they
had scant sympathy with doctrines which reflected the spirit of
mutual aid not unnatural in the small circle of neighbours who

---

[22] See R. Ashton, *The Crown and the Money Market* (Oxford 1960).
[23] *Tudor England*, p. 288.

formed the ordinary village or borough in rural England.'[24] The
facts of the financial operations in trade and industry in continental
Europe charted by Richard Ehrenburg in *Capital and Finance in the Age
of the Renaissance* indicate how sophisticated and complex were those
systems of credit and capital, whereas Lawrence Stone (in *The Crisis of
the Aristocracy*) charts a corresponding English situation where rates
of interest were near *double* those of mercantile communities such as
Holland and Genoa; even though English interest rates dropped from
12–15 per cent in 1550–1570 to 8 per cent in 1624, they remained
far higher than Holland's.[25] Such high interest rates obviously must
have slowed economic growth and show that popular strictures
against moneylending could only help to obstruct the development
of easier credit facilities. Obstructions to new credit and capital
systems merely damaged trade and industry, with little corresponding improvements to 'usury'.

Though it is true that the huge capital required to set up and sustain
manufacturing industry in mass production was not in demand until
the mid-eighteenth century, yet the full industrial revolution was
only an acceleration of developments, and a logical extension of
methods, explored and utilised by sixteenth and seventeenth
century industrialists, stockbrokers and capitalists. It is inappropriate
to describe mid-sixteenth century England as an 'organic society'
merely 'threatened' by capitalism. The network of European stock
exchanges already functioning in the early Tudor period was a
sophisticated and complex machine. Certainly it is also true that
business life at this period must have been harsher because the law
was less extensive and less efficiently executed, government control
less competent and, like financial knowledge, theory and skill, often
ill informed or crude in particular instances. Given that risk and
reward in business are so high that they deter the highly scrupulous
hand and the tender conscience, it may be worth dwelling on the
plain courage which attended investment in a venture which had
already failed once, in the middle of what most merchants thought
was an irrevocable state of depression: for this was what the group
did when they invested in the Sunderland salt pans, as we saw.
Again, what strength must have been demanded to set up, in those
days of experiment in the still little known sciences of geography,

[24] Op. cit., pp. 181–182.
[25] Stone, *The Crisis*, pp. 530, 544, 546.

navigation, business management and capital investment, companies such as the Muscovy and East India Company. Doubtless luck played a part, but risk and even danger were severe; it was not only great merchants who invested, but small ones like the one studied by W. G. Hoskins (in *Elizabethan Government and Society*) who had money in 'adventures abroad' both 'in the Isles' and in Spain;[26] that merchant lived not in London, but in Exeter. Lawrence Stone's lively biography shows Pallavicino as a man who behaved criminally in financial affairs yet prospered, but A. H. Dodd's account (in *Elizabethan Government and Society*) of Myddleton's achievements in varied fields, despite the slowness of communications, the inefficiency and inadequacy of theory and factual data — of the kind now found in economic statistics, for example — suggests that high success in business could also result from intelligence, courage, perseverance and readiness to experiment with new methods. Machiavelli's use of the scientific method in political theory was a guide to its possible use in other areas of practical life.

Successful merchants and capitalists were of course frequently blamed for social upheaval and the decay of 'the old order'. L. C. Knights recalled[27] that Sir Simonds D'Ewes was disgusted at the fact that Lionel Cranfield 'started up suddenly to such great wealth and honour from a base and mean original', and Knights implied that the popular quotation from Ulysses' speech on 'degree' (*Troilus & Cressida* I, iii) might aptly be invoked. But D'Ewes is merely invoking a familiar 'nowadays' lament from Complaint tradition, often used completely disingenuously, as Sylvia Thrupp shows (in *The Merchant Class of Medieval London*, chapter VII) if not unrealistically: 'Families of the fourteenth and fifteenth centuries actually knew very little about their ancestry. They had few deeds or seals antedating the twelfth century, few hereditary arms ran back any further, and there were no early portraits. There is no genealogical information on the medieval rolls of arms. The pedigrees of which people boasted were passed on orally through the memories of the aged, a process which allowed fairly free play to the imagination. In the late fourteenth century several friends of the first baron Scrope testified on hearsay, without having seen any written record professing to prove it, that he was

---

[26] *Elizabethan Government and Society*, ed. S. T. Bindoff et. al. (London 1961), p. 176.

[27] *Drama and Society in the Age of Jonson*, p. 83.

descended from great gentlemen of the time of the Norman Conquest.' It is certainly unwise to suppose that D'Ewes sees Cranfield as a
new kind of bourgeois-capitalist entrepreneur in a Chivalric society.
The Elizabethan and Jacobean social structure is better understood in
terms of ranks. Movement up or down the scale occurred constantly
but the rights, functions, and habits of each rank remained largely
unaltered. If a knight was promoted to the nobility he was treated as
a noble and his acquaintances had to adjust themselves to his new
dignity and prestige. G. R. Elton has summarised the situation[28] by
observing that the upper ranks of sixteenth century England included
men without titles as well as those with them; traffic between titled
and untitled was brisk because the principle of primogeniture forced
younger sons downward (even sons of gentlemen down to tradesmen, as in the case of Quicksilver in *Eastward Ho*), while the crown
could and did promote up into the ranks of gentry and nobility.
We may recall the king's speech in *All's Well That Ends Well* II, iii:

> 'Tis only title thou disdain'st in her, the which
> I can build up . . .
>   If she be
> All that is virtuous, save what thou dislik'st,
> A poor physician's daughter, thou dislik'st
> Of virtue for the name; but do not so:
> From lowest place when virtuous things proceed,
> The place is dignified by the doer's deed:
> Where great additions swell's, and virtue none,
> It is a dropsied honour. . . .
>   . . . honours thrive
> When rather from our acts we them derive
> Than our foregoers. The mere word's a slave
> Debosh'd on every tomb, on every grave
> A lying trophy, and as oft is dumb
> Where dust and damn'd oblivion is the tomb
> Of honour'd bones indeed. What should be said?
> If thou canst like this creature as a maid,
> I can create the rest.

There were indeed many complaints in the Elizabethan and Jacobean
period that traditional landowning families were decaying, that the
ordered rural society was breaking up and that customary hospitality

---

[28] Elton, p. 256.

was in decline. These lamentations are so numerous partly because the recent introduction of printed books vastly increased writings of all kinds and has preserved them as never before. The great majority of such complaints derive from London, the capital city and centre of journalism, beset by the seriously increased numbers of landless men and vagrant sturdy beggars, also the centre of expanding manufacturing industries, and hence plagued by new buildings, suburban growth and overcrowding, and furthermore a major port and within easy reach of the southern and eastern ports where sporadic mass demobilisations of soldiers and sailors took place; the latter must have swelled the numbers of petty criminals who found London an excellent place in which to steal, dispose of their goods and evade detection. The contemporary observer must have been prejudiced by these circumstances even if he was not committed to Tudor policies of stratification and the enforcement of social stability, as was the Recorder of London, William Fleetwood, whose memoranda to Burghley about London's thieving vagrants are full of righteous indignation,[29] or John Stow, whose history of the City so often deplores the new building taking place all round its boundaries.

John Stow indeed shows how attractive the theme of dying traditions of hospitality can be, especially in the hands of an old chronicler. In *The Survey of London* we read how in Henry VI's reign 'Richard Nevill, Earl of Warwick, with six hundred men, all in red jackets, embroidered with ragged staves before and behind . . . was lodged in Warwicke lane; in whose house there was oftentimes six oxen eaten at a breakfast, and every tavern was full of his meat; for he that had any acquaintance in that house, might have there so much of sodden and roast meat as he could prick and carry upon a long dagger'.[30] Stow is characteristically at his best with events, like this one, some distance away. There is a perceptibly elegaic note to his final instance of the old order's custom: 'The late Earl of Oxford, father to him that now liveth, hath been noted within these forty years to have ridden into this city, and so to his house by London stone, with eighty gentlemen in a livery of Reading tawny, and chains of gold about their necks, before him, and one hundred tall yeomen, in the like livery, to follow him without chains, but all having his cognisance

---

[29] See *Queen Elizabeth and her Times* (London 1838), pp. 164–166 especially.
[30] *The Survey of London* (Everyman edition, London 1956), p. 81.

of the blue boar embroidered on their left shoulder.'[31] It is perhaps a
subject more interesting as colourful romance than as objective
history. It is true that some great aristocratic houses dwindled in
riches and pomp during this period, but it should be remembered
that James I and Buckingham gave to the aristocracy a sum equivalent
to half the total cost of Elizabeth's war with Spain from 1585–
1603,[32] while many landowning families did not decline or crumble
through the undermining by merchants and city usurers. The origins
of landowning families must frequently have been successful
merchants, citizens and tradesmen, in the reigns of Elizabeth's
ancestors no less than in her own. Thus Stokesay Castle, which still
stands in Shropshire, was built as a fortified manor house some time
between 1240 and 1290 largely to call attention to the improved
social status of an enriched successful merchant named Sir Lawrence
de Ludlow.[33]

G. R. Elton warns that we ought to beware of imposing on the
Tudor period theories of class derived from the sociology of the
early nineteenth century, and theories of the rise of new men which
have been applied to the fourteenth and sixteenth centuries as well
as the seventeenth centuries. The literary critic who applies such
unguarded generalisations to complex artistic works is in danger of
actual error, like that of J. F. Danby, discussing Edmund's words in
King Lear I, ii. Edmund declares

> Legitimate Edgar, I must have your land

and Danby (in *Shakespeare's Doctrine of Nature*) comments as follows:
'this society is that of the medieval vision. Its representative is an old
king . . . The other society is that of nascent capitalism. Its representative is the New Man'. To this we might begin by opposing the
comment of Elton that 'at all times men try to better themselves by
approximating to a social ideal. Those that succeed (always a
minority of those that try) come as new men into established ranks,
but in a society as flexible as that of England they generally get
established in a generation or two, just in time to bewail in their
turn the arrival of others from below. Now the social ideal of Tudor
England was the landed gentleman . . . if a vaster generalisation still

---

[31] Ibid., p. 82.
[32] Stone, *The Crisis*, p. 273.
[33] Ralph Dutton, *The English Country House* (London 1962), p. 35.

may be hazarded it is this: from the decay of feudalism proper round the year 1300 to the rise of an industrial and urban society round about the year 1850, the social ideal of England was that of the landed gentleman.'[34] The gentry probably refuses to acknowledge itself dead even today, and Evelyn Waugh was forced to admit that his novel *Brideshead Revisited*, written in 1944 to mark the spoliation of those 'ancestral seats which were our chief national artistic achievement', seems rather an over-anticipation. 'The English aristocracy has maintained its identity to a degree that then (1944) seemed impossible,'[35] Waugh declared.

Returning to the Tudor period, it might be noted that there had been rich merchants before Henry VII was crowned. That is to say, enterprising individualists manipulating capital and trade had grown rich for long years before Henry VIII caused the monasteries to be dissolved. Nor, indeed, was the sale of peerages and knighthoods by James I and Charles I an abuse because no previous monarch had rewarded with titles those who gave him money and other pedestrian services of the kind. The sale of honours was an abuse because it was performed too often and for too trivial reasons, not because it mocked Chivalric ideals still vigorously, exclusively guarded by valorous gentlemen and knights. In Elizabeth's reign New Men were not new. Capitalism was not nascent. That is hardly the word at the end of the Age of the Fugger.

---

[34] Elton, pp. 257–8.
[35] *Brideshead Revisited* (Penguin edition 1962), p. 8.

D

3   The Approaching Equinox

Politics and City Comedy

AFTER ELIZABETH'S DEATH plays at Blackfriars, Paul's, and, increasingly, the Globe, register a note of discontent with public affairs, including the King's own actions, while the other adult companies at the Red Bull, Swan, Rose and Hope largely continue to evoke an air of cheerful patriotism and national self-satisfaction. It has been surmised that this divergence in attitudes to government and monarchy reflects a progressive split in the political attitudes of the two audiences: the first includes lawyers, members of the Commons, merchants and Inns of Court students, nobility and gentry, the second more predominantly tradesmen, citizens, labourers, carriers, apprentices, servingmen.

The proliferation of satiric literature has often been cited as evidence of the widening split in Jacobean society, ultimately to end in Civil War and the execution of Charles I. However satiric literature is always concerned with the corruption and mismanagement of affairs — in Jonson's words 'the times deformitie' — and in fact there is continuity between Elizabethan and Jacobean political and social satire. There is also continuity between the two centuries in the realm of social and political conflict, which is in vital respects related to economic history. The period is one of progressive alteration in the balance of power; as, in an hourglass, the sand pours from the upper bowl to the lower, so gradually power drained from James

50

to the Commons, as his income dwindled and his policy failed to adjust itself to changing situations, and as their understanding of the situation grew and their control of finances tightened. The Jacobeans did not know and hardly would have guessed that one day James's successor would die under the axe; but the parliamentary opposition to James directly developed into that opposition which Charles knew and feared. As R. Ashton remarked in *The Crown and the Money Market* Charles found the economic situation desperate in 1640, and the Commons knew how to wield it as a weapon: 'there is no better index of the weakness of the royal financial position in 1640 than the recourse to the pepper loan, the threat to coin brass money, and — most desperate of all — the calling of Parliament.'[1]

In politics, as in social and economic affairs, it is the deeper issues which the dramatists intuitively grasp as important and it is their concern with these that makes their work significant as a criticism of society. Dominating the political scene, as I have indicated, was the progressive redistribution of power from the monarchy to the Commons; and the importance of this is indicated in the warning of Francis Bacon:[2]

> Shepherds of people had need know the calendars of tempests in state; which are commonly greatest when things grow to equality; as natural tempests are greatest about the *Equinoctia*.

The fact that James I, by his own claim king by divine right, could be referred to on the stage, less than two years after his coronation, as one of

> a few industrious Scots
> (*Eastward Ho* III, iii. 41–42)

suggests how the mood of general cynical pessimism about king, court and government, expressed in City Comedy, is related to political history.

In this chapter we shall see the questioning empirical approach, which is so important in the economic developments of the period, in use by the politicians. The fundamental questions are about the nature of the state: Is the state a family, a commonwealth, or is it

---

[1] R. Ashton, *The Crown and the Money Market*, p. 176.
[2] *Of Seditions and Troubles* in Bacon's *Works*, ed. Spedding *et al.*, Vol. VI, p. 406.

based on a contract between the head (the king) and the members? Is the head appointed by divine right, or because the members agree that he is fit? If private property is an inalienable right of the individual, is it right for the head, and is it legal for him, to take away private property without consent? If the members are vitally affected by the mercantile laws and the foreign policy of the head, and if these decisions are arrived at by logical deductions from the empirically assembled evidence, should not the decisions of the head be open to logical analysis and, if necessary, correction? Is not government a science rather than a divine mystery? Is not the king only a man accepted by the members of the state as its head?

These issues are focused in the Jacobean constitutional conflict. In the late Tudor period royal authority was growing stronger and the concept of the divine right of kings was being exalted. However, Tudor absolutism did not develop into complete absolutism in the early Jacobean period, although the divine right concept was by no means abandoned. The problem facing James I and Charles I was that the cost of government, which was their responsibility, was rising while the royal income was falling, and at the same time their power did not extend to control of their subjects' private property. Indeed as the Tudor concept of divine right became strong, so simultaneously the growing amount of private property owned by influential subjects strengthened the medieval concept that property was a right belonging to subjects.

The royal aim was therefore to achieve recognition of absolute prerogative in Council and star chamber, and legal sanction in common law courts, so that funds could be levied for government without the recourse to the Commons which Elizabeth had been forced to make. It is characteristic of the complexity of the situation that at the same time as the decision in the ship money case or Sir Thomas Fleming's decision in Bate's case (1606) upheld the royal prerogative against subjects' rights over private property, many common law cases were decided in favour of subjects' property rights even against private royal prerogative.[3] It was not simply a matter of whether the lawyers were traditionally on one side or the other, nor was it that there were two clear legal arguments, either of which could be used to find for or against. Even the upholders of

---

[3] M. A. Judson, *The Crisis in the Constitution* (Rutgers, U.S.A. 1949), p. 36.

royal prerogative at the early stage of 1606, in Bate's case, agreed in the 1610 Parliamentary discussion that actual taxes could only be granted by Parliament. There was also the notion that the system where the monarch depended on his subjects' agreeing to grant him funds truly reflected the divinity and justice of God, who had ordained and exalted the king but had also given rights of property to the subjects.[4]

James I and Charles I needed, more urgently than the Tudors, to rely on prerogative institutions to govern the country, because they were unable to carry out their policies smoothly through Parliament as the Tudors had. Of course the Tudor concern to extend and improve local government had demanded the assistance of country magnates who thus expected, and demanded to be, consulted. The Tudor method of government through an admittedly controlled Parliament meant that its members became more active, and that the House of Commons was certain to demand power sooner or later.[5] The growth of Puritanism, emphasising as it did the importance of the individual, his personal judgement and the rewards attending zealous right conduct (grace through works) further contributed to a general movement of the subjects away from submissiveness and towards active participation in politics. Thus James I inherited a Parliament which was from the outset less inclined to submit to absolute government.

As the Jacobean age continued, lawyers became the spearhead of the opposition to absolute government. By the 1620s lawyers were wellnigh the most powerful class in the country.[6] They clearly realised the importance of the royal legal victories in Bate's and the ship money case and concentrated on opposing the legal views of royalist judges and counsellors, ignoring the talk about divine right from James himself. In 1628 Wentworth summarised their attitude by observing 'that which passes from White Hall is but a gust . . . but that which is legally done stinges us'.[7]

In the long conflict both sides argued inconsistently, neither defined the crucial point, the 'general welfare'; royalists argued that

---

[4] Ibid., p. 42.

[5] W. Notenstein, *The Winning of the Initiative by the House of Commons* (London 1924), pp. 47–48.

[6] Ibid., p. 50.

[7] Cit., Judson, p. 142.

the king in levying taxes to finance government did so for the
'general welfare', opposition argued that private property must be
protected for the 'general welfare'. Royalist judges inconsistently
pronounced that the royal prerogative did not come within the
competence of the law, but simultaneously pressed for legal decisions
confirming that prerogative.[8] Opposition appealed to their position
as trustees of the country's good, a merely political argument, in a
dispute over law and rights, and they used this political argument to
encroach on royal prerogative in foreign affairs and to justify new
aggressive procedures. Thus on both sides old traditional principles
are subjected to what looks suspiciously like sceptical analysis, and
then disingenuously used to cover new schemes for political power.
Neither side is really concerned with attaining that situation where
'mutual respect and love between king and people maintain a
proper balance',[9] both sides are struggling for control of the
government, although the opposition never formulated their aim so
specifically as that. So in the 1628 Parliament Hoskins declared 'we
come not in this assembly but to preserve the liberties of the
kingdom',[10] and in critical moments members made such appeals as
'If wee should now retourne into our country with nothing for the
good of the comon wealth they would say that [we have] bene all
this while like children in ketching butterflies' (1610) and 'Wee
serve here for thousands of tenn thowsands' (1621).[11] The opposition encroached on royal prerogative in foreign policy, while the
very insistence of royalists on the divine right theory 'exposed the
glaring contrast between their conception of monarchy and the
actual kings, James and Charles, who sat upon the throne'.[12]

The royalists knew that co-operation must exist between ministers
and Parliament, and they knew that much of the Tudor success in
strengthening and unifying the nation had been done in Council
and Star Chamber, and all of it under powerful rulers. Faced with
work to do, many could have justified absolutism on practical
grounds alone. They saw that the king must maintain his authority
over his subjects. It is striking indeed that Francis Bacon's advice to

---

[8] Judson, p. 127.
[9] Judson, pp. 154–155.
[10] Judson, p. 280.
[11] Cit., Notenstein, p. 43.
[12] Judson, p. 159.

James in 1613 to deal differently with the Commons, to 'put off the person of a merchant and contractor and rest upon the person of a king'[13] exactly anticipates the social theory of Thomas Hobbes — and interestingly relates to Rochester's ridicule of Charles II in The *History of Insipids* as a 'Lewd King' —

> But wonder not it should be so, Sirs,
> When Monarchs rank themselves with Grocers.

As the struggle between royalists and Parliamentary opposition develops, both sides progressively exploit pragmatic methods in arguing for the disputed prize of political control. Older philosophies of kingship and government are still gestured to — but with decreasing seriousness.

It is paradoxical that the entrenched attitude of opposition to innovations which characterises Complaint tradition, and provides City Comedy with its criteria, should censure policies and actions of the king and hence align itself with the Parliamentary opposition.[14] A document such as The *Secret History of the Reign of James I*, though written in thoroughly conventional Complaint style, is disrespectful of authority and discusses the royal administration with attention to the actions themselves and the king as a man like other men. Though arguing for a return to traditional methods of government, and therefore still opposed to innovation, these satirists inevitably aligned themselves with those thinkers who wanted change of another sort, though at this stage (before 1620) few protestants yet contemplated revolution.

In the Jacobean age the drama registers a split in the social fabric and an uneasy dissatisfaction with political affairs; it is character-

---

[13] Cit., Judson, p. 75.

[14] Corruption at Court was a fact as well as a traditional preoccupation of satiric art. Stone in The *Crisis of the Aristocracy* notes that heavy debts contracted by the courtiers in the 1590s caused many to resort to corruption to maintain themselves, and thereafter bribery seems to have become an accepted part of Court routine. In the 1620s Stone calculates an unrecorded revenue of the Crown in bribes, fees, favoured rents and gifts of about £500,000 — a vicious burden exacted in an obnoxious and inequitable way. The financial ethics of such serious public men as Salisbury, Cranfield, Strafford, being involved in the grant and fee system of reward for governmental service, differed only in degree from those of the parasites they attacked (pp. 490–495).

istic of the confused atmosphere that the satire should attack the
king and yet resist change; perhaps it is too much to ask that the
dramatists, having articulated the conflict, should not reflect its confused, inconsistent, fragmentary and ambiguous manifestations as
they occurred. It was only with hindsight that the central issues were
formulated clearly, by Hobbes.

Unlike James, Elizabeth I, though never relaxing her hold on
Parliament through Burghley, yet knew how to accede to the
petitions of her subjects in a way that bound them irresistibly to her.
When the outcry against monopolies in 1601 persuaded her to
withdraw them, she took the opportunity to evoke with brilliant
eloquence the ideal of Tudor monarchy: in her speech to the Commons stands revealed a great orator, and a great politician: 'Though
God hath raised me high, yet this I count the glory of my crown, that
I have reigned with your loves . . . Though you have had and may
have many mightier and wiser princes sitting on this seat, yet you
never had nor shall have any that will love you better . . . And I pray
you, Mr Comptroller, Mr Secretary, and you of my council, that
before the gentlemen depart into their counties you bring them all to
kiss my hand.'[15] James I did not win the hearts of the Commons, and
I think it is probable, judging from Notenstein's account of James's
manner with the Commons,[16] that Francis Bacon had James in mind
when he wrote his essay Of Great Place and observed: 'Preserve the
right of thy place; but stir not questions of jurisdiction: And rather
assume thy right, in silence and de facto, than voice it with claims and
challenges. Preserve likewise the rights of inferior places; and think it
more honour to direct in chief than to be busy in all. Embrace and
invite helps and advices touching the execution of thy place; and do
not drive away such as bring thee information, as meddlers; but
accept of them in good part.'[17] James disobeyed every item of this
advice, and Notenstein ascribes the sudden flowering of the opposition in the Commons to precisely this neglect. In a situation where
the new monarch was all too unfavourably compared with his predecessor, it was unfortunate for him that economic difficulties and
certain abuses should have put the Commons on the offensive, and

---

[15] Cit., England Under the Tudors, p. 465.
[16] Op. cit., pp. 32–33.
[17] Of Great Place in Works ed. Spedding et al., Vol. VI, p. 400.

that he did not ensure that his wishes were well represented, numerically, in the lower House. The progressive alienation of the Peers meant that local elections, which he did not trouble to nurse like the Tudors, were not dominated by a royalist nobility either. Thus the two Houses quickly grew in numerical opposition, and the growth of the Whole House Committee progressively annihilated the effectiveness of royal Councillors in the Commons.[18]

James's interest in government was from the outset notoriously unzealous. Here is what the Venetian ambassador communicated to the Doge on February 10th 1605: 'I hear the King has written a letter to the Council, in which he tells them that having been recently for nearly three weeks in London he finds this sedentary life very prejudicial to his health; for in Scotland he was used to spend much time in the country and in hard exercise, and he finds that repose robs him of his appetite and breeds melancholy and a thousand other ills. He says he is bound to consider his health above all things, and so he must tell them that for the future he means to come to London but seldom, passing most of his time in the country in the chase; and as he will be thus far away from court he cannot attend to business, and so he commits all to them . . . Many who went to him with petitions and grievances have been told to go to the Council, for they are fully authorised . . . This is the cause of indescribable ill-humour among the King's subjects.'[19] Making allowances for the exaggeration of second hand information ('I hear . . .') it is still significant that the ambassador has heard the rumour slanted in this direction. The king, it was plainly well known, cared nothing for the Commons. On the other hand there was sufficient popular interest in Parliamentary business to arouse demand for copies of speeches and the subsequent introduction of Parliamentary newsletters. Beaulieu wrote in February 1610 'the Parliament here doth chiefly now occupy the Minds of our Court and the Tounges of our Exchange',[20] and the Venetian ambassador notes in 1605 how affairs were discussed in public: '*many members openly declare* that as there is no war with Spain, no war with Holland, no army on the Scottish border (!) . . . they cannot understand why the king, who has the revenues of Scotland should

---

[18] Notenstein, p. 26.
[19] *Calendar of State Papers Venetian* (1603–1607) no. 341.
[20] Cit., Notenstein, p. 49,n.

want money. They add that the people are far more heavily burdened . . . for the king stays so continually and so long in the country . . . and whenever he goes a-hunting the crops are ruined.'[21] It is only necessary to glance at The Secret History of the Reign of James I to see how scandalous rumours might turn country gentlemen and nobility over to the opposition. In addition to the scandals of his Court and his actions once he was crowned, James had begun to alienate the nobility as soon as he set foot in England. On his way south had he not created forty-six new knights at a go before breakfast at Belvoir?[22] Did not the displeasure at his indulgence to Scottish nobility above the English nobility register almost as soon as he arrived in London?[23]

Personal grievances among the nobility arising from the king's failure to favour their allies or kinsmen at Court were soon aggravated by the prolific sales of knighthoods (and peerages after 1615). Since the ordinary resources of the money market were quite inadequate it was inevitable that the crown should seek special expedients. These fell into the categories of forced public loans, private loans from rich merchants, ordinary public loans, the sale of monopolies, favouring of informers as a cheap instrument of government, and the sale of peerages, baronetcies and knighthoods. The impersonal credit system was not yet functioning satisfactorily for government requirements, and these royal attempts at solvency seriously affected relations with the Stuarts' subjects. James having debased the dignity of knighthood until it was hardly worth having, Charles fined large numbers of the gentry the total of £173,537[24] for spurning it. The price of a baronetcy dropped from £700 in 1619 to £220 in 1622; even in 1606 Cranfield was able to buy 'the making of six knights' for £373 1s 8d. Finally in 1641 when Charles made 128 baronets, more of them joined the opposition than the royalist side, so base had the honour become! There were earlier instances of the unpopularity of James's sale of honours; the York herald in 1616

---

[21] C. S. P. Ven., no. 440.

[22] Stone, 'The Inflation of Honours 1558–1641' Past & Present XIV (London 1958).

[23] See C. S. P. Ven., 1603–7 no 55: 'no Englishman, be his rank what it may, can enter the Presence Chamber without being summoned, whereas Scottish lords have free entree of the Privy Chamber' (May 1603).

[24] Stone, 'The Inflation of Honours 1558–1641'.

tricked the Garter King of Arms into granting a coat of arms to Gregory Brandon the common hangman. C. R. Mayes has remarked that 'the sale of peerages (was) a practice wholly offensive to the landed classes and one which contributed significantly to the growing opposition to the crown'.[25] The broader significance of the prolific references in City Comedy to this practice is perhaps apparent.

Finally there was the reaction to James's foreign policy and his longstanding but very unpopular friendliness to the Spanish ambassador Gondomar, about which Middleton wrote a tremendously popular play, the *Game at Chesse*. It was not only the London apprentices who distrusted Gondomar, as Sir Simonds D'Ewes testifies in his autobiography, though he attempts objectivity: 'Tuesday, the 1st day of May, the Count of Gondomar fearing some mischief from the apprentices of London, there were divers companies of soldiers appointed to guard, and watch in several quarters of the City, which still did more and more argue the potency this Spanish Ambassador had in the English Court.'[26] Not only was there a general distaste for Spain and Roman Catholicism, especially among those who looked back to Elizabeth's reign with pride and affection; but there was a growing disquiet born of doubt about James's ability and judgement in foreign affairs. Was it relevant that he was king 'by divine right' if he could not do his job and brought the nation to its knees by mismanagement?

James was a bad politician not because he was too practical and ignored irrelevancy and display before the people, but because he was not practical enough. He did not cast a calculating eye over his new kingdom, he did not observe the tastes of the people, he did not attend to experienced counsel. He fatally weakened the royal control in both Houses of Parliament and failed to grasp why his own revenues were decreasing — though he must have understood his authority was decreasing proportionately. It is important to note that James's policy of appealing to a medieval doctrine of royal authority seems to have been conclusively unsuccessful; if he did not concern himself with the shift of power in his realm, his subjects were sharply aware that they were more powerful and that government, so far from

---

[25] C. R. Mayes, 'The Sale of Peerages in Early Stuart England', *J. Mod. Hist.* xxix, 1957.

[26] *The Autobiography of Sir Simonds D'Ewes* (London 1845), Vol. I, p. 187 — for 1621.

being a mystery, was a matter in which their Parliamentary representatives had a permanent and useful part to play, but where it
seemed that the king exercised skills demonstrably inadequate for
the task.

The single most significant political development in the Jacobean age
was the gradual realisation by many Englishmen that the king was not
a man whom they could respect and obey as they had respected and
obeyed Elizabeth. It is with such a situation in mind that Bacon
wrote 'tempests in state . . . are commonly greatest, when things
grow to equality'. Satiric drama with political slants had been written
in the late Elizabethan period — Nashe and Jonson had written *The
Isle of Dogs* in 1597 — but it is the general atmosphere of political
cynicism, unrest, the constant implication met with in City
Comedy that the Court is squalidly corrupt, which marks Jacobean
satiric drama off from Elizabethan. City Comedy, we must conclude,
presents a pessimistic picture of urban life in James's kingdom even
when we have made all allowances for the fact that the attitude to
economic individualism of the satiric dramatists is inherited from
medieval Complaint and that targets such as usury, upstarts, enclosures were in part the drama's new guise for the Deadly Sins,
Avarice and Pride, characters in the older Morality drama. The satire
of Court and King, too, was partly Satire's new guise for the literary
models of imperial Rome, and indeed some of the non-dramatic
verse satire was straight translation of Horace and Juvenal; but in
politics, of which the patterns and the personalities are less subject to
variation through time, Jacobean satire was more accurate, and its
choice of targets is a more reliable guide to the age's political history.
In both social and political history the mood which is called
Jacobean derives from the conflict which provides, also, the dynamic
for City Comedy; it is this which most vitally relates City Comedy to
the early Jacobean age.

4 To Strip the Ragged Follies of the Time

The Comical Satyres

THERE IS A DANGER of distortion in any attempt to interpret events of a period in terms of one major issue. England from the beginning of Elizabeth's reign to the end of James I's remained predominantly rural and patriotic; even the opposition to James's government looked back to Elizabeth as an ideal rather than forward to a revolution against monarchy. Some elements in the nation wanted more say in government and scorned the king's incompetence; some wanted to secure more power for the king and resist the ambitions of the Commons; but there is insufficient evidence whether the common people were politically alive to the complex struggle in the Jacobean House of Commons, and though Puritanism was spreading throughout the reigns of James I and Charles I, nevertheless determined opposition to the crown did not harden until late in the day, and even then the picture remained confused. The two titles familiarly applied to the period are contradictory, in fact, for though 'Jacobean' suggests a mood of pessimism arising from decadent faith and government, producing sardonic comedy and violent, at times lurid, tragedy, 'Early Seventeenth Century' on the other hand suggests, with perhaps equal validity, new stimulating ideas in science, politics and economics, energetic experimental thought, bustling Puritanism, an ably intelligent House of Commons, Harvey, Bacon, the new cosmology.

Jacobean drama reveals a comparable disturbance and ambivalence: it cannot be insignificant that the tragic drama of the Age is
violently disturbing and yet contains comic and farcical elements,
while comedy is often savage and aggressive, its closing harmony
often torn by discords.

It is tempting to over-emphasise the significance of the rise of
satiric comedy, in the intellectual and social climate of the late
1590s, and it is worth insisting on the limited scope of the first
experimental plays of Ben Jonson in this mode, *Every Man Out of His
Humour*, *Cynthia's Revels* and *Poetaster*. It is arresting to notice that the
spread of satire in verse and drama was contemporaneous with the
overthrow of the old Ptolemaic concept of the universe; the earth, it
seemed, was no longer the centre: on the contrary, it circled the
sun. Satire too often turns the familiar upside down to reveal unexpected truth, however unwelcome and hostile to custom and
propriety; so Thersites describes Ajax as one who 'wears his wit in
his belly and his guts in his head', so too he suggests how acute, if
bitter, the insight of satire can be, when he impudently enquires
'Agamemnon, how if he had boils? full, all over, generally? . . . were
not that a botchy core?' We may recall Bacon's remark that we are
beholden to Machiavelli and other writers who 'openly and un-
feignedly declare or describe what men do, not what they ought to
do', though we recognise the repellent perversity of Thersites' wholly
diseased vision. Such extremity of pessimism is rare in Jacobean
comedy, perhaps because it is partly traditional for the anarchic
spirit of comedy to mock social and moral values; at all events, the
beginnings of the genre City Comedy do not lie in an apocalyptic
vision so much as in the particular, local critical observation of folly
by bitter jesters and more academic writers of Horatian satiric verse.

To trace the emergence of the form, conventions and themes of
City Comedy, we must begin by studying the early experimental
comedies of Jonson, and also Marston and Middleton. This is the
subject of the present chapter and of the two following. I have
restricted the discussion mainly to close critical engagement with
individual plays in order to show as clearly and directly as possible
the rise of City Comedy. Once this is clear, some review of the early
plays' treatment of Jacobean social and political affairs will be more
meaningful and appropriate. Meanwhile, we may keep this question
of realism in mind — it is inevitably raised by reading the quotations

from Donne's satires in this chapter, for instance — though the discussion will focus here on the satiric and dramatic art, and will take up the wider questions in chapter VII. The present purpose is to locate and trace the emergent form of the Genre, and this will involve consideration of certain plays not at first sight relevant, such as *Antonio and Mellida* and *The Malcontent*. But this is to anticipate, and we may now begin with Jonson.

The tone of Jonson's first plays is in part genially Elizabethan, in part ebulliently critical (following Sidney but in the accent of Nashe), and in part severely censorious in the manner of Donne. There is some uncertainty in purpose, emphasis and manner firstly because the plays are experimental and secondly because Jonson seems to have written with more felicity and facility in the traditional fashion of Popular Elizabethan comedy in these early years. The characteristic Jonsonian style was yet unformed.

In the Prologue to *Every Man In His Humour* we find strong echoes of Sir Philip Sidney's criticisms of the popular stage, and Nashe too had already ridiculed Popular playwrights, 'a sort of shifting companions, that runne through every arte and thrive by none, to leave the trade of *Noverint* whereto they were borne, and busie themselves with the indevors of Art, that could scarcelie latinize their necke-verse',[1] but the Humour plays display everywhere close sympathy with Sidney's question 'for what is it to make folkes gape at a wretched Begger, or a beggerly Clowne, or . . . strangers, because they speake not English so well as wee doe? What doe we learne',[2] and Jonson's ridicule of such comedy (in the character Antonio Balladino in *The Case Is Altered*) prepares us for the style of his subsequent plays, accommodating Sidney's recommendations in *The Apologie for Poetrie*: there Sidney's preferred comic figures were 'rather a busy loving Courtier, a hartles threatening *Thraso*, a self-wise-seeming schoolemaster, a awry-transformed Traveller' which 'if wee sawe walke in stage names, which wee play naturally, therein were delightfull laughter, and teaching delightfulnes'. It is a paradox that a newly experimental drama was begun to put into effect such well known precepts and to affirm traditional social values.

The didactic and satiric elements in Sidney's concept of comic drama may remind us of the highly *dramatic* quality of verse satire in

[1] Preface to Greene's *Menaphon* ed. Arber (London 1880), p. 9.
[2] Sidney, *The Apologie for Poetrie* ed. Collins (Oxford 1907), p. 56.

the late 1590s, oddly enough. It has often been remarked that Donne's
poetry is marked by dramatic influence, yet the verse of Donne's
Satires of the 1590s is more assuredly vigorous and supple than
Jonson's. In Donne's first satire[3] we see the satirist's sharp eye
bringing a scene vividly to life in a dramatic situation:

> Oh monstrous, superstitious puritan,
> Of refin'd manners, yet ceremoniall man,
> That when thou meet'st one, with enquiring eyes
> Dost search, and like a needy broker prize
> The silke, and gold he weares, and to that rate
> So high or low, dost raise thy formall hat:
>
> (Satyre I, 27–32)

This presents a convincingly realised dramatic character and attacks
him with the verse's sinewy masculine movement, the vigorous
scorn in the harsh consonants and heavy rhythmic emphasis on
verbs. The immediacy with which this character comes alive is also
due to the clarity with which he is visualised; and in Satyre IV
Donne gives us a series of such small dramatic episodes in a survey
of court and city. The poet adopts the persona of satiric observer;
his companion is an unwelcome and ridiculous chatterer, whose

> cloths were strange, though coarse; and black, though bare;
> Sleevelesse his jerkin was, and it had beene
> Velvet, but 'twas now (so much ground was seene)
> Become Tufftaffatie; and our children shall
> See it plaine Rashe awhile, then nought at all.
>
> (30–34)

This 'thing' appears and is treated with satiric scorn:

> Towards me did runne
> A thing more strange, then on Niles slime, the Sunne
> E'r bred; or all which into Noahs Arke came;
> A thing, which would have pos'd Adam to name;
> Stranger then seaven Antiquaries studies,
> Then Africks Monsters, Guianaes rarities.
>
> (17–22)

When he speaks, he disgusts the poet (as Crispinus does Horace in
Poetaster III, 1). He is not ridiculed playfully, like Osric in Hamlet, but
harshly:

---

[3] The Poems of John Donne ed. H. J. C. Grierson (Oxford 1912).

> Then, as if he would have sold
> His tongue, he prais'd it, and such wonders told
> That I was faine to say, If you 'had liv'd, Sir,
> Time enough to have beene Interpreter
> To Babells bricklayers, sure the Tower had stood.
>   (61–65)

Donne's interest in this garrulous fool is incidental, for his main purpose is to shape the conversation to survey a variety of court and city themes; yet the dialogue is unmistakably that of a good playwright in satiric comedy.

The form of Satyre IV provides a series of scenes in court and city exemplifying folly and corruption in various guises. The satirist's interlocutor is himself a kind of compendium of folly, his ugly mixture of style and vocabulary illustrating how completely he is a thing of shreds and patches, botched up, a creature of the times and the town. His social pretensions are representative: he is ludicrously snobbish:

> More then ten Hollensheads, or Halls, or Stowes,
> Of triviall houshold trash he knowes; He knowes
> When the Queene frown'd, or smil'd, and he knowes what
> A subtle States-man may gather of that;
>   (97–100)

but as he talks on he ranges over many abuses and evils

> He names a price for every office paid;

and pretends to know

> Who loves whores, who boyes, and who goats.

He departs with money politely extorted from the satirist, who is left with a bitterly working imagination, and surveys the town with the hostility of the religious Complaint writer:

> 'Tis ten a clock and past; All whom the Mues,
> Baloune, Tennis, Dyet, or the stewes,
> Had all the morning held, now the second
> Time made ready, that day, in flocks, are found
> In the Presence, and I (God pardon mee.)
> As fresh, and sweet their Apparrels be, as bee
> The fields they sold to buy them; For a King
> Those hose are, cry the flatterers; and bring
> Them next weeke to the Theatre to sell;

E

> Wants reach all states; Me seemes they doe as well
> At stage, as court; All are players; who e'r lookes
> (For themselves dare not goe) o'r Cheapside books,
> Shall find their wardrops Inventory.
>
> (175–187)

Donne's mounting disgust is further sharpened by the entry of court
ladies, and the poem's climax is provoked by the bold lord Glorius,
a vigorous dramatic creation no less vigorously scourged by the
satire:

> Whose cloak his spurres teare; whom he spits on
> He cares not, his ill words doe no harme
> To him; he rusheth in, as if arme, arme,
> He meant to crie; And though his face be as ill
> As theirs which in old hangings whip Christ, still
> He strives to wook worse,
>
> (222–227)

The satirist gratefully escapes through the Great Chamber which, he
notes, is hung with ironically appropriate pictures of the seven
deadly sins, and the poem ends.

Donne's satiric persona has a distinct effect on the response of his
readers; it differs obviously from the response to songs and sonnets,
it establishes a distance between reader and subject, invites astringent,
intelligent glee or disgust rather than sympathetic identification
with character, scene and experience. When Ben Jonson set out to
write comic drama incorporating satire he became immediately
involved in establishing a new relationship between the play and the
audience which corresponded to that between satiric poetry and its
readers. Jonson's first plays are highly, even excessively self-conscious
about form and style partly for this reason, and partly because
Elizabethan satire felt the need to insist on its morally corrective
purpose and political impartiality.

The first experiment in satire-dramatised which concerns the rise of
City Comedy appeared in 1597; it was Chapman's *An Humourous
Day's Mirth*. This play is slight in content and weak in comic
art, but it does give dramatic articulation to foolish characters
without employing a causally connected plot; instead, like a verse
satire, it offers a survey of types of folly, dramatically displayed and
ridiculed. The form owes something to the Interlude, too, and

Chapman's dramatic manner makes a virture of unconcealed exposition, is frankly theatrical. The character Lemot tells the audience plainly how and why the play adapts the older dramatic form:

COLINET The sky hangs full of humour, and I think we shall have rain.

LEMOT Why, rain is fair weather when the ground is dry and barren, especially when it rains humour, for then do men, like hot sparrows and pigeons, open all their wings ready to receive them.

COLINET Why, then, we may chance to have a fair day, for we shall spend it with so humorous acquaintance as rains nothing but humour all their lifetime.

LEMOT True, Colinet, over which will I sit like an old king in an old-fashion play, having his wife, his council, his children, and his fool about him, to whom he will sit, and point very learnedly, as followeth:
'My council grave, and you, my noble peers,
My tender wife, and you, my children dear,
And thou, my fool —'

COLINET Not meaning me, sir, I hope!

LEMOT No, sir: but thus will I sit, as it were, and point out all my humorous companions.[4]

Lemot is the Presenter of the humorous or foolish characters, and his role is to become a vital convention in Jacobean dramatic satire, taken up by Thersites in *Troilus and Cressida*, and by Pandarus when he points out the armed heroes to Cressida in I, ii, by Edmund in the speech in *King Lear* beginning

This is the excellent foppery of the world

by Vindice in the first scene of *The Revenger's Tragedy*, and very frequently in the plays of City Comedy.

Chapman's Presenter Lemot points out somewhat crudely explicit foolish behaviour in naive style:

LABERVELE I marvel much at my son's sudden strange behaviour.

LEMOT Bear with him yet my lord 'tis but his humour.

(vii. 218–220.)

More importantly, Lemot's function is also to effect the isolation of a character, from his stage companions and from the audience's

---

[4] *An Humorous Day's Mirth* ii 3–21 in *The Plays of George Chapman* ed. T. M. Parrott (London 1913 repr. New York 1961).

sympathy. Such characters are to be viewed analytically, we are to
see them with the satirist's critical eye, and Lemot's commentary on
the action from which he is detached invites a similar detached
attitude from the audience. For example in one sequence the
audience watches Lemot and Florilla meet Labervele, whom they
have both planned to gull. But Labervele privately takes the audience
into his confidence to assure them that Florilla is faithful to him
alone. The audience is involved in a three-cornered pattern of deceit;
it must conceal its glee at Labervele's egotistic absurdity which
allows him to be gulled. However the effect is not only to isolate
Labervele and ridicule him, but to expose the motives and conduct
of Lemot and Florilla. The participation is not sympathetic:

LABERVELE I long to see the signs that she will make (*Aside*)
FLORILLA   (*Aside* to LEMOT) I told my husband I would make these signs:
            If I resisted, first, hold up my finger,
            As if I said 'i'faith, sir, you are gone',
            But it shall say, 'i'faith, sir, we are one'.
LABERVELE [*Aside*] Now she triumphs, and points to heaven, I warrant you![5]

So, in a subsequent sequence, Lemot produces a witty, epigrammatic
description of a character, who then speaks, provoking Lemot to
criticise the speech in an aside to other detached observers. Lemot
tells these observers that he will demonstrate another aspect of the
character's folly; he does so absolutely as he predicted, and observers on stage applaud this entertainment elicited from the gull.[6]

Here then is the verse satire of Donne, in form at least, transferred
to the stage where the medieval and Tudor conventions of didactic
drama could be readily adapted to its basic needs. Chapman's
experiment is poor stuff, perhaps; but it has relevance to Jonson's
search for a dramatic form in which 'to strip the ragged follies of the
time'. For the sequences in Chapman's play may be distinguished
from Popular Elizabethan drama by their lack of relation to a main
theme or main plot. Whereas, even in early Shakespearean comedy a

---

[5] The subsequent sequence in which Lavel enters 'with a picture, a pair
of large hose, a codpiece, and a sword' intended to provoke Dowsecer's
humours ('To put him by the sight of them in mind of their brave states
that use them') clearly illustrates the rudimentary basis of comedy in Chapman's play.
[6] See scene viii, lines 185–251.

sequence of gullery, like that in Love's Labour's Lost IV, iii, where the three young nobles and the king in turn overhear each other's confessions and unmask and ridicule each other, is organically related to the main themes of the play and the development of the complex intrigue. Again, in Twelfth Night II, v, the gulling of Malvolio in the orchard may be harsher comedy directed to ridicule, but it is integrally related to the main intrigue and illuminates the deeper themes of the play imaginatively.

Jonson himself was sufficiently aware of the different formal nature of Humour comedy to cause the character Antonio Balladino — a burlesque of a Popular repertory hack such as Chettle, or Munday — to complain about the new plotless style of comedy. Balladino speaks of the old decorum before satire-dramatised; it is worth incidental inclusion here because Jonson shows his mastery of Popular comic style in the act of mocking that style: Balladino expostulates

> Why looke you sir, I write so plaine, and keep that old Decorum . . . mary you shall have some now (as for example, in plaies) that will have every day new trickes, and write you nothing but humours: indeede this pleases the Gentlemen: but the common sort they care not for't, they know not what to make on't, they looke for good matter, they, and are not edified with such toyes.
>
> (The Case is Altered I, ii. 58–65)

Here, early on in his career, Jonson reveals his love-hate relationship with Popular comedy in the vitality of this character whose stupidity and incompetence he ostentatiously despised.

Every Man In His Humour was performed at the Globe in 1598 and was successful. Although the 1616 version of the play was set in London, the original scene was Italy, and the closeness to Italian popular comedy of some of the characters and trickery episodes is apparent. Jonson followed Chapman in using a modified morality form for the play. The young gallant (Prodigality) sets out for the City (the World of Temptation) while warned of the dangerous New Guise which waits to snare youth. These warnings are phrased in dignified blank verse, the father lamenting the prevalence of 'geering follie, and fantastique humour'. True to type, the father calls in his servant Musco, who turns out to be the chief trickster. His devices have much in common with those of Ambidexter in Cambises, and the whole play reveals a familiar exemplary pattern. The two

aimable young prodigal-gallants Lorenzo and Prospero, aided by
their witty servant Musco, observe and devise tricks, and are in turn
caught by tricks; their experiences instruct them in the avoidance of
folly. Stephano the gull, Bobadilla the braggart, Matheo the poetaster,
and Thorello the jealous man act out their humours in a series of
episodes which conclude in correction or ridicule. Dr Clement
distributes judgement in the conclusion where the varied groups at
last are brought together. The atmosphere is genial and lively, sustained by richly varied Elizabethan popular prose dialogue, and great
physical immediacy of language. Yet it is worth looking closely at the
way Jonson uses the didactic dramatic form and gives coherence to
the otherwise accidental and unrelated series of episodes.

The third scene of Act II begins with the casual appearance of three
characters engaged in trying to impress each other; Bobadilla's
rare expressions outrun Matheo's citizen speech, but Prospero's
erudition makes its mark as truly witty:

BOBADILLA *Giuliano?* Signior *Prospero,* I know not in what kinde you value
          me, but let me tell you this: as sure as God I do hold it so much
          out of mine honor & reputation, if I should but cast the least
          regard upon such a dunghill of flesh; I protest to you (as I have
          a soule to bee saved) . . . I should not fancie him by *Phoebus.*
MATHEO   Troth nor I, he is of a rusticall cut, I know not how: he doth
          not carrie himselfe like a gentleman.
PROSPERO Oh Signior Matheo, that's a grace peculiar but to a few; *quos*
          aequus amavit Iupiter.
MATHEO   I understand you sir. (lines 6–18)

The true standard of witty speech is registered by Prospero the young
gallant, who is lively and spirited as befitting an Inns of Court or
University man; Prospero's conversation, like Lorenzo's, recalls
Thomas Nashe above all:

          how doest thou sweet raskall? my Genius? S'blood I shal love
          Apollo, & the mad Thespian girles the better while I live for this;
          my deare villaine, now I see there's some spirit in thee:
                                                              (20–23)

Prospero points out to Lorenzo the two gulls he has brought along,
and they delight in the *exemplum* which is about to begin:

PROSPERO . . . I pray thee be aquainted with my two *Zanies* here, thou wilt
          take exceeding pleasure in them if thou hearst them once, but
          what strange peece of silence is this? the signe of the dumbe
          man? [*points to Stephano*]

LORENZO Oh sir a kinsman of mine, one that may make our Musique the fuller and he please, he hath his humor sir.   (52–58)

The foolish characters now take the centre of the stage, Bobadilla's rare expressions and fine oath 'by the host of Egypt' competing with Stephano's humour of melancholy, which Stephano finds hard to keep up and asks for reassurance: 'Cousin, is it well? am I melancholie inough?' Matheo meanwhile has carelessly informed the company how 'true melancholy, breedes your perfect fine wit sir' and confesses

> I am melancholie my selfe divers times sir, and then do I no more but take your pen and paper presently, and write you your halfe score or your dozen of sonnets at a sitting.   (78–81)

Noticing the inactivity of Bobadilla the two Presenters urge the braggart into action. Bobadilla launches into a splendid military fantasy, the high absurdity of which recalls the wildly exaggerative style of Nashe's military burlesque in The Unfortunate Traveller. Jonson gives Bobadilla a speech wrought in almost rococo patterns of rhythm and syntax, where every clause seems to be the climax until the last moment, when it curves back to engender yet another flourish of ornate, non-functional decoration to the fantastic design:

BOBADILLA . . . ile tell you gentlemen, it was the first, but the best leagure that ever I beheld with these eyes, except the taking in of Tortosa last year by the Genowayes, but that (of all other) was the most fatall & dangerous exploit, that ever I was rang'd in, since I first bore armes before the face of the enemy, as I am a gentleman and a souldier.

STEPHANO So, I had as liefe as an angell I could sweare as well as that gentleman.

LORENZO Then you were a servitor at both it seemes.

BOBADILLA Oh Lord sir: by Phaeton I was the first man that entred the breach, and had I not effected it with resolution, I had bene slaine if I had had a million of lives. . . . Observe me judicially sweet signior: they had planted me a demy culvering, just in the mouth of the breach; now sir (as we were to ascend) their master gunner (a man of no meane skill and courage, you must thinke) confronts me with his Linstock ready to give fire; I spying his intendement, discharg'd my Petrinell in his bosome, and with this instrument my poore Rapier, ran violently upon the Moores . . . it is the most fortunate weapon, that ever rid on a

poore gentlemans thigh: shall I tell you sir, you talke of
Morglay, *Excaliber*, *Durindana*, or so: tut, I lend no credit to that is
reported of them,

(104–116, 123–130, 136–139)

Bobadilla's reiterated superlatives explode the bubble of bombast;
his oath 'by *Phaeton*' is ironically apt.

The tale of Bobadilla's sword allows Stephano the chance of
showing off the sword sold him earlier by disguised Musco. Both
Matheo and Bobadilla can now show off by ridiculing the prized
acquisition — 'This a *Toledo*? pish' — and when Musco appears to
give Stephano a chance of fighting, the poor gull's exposure is
complete, and the Presenters advise him to avoid further ridicule.
The *exemplum* concludes with Prospero's witty comparison of Stephano to a barber's virginals ('every one may play upon him') and
the two Presenters, well satisfied, go off with Musco to lay new
schemes.

There is assured dramatic art in Jonson's shaping of such comic
episodes, but we should notice that the play's freshness and vitality
derive also from what might be called mimetic syntax. The speech
of a character often seems to reveal the process of thought coming
across into words, and, as in the case of Musco's parody of a braggart
(in II, i) the effect can be very complex. Musco in this scene deliberately offers the gallants a chance to mock his huff-snuff boasting,
so he includes farcical improbabilities in his patter. But the whole
speech brings out the movement of a braggart's thought, jerking
awkwardly from one plausible bit of detail to the next, grabbing at
them anyhow in the effort to make an impression. Like a blind man
who has lost his stick, the braggart is so relieved to grab the next
idea or image that he certainly has no resources to spare for observing
other people or detecting their reactions. Musco's syntax in the
following passage acutely parodies the mental processes of Bobadilla,
while the ludicrous boasts and emphatic diction imitate more
obvious aspects of the 'humour':

I was twise shot at the taking of *Aleppo*, once at the reliefe of *Vienna*; I
have beene at *America* in the galleyes thrise, where I was most danger-
ously shot in the head, through both the thighes, and yet being thus
maim'd I am voide of maintenance, nothing left me but my scarres,
the noted markes of my resolution.

(II, i. 59–64)

In the final moments of the play, however, Jonson falls back on a boldly simplified technique where even comic ridicule gives way to a severe and harsh note of invective as the poetaster-dunce Matheo, like other foolish debasers of standards in social, moral and literary tradition, receives judgement. Disrespect for the rules of art, like disrespect for law, must be censured with the authority and weight of a whole society. Here the accent of Jonson's next three plays is heard clearly for the first time: the punishment of sackcloth and fool's motley is a taste of crueller mockery to come. The dialogue charts the transition from the mood of *Every Man In His Humour* to that of *Every Man Out Of His Humour*: Dr Clement examines the evidence of Matheo's poems:

CLEMENT   *In Sommer time when Phoebus golden rayes.* You translated this too? did you not?
PROSPERO   No this is invention; he found it in a ballad.
MATHEO   Fayth sir, I had most of the conceite of it out of a ballad indeede.
CLEMENT   Conceite, fetch me a couple of torches, sirha, I may see the conceite: quickly! its very darke!
GIULLIANO Call you this poetry?
LORENZO   Poetry? nay then call blasphemie, religion . . .
           Let all things be preposterously transchangd . . .
           But that this barren and infected age,
           Should set no difference twixt these empty spirits,
           And a true Poet: then which reverend name,
           Nothing can more adorne humanitie.
                              (*V*, iii. 297–305, 307, 340–343)

Jonson's more determined didactic purpose in *Every Man Out Of His Humour* dominates the atmosphere. The Induction, ostentatiously casual and negligent of the audience's wishes, gives the over-severe satirist Asper scope to express his scorn for the follies of the age, for poetasters 'plagued with an itching leprosie of wit', those who abuse the term 'humour' and especially those who threaten or seek to stifle the satirist's freedom to lash and scourge abuses. The tone of relentless severity insistently declares that Asper has read the Elizabethan satiric poets, but though there is a hint of parody in Jonson's portrayal of the satirist's *furor poeticus*, we are warned by the two critical observers Cordatus and Mitis that any such attitude of disrespect for satire can only arise from envy. It is the more re-assuring, therefore, when Carlo Buffone strolls on, glass in hand, and his genial wit 'places' the over-serious and reverential comments of Cordatus and Mitis.

These two detached observers provide a running commentary on nearly every one of the self-sufficient episodes, the *exempla*, which are otherwise not unlike those in *Every Man In His Humour* in form. Here however Jonson sets the whole comic substance of the play in a firmly shaped critical perspective to insist that the audience adopt a self-conscious stance of observant detachment. The search for a new comic form to replace the genially inconsequential romantic tale or knock-about farce, so popular on the Elizabethan Stage, was also a search for a new audience; if they did not exist, they must be created. The revolutionary fervour of Jonson dominates all other considerations in this play and in his next, *Cynthia's Revels*, and only in *Poetaster* is he again confident enough to give his comic imagination freedom.

The discussion in the Induction to *Every Man Out Of His Humour* shows Jonson taking account, publicly, of the demands made on comedy by educated and serious scholarly spectators, typified by Sidney in the *Apology*. Jonson accommodates their wishes but he also asks for artistic freedom to modify and to innovate. He reveres and imitates the Classics but, as he wrote in the *Discoveries*, 'to all the observations of the *Ancients*, we have our own experience: which if wee will use, and apply, wee have better meanes to pronounce'; Classical writers are best used as 'Guides, not Commanders'. To refresh Elizabethan comic art Jonson invoked the older tradition of Aristophanes against what seemed to him the hopelessly shapeless Romantic comedy of, say, Greene, the debased and clumsy stuff of Munday and Dekker, and the too exclusive and limited convention of Plautus and Terence. The new kind of comedy was to be more freely flexible and inclusive than the tone of Asper or Cordatus or indeed this play as a whole might lead us to expect.

The comic atmosphere of *Every Man Out Of His Humour* is not only interrupted by the comments of the observers, but is itself controlled by more sternly shaped language and incident. In the second scene of the play, for example, we have the encounter of envious Macilente with would-be gentleman Sogliardo, whom Buffone is preparing to gull. Their dialogue clearly reveals their contrasting Humours, but their roles imprison them so effectively that they are isolated from each other; the episode is more like a tableau, each figure can be

examined separately for the attitude he embodies. There is a minimum of interplay; they manipulate each other's humours:

MACILENTE I meane simply. That you are one that lives not by your wits.
SOGLIARDO By my wits? No sir, I scorne to live by my wits, I. I have better
          meanes, I tell thee, then to take such base courses, as to live by
          my wits. Sbloud, doest thou thinke I live by my wits?
MACILENTE (to BUFFONE) Me thinkes, Jester, you should not relish this well.
BUFFONE Ha? does he know me? . . . .
          Sbloud 'tis MACILENTE! Signior, you are well encountred, how
          is't? (Aside to SOGLIARDO) O, we must not regard what hee saies
          man, a trout, a shallow foole, he ha's no more braine then a
          butterflie, a meere stuft suit, he looks like a mustie bottle, new
          wickerd, his head's the corke, light, light. (to MACILENTE) I
          am glad to see you so well return'd, Signior.
MACILENTE You are? Gramercie, good JANUS.
SOGLIARDO Is he one of your acquaintance? I love him the better for that.
BUFFONE Gods precious, come away man . . . and you knew him as I doe,
          you'ld shun him, as you'ld doe the plague?
SOGLIARDO Why, sir?
BUFFONE O, hee's a black fellow, take heed on him.
SOGLIARDO Is he a Scholler, or a Souldier?
BUFFONE Both, both; a leane mungrell, he lookes as if he were chap-falne,
          with barking at other mens good fortunes: 'ware how you offend
          him, he carries oile and fire in his pen, will scald where
          it drops: his spirit's like powder, quick, violent: hee'le blow a
          man up with a jest: I feare him worse then a rotten wall do's
          the cannon, shake an houre after, at the report. Away, come not
          neere him.
SOGLIARDO For Gods sake let's be gone, and he be a Scholler,
                     (I, ii. 182–190, 197–219)

This dialogue charts the course of each obsessively intent mind as it
avoids or collides with obstacles in pursuit of its goal. The characters
come to seem so isolated and so incapable of sympathetic communi-
cation that they actually resemble the objects, composed of such a
variety of materials with hard, impermeable surfaces, to which they
are insistently compared. These evocative details insist on the surfaces, but they are usually dead, immobile, frozen or stylised:
Sogliardo is advised that he should 'looke with a good startch't face,
and ruffle your brow like a new boot' (I, ii. 58–59), while Buffone
later evokes with graphic immediacy the scene — from the theatre

audience's viewpoint — of Sogliardo's visit to an ordinary: the
choice gallants, 'when any stranger comes in among'st 'hem, they all
stand up and stare at him, as he were some unknowne beast, brought
out of *Affrick*'. The extent to which Jonson has frozen the surfaces, so
as to turn the event into a tableau, may be gauged by comparing the
passage in Donne which I quoted earlier: there, all was movement:

> Towards me did runne
> A thing more strange, then on Niles slime, the Sunne
> E'r bred; . . .
> Stranger then seaven Antiquaries studies,
> Then Africks Monsters, Guianaes rarities.

If the characters in the play have immediacy, it is not a life arising
from their mental processes; we do not see thoughts coming over
into speech. It is a life which may scintillate on the surface but which
rarely has organic vitality; beneath the surfaces there is vacancy.
This exactly parallels the traditional satiric habit of caricature, and
Donne himself frequently uses pictorial methods, as in the depiction
of Glorius:

> And though his face be as ill
> As theirs which in old hangings whip Christ, still
> He strives to looke worse,
>
> (*Satyre IV*, 225–227)

The problem of dramatising verse satire was primarily formal, since
the verse satirist focuses closely on details of behaviour in a social
situation, moving curtly and without much ceremony from one point
of focus to the next. The weight is concentrated on the independent
episodes which are related by their function of illustrating the
satirist's thesis. The satire's conclusion comes with the statement
of this thesis or with a climax of absurdity or viciousness, but
nevertheless the weight of interesting detail lies distributed in the
episodes and produces an inertia — the Elizabethan use of heroic
couplets for satire acknowledges this fact: the rhyme scheme
happily accommodates a series of epigrams or critical comments,
and brief crisp units add strength, vigour, and bite, especially when
syntax reinforces rhyme words. Jonson's difficulty in both *Every Man
Out Of His Humour* and *Cynthia's Revels* lies in trying to give movement
and dramatic life to a series of episodes, each self-sufficient and lacking causal connection to some main plot (strikingly in contrast to

those in a contemporary work of Shakespeare, *Henry IV*). In neither of his experimental comedies does Jonson overcome the inertia fully, and in fact the second play, *Cynthia's Revels*, becomes so hamstrung by the difficulty of setting static episodes in motion that it frequently grinds to a halt.[7] This characteristic pattern may be readily found in the movement of the play as a whole, in the movement of individual episodes, and in individual speeches. The set-piece of Amorphus on the hat in Act I Scene iv recalls similar fantasies of Bobadilla, Musco, and of course Nashe; but the rhythmic pattern alters half-way through, becoming terse, broken into wedgy segments; the weight of inertia seems to bring it to a halt more insistently as it nears the conclusion, and the tone lacks ebullience and exuberance:

> Sir, shall I say to you for that hat? be not so sad, be not so sad: it is a relique I could not so easily have departed with but as the *hiero-glyphicke* of my affection; you shall alter it to what forme you please, it will take any blocke; I have receiv'd it varied (on record) to the three thousandth time, and not so few: It hath these vertues beside; your head shall not ake under it; nor your braine leave you, without licence; It will preserve your complexion to eternitie; for no beame of the sunne (should you weare it under *Zona torrida*) hath power to approach it by two ells. It is proofe against thunder, and inchantment: and was given mee by a great man (in *Russia*) as a especiall-priz'd present; and constantly affirm'd to bee the hat, that accompanied the politike ULYSSES, in his tedious, and ten yeeres travels.
>
> (I, iv. 182–196)

Of course this is mere repetition of an earlier comic effect in the first humour play; but Jonson's inventive fire is low. Similarly, the sequence in which Amorphus gulls Asotus out of his new clothes parallels that in *Every Man In His Humour* II, i, where Musco sells the rapier to Stephano. But in *Cynthia's Revels* Jonson does not let the implications emerge from the action, instead the whole thing is laid out in a shroud, so deliberately and intrusively does the didactic

---

[7] Brecht notes this problem when discussing *The Threepenny Opera*, and remarks that the need is to avoid the shapeless inconsequence of a revue-like series of sketches and instead to create a form incorporating the experimental: 'it must be able to utilise associations in all directions; it needs static energy and has a tension which prevails in its individual parts and which "charges" these antithetically.' *Brecht Plays* trans. D. Vesey (London 1963), Vol. I, p. 188.

form restrict Jonson's invention: we see dramatist and characters
preparing for the incident, as it were, but Jonson-Crites lacks
vitality and glee:

AMORPHUS Ha! A prettie formall yong gallant, in good sooth: pitty, he is
          not more gentilely propagated. Harke you, CRITES, you may say
          to him, what I am, if you please: though I affect not popu-
          laritie, yet I would be loth to stand out to any, whom you shall
          vouchsafe to call friend.
CRITES   Sir, I feare I may doe wrong to your sufficiencies in the reporting
          them . . . O heaven! that any thing (in the likenesse of man)
          should suffer these rackt extremities, for the uttering of his
          sophisticate good parts.
ASOTUS   CRITES, I have a sute to you; but you must not denie mee: pray
          you make this gentleman and I friends.
          . . . .
CRITES   What ridiculous circumstance might I devise now, to bestow
          this reciprocall brace of butter-flies one upon another?
AMORPHUS Since I trode on this side the *Alpes*, I was not so frozen in my
          invention. Let mee see: to accost him with some choice rem-
          nant of *spanish*, or *italian*?

                          (I, iv. 34–40, 46–51, 76–81)

The absurdities and affectations of speech and pretentious behaviour
which Jonson ridicules in Cynthia's Revels are so intricate and so
trivial that they seem to have bored Jonson himself; the texture of
Amorphus' speech is an index to his substance as a character; it is to
break a butterfly upon a wheel, to spend a whole five acts exposing
such trifles. As the spectators remark on the entertainment in Act V,
'Tis too full of uncertaine motion. He hobbles too much;' it is
aptly 'call'd your *court-staggers*'. The experiments begin to bear fruit in
Jonson's next play, however; for in Poetaster there was a subject which
absorbed Jonson's central interests.

   There is a vigour and freshness in the conflict between affected,
humourous characters and sober, sane upholders of order, good
conduct and true poetry, in this most successful of the three so-called
Comical Satyres of 1599–1601. The approved normal character is
himself full of positive vitality, but Jonson's self-portrait as Horace is
successful also because of the equally positive energies embodied in
the rebelliously individual, perpetually explosive rival and anarchist,
Captain Tucca. Demetrius, too, is far from lacking comically

erratic attractiveness: his ridicule of Horace-Jonson is in the great
tradition of *Every Man In His Humour* and Elizabethan comic art:

> Alas, sir, HORACE! hee is a meere spunge; nothing but humours, and
> observation; he goes up and downe sucking from every societie, and
> when hee comes home, squeazes himselfe drie againe. I know him, I.
>
> (IV, iii. 104–107)

It is in releasing his creative energies in such characters that Jonson
reaches his full stature as a poet and dramatist; we may recall
W. B. Yeats' remark[8] 'that all happiness depends on the energy to
assume the mask of some other self; that all joyous or creative life is
a re-birth as something not oneself'. When Horace confronts Tucca
finally it is to witness his purgation, but Tucca has previously made
us closely acquainted with a wonderfully distorted and fragmentary
image of the poet: 'Hang him fustie *satyre*, he smells all goate; hee
carries a ram, under his arme-holes, the slave' and, more perceptively,
'A sharpe thornie-tooth'd *satyricall* rascall, flie him; hee carries hey in
his horne: he wil sooner lose his best friend, then his least jest.
What he once drops upon paper, against a man, lives eternally to
upbraid him in the mouth of every slave tankerd-bearer, or water-
man'. Instead of the pedestrian and clumsy didacticism of *Cynthia's
Revels* (where Crites-Jonson receives the praise and admiration of
fools and hypocrites in his absence, and is their model), here in
Poetaster such satiric schemes are assumed into the richer fabric of
characterisation. Tucca's aggressive ridicule of Horace-Jonson is a
mixture of shrewdness and nonsense; when his comments are not
objective, their reflection of Tucca's own mind and character is
both illuminating and comically effective; Tucca reveals his own
fear of being made ridiculous in a satire or satiric comedy, and
obliquely, unintentionally admits the justice and skill of Horace-
Jonson. The wild aggression frequently modulates into self-con-
gratulation, or changes direction to gain the favour of whoever is
present. It is a spendid moment when Tucca assumes equal authority
with Caesar, Virgil and Horace:

> Thou twang'st right, little HORACE; they be indeed a couple of chap-
> falne curres. Come, We of the bench, let's rise to the *urne*, and con-
> demne 'hem, quickly.
>
> (V, iii. 340–342)

---

[8] Cit. R. Ellman, *Yeats: the Man and the Masks* (London 1961), p. 177.

and no spectator can be without a regret when he is punished by being forced to wear a pair of vizards to emblemize his duplicity.

As in the scene where Tucca meets the players, Jonson combines his Popular comic genius with the newly adapted satiric form and discursive theme. The 'Parnassus' of two boy players, one standing on the other's shoulders, mimicking the old-fashioned tragic style, pleases the Popular taste of the captain, who dislikes 'humours, revells, and satyres, that girde, and fart at the time'. Yet the sympathy and assured skill with which Popular comic technique is used in this scene is representative. It is noticeable in the broad strokes of farcical humour — 'what's he, with the halfe-armes there, that salutes us out of his cloke, like a motion? ha?' — and the conventionality of the whole incident, and it also alerts us to other episodes based on such broad, familiar and traditional convention. The citizen Albius and his wife Chloe speak and act in a way highly reminiscent of Dekker's citizens in The Shoemakers' Holiday. The deft handling of Chloe's moment of fashionable behaviour has Popular convention to support it. Chloe has been instructed by Crispinus that she ought to seem bored and irritated, should stylish people visit her; but her husband lacks polite education:

ALBIUS   O wife, the coaches are come, on my word, a number of coaches, and courtiers.
CHLOE   A poxe on them: what doe they here?
ALBIUS   How now wife! wouldst thou not have 'hem come?
CHLOE   Come? come, you are a foole, you: He knowes not the trick on't.
                                                                    (II, i. 153–159)

Similarly, there is Popular convention behind the farcical comic reversal which reveals Captain Tucca's cowardice (in fact it echoes the discomfiture of Bobadilla in Every Man In His Humour IV, ii):

TUCCA   Valiant? so is mine arse; gods, and fiends! I'le blow him into aire, when I meet him next: He dares not fight with a puck-fist.
PYRGUS   Master, here he comes. (HORACE passes by)
TUCCA   Where? JUPITER save thee, my good poet; my noble prophet; my little fat HORACE. I scorne to beate the rogue i'the court; and I saluted him, thus faire, because hee should suspect nothing, the rascall:
                                                                    (IV, vii. 19–26)

The argument between Albius and his wife Chloe begins in the atmosphere and speech of Dekker, but as it develops their snobbish façades crumble in the heat and their 'hospitality' is exposed as social ambition, their 'love' as a contract. The situation — a domestic row in front of guests — is traditional comic material; but Jonson's adaptation of it to satiric purposes is original, and the ironic use of the manner and tone of Dekker fully realises the potential in the new form, and looks forward to his next successful play, the collaborative *Eastward Ho* of 1605.

As *Poetaster* draws to a close the serious theme finds expression through the form: it is not imposed upon it from outside. Indeed the purgation administered to Crispinus is not merely a memorable dramatic *jeu d'esprit*; it has the visual wit and the underlying serious-ness of Jonson's Classical predecessor Aristophanes himself. It is the climax of the theme that absurd and vicious speech, like absurd and vicious thought, conduct and feeling, must be castigated and corrected, because they are all interrelated; traditional rules nurture the mind, the language and the body politic; the satirist's highest purpose is enacted and emblemized by the purging of Crispinus:

CRISPINUS O — *oblatrant* — *furibund* — *fatuate* — *strenuous* — ... O — *clutcht.*
HORACE Now it's come: *clutcht.*
CAESAR Clutcht? It's well, that's come up! It had but a narrow passage.
CRISPINUS O —
VIRGIL Againe, hold him: hold his head there.
CRISPINUS Snarling *gusts* — quaking custard.
HORACE How now, CRISPINUS?
CRISPINUS O — *obstupefact.*

(I, ii. 499, 519–527)

Poetaster as a whole reveals also the ambiguous attitude of Jonson to folly. No man could fill his plays with such braggarts, rogues, poetasters, fools, gulls, coney-catchers and puritans without delight-ing in them also. The creator acknowledges the liveliness, as he castigates the folly of his creatures. It is characteristic that Jonson should allow Tucca to burlesque Homer himself, the rock on which Classicism stands; and it is characteristic too that Tucca should take the opportunity with both hands: Homer? —

Mary, I'le tell thee, old swaggrer; He was a poore, blind, riming rascall, that liv'd obscurely up and downe in boothes, and tap-houses, and scarce ever made a good meale in his sleepe, the whoorson hungrie begger.

(I, ii. 84–87)

F

In creating such a character as Tucca, Jonson shows the truth in Malraux's remark on realism: 'les grands artistes ne sont pas les transcripteurs du monde; ils en sont les rivaux'.[9]

[9] Quoted by Jonas Barish in his excellent study *Ben Jonson and the Language of Prose Comedy* (Cambridge, Mass. 1960).

5 The Giddy Sea of Humour

Marston's First Contribution

WE HAVE SEEN how Jonson explored the possibilities of a new, flexible comic form in which the discursive manner and wide-ranging preoccupations of verse satire could be expressed. In the early Comical Satyres Jonson tried to subdue the interest in mere story and the articulative function of plot in Popular comedy; instead, he strove to achieve a form in which satiric-didactic episodes, or *exempla*, could be articulated to illuminate a general thesis about respect for Art, the authority of tradition in social conduct, and the pernicious effect of fools, fops or poetasters on the commonwealth of men and of letters. In *Poetaster* Jonson had considerable success in this attempt partly because he did not scorn to absorb into his new style some of the rich vitality of Popular comedy and some of the dramatic excellence stored in that tradition.

Jonson's achievement may be seen more sharply by contrast with two dramatists who wrote under his dominant influence at this early stage. The comparison reveals how a traditional Popular playwright, Dekker, failed to grasp the fruitful possibilities of Jonson's experiment, whereas the young, but already somewhat notorious university wit, Marston, experienced in verse satire, was able to learn from Jonson's Comical Satyres and build upon their foundations.

Dekker's *Satiromastix*, though a cursory glance might suggest otherwise, is constructed on wholly Popular conventional lines, and is in

83

essence a romantic comedy in which the main plot, with verse
dialogue, deals with the love test, and its happy outcome, imposed on
the young couple Walter Terrill and Caelestine. The climax is the
melodramatic revelation that poor Caelestine, apparently dead, has in
fact merely had

> . . . ministred to her chaste bloud,
> A true somniferous potion,
>
> (V, ii. 99–100)[1]

so that the proven love of Terrill may be rewarded. The satiric matter
in the play is expressed in the low sub-plot of the gulling of Horace.
Most of this satiric matter surprisingly lacks the critical flavour of
Jonson and actually recalls more readily Shakespearean comedy, in
particular *Henry IV* and, suggested to Dekker perhaps by the similarity
in main plot, the comic elements in *Romeo and Juliet*. In *Satiromastix*
Dekker reproduces Jonson's character Captain Tucca, but here even
he vacillates between his Jonsonian original and that less coherent
braggart, Ancient Pistol:

> I know thou didst, and therefore whilst we have Hiren heere, speake
> my little dish-washers, a verdit Pisse-kitchens.
>
> (IV, iii. 243–244)

The play is firmly articulated by causal plotting, Jonson's experiments
in self-sufficient scenes in suspension are ignored by Dekker, perhaps because he sensed the demands made on the dramatist by the
new form, perhaps because the Horace-Tucca sub-plot was added as
an afterthought. It is certainly un-Jonsonian to find casual explanations
for the entry of Tucca:

> *Enter Tucca brushing of the crumbes.*
>
> TUCCA   Wher's my most costly and sumptuous *Shorthose?*
> SIR QUINTILIAN Is the King risen from table Captaine *Tucca?*
>
> (III, i. 99–100)

The characters in *Satiromastix* derive similarly either from the common
stock of Elizabethan popular romantic comedy or they are lifted from
Poetaster and modified, their most striking individual vitality now
anaemic: they join the ranks of stock figures in popular repertory.

---

[1] *Satiromastix* ed. F. T. Bowers in *The Dramatic Works of Thomas Dekker* (Cambridge 1953).

Horace speaks here only empty bombast, vulgar in tone, lacking in sinew or acerbity:

> dam me if I bring not's humor ath stage: and — scurvy lymping tongu'd captaine, poor greasie buffe Jerkin, hang him:
>
> (I, ii. 132–134)

while thinness in texture, in invention and in wit reduce Tucca to a mere braggart: Dekker has borrowed the most obvious tricks of speech, but produces only a veneer:

> Goe too, thou shalt now King Gorboduck, thou shalt, because Ile ha thee damn'd, Ile ha thee all in Sattin: *Asper, Criticus, Quintus, Horatius, Flaccus,*
>
> (I, ii. 339–341)

When Dekker apes Jonson's habitual manner of pictorial, epigrammatic description, his inadequacies stand revealed:

> hange her she lookes like a bottle of ale, when the cork flyes out and the Ale fomes at mouth, shee lookes my good button-breech like the signe of Capricorne, or like Tiborne when it is cover'd with snow.
>
> (III, i. 109–112)

the pile of words is a hurried attempt to catch the broad accent of a stage-dominating, salty braggart; it is too much to hope that Dekker intends to suggest, through parody, the potential absurdity in Jonson's most characteristic physicality in prose style, e.g.:

> the vitious Language is vast, and gaping, swelling, and irregular; when it contends to be high, full of Rocke, Mountaine, and pointednesse: as it affects to be lowe, it is abject, and creeps, full of bogs, and holes.[2]

Dekker only achieved the Jonsonian pose of critical analyst of manners in one place, the *Gulls Horn Book*: here wit is rare indeed; instead we find bald statement of faults, though not without real liveliness:

> th'ast entred Actions of assault and battery, against a companie of honourable and worshipfull Fathers of the law ... thy sputtering chappes yelpe, that Arrogance, and Impudence, and Ignoraunce, are the essentiall parts of a Courtier ... thou cryest ptrooh at worshipfull Cittizens, and cal'st them Flat-caps, Cuckolds, and banckrupts, and modest and vertuous wives punckes and cockatrices.
>
> (IV, iii. 184–186, 189–190, 194–196)

---

[2] Jonson, *Discoveries*, lines 2047–51.

This straightforward appeal to good sense and brotherhood lacks
any defence against the quick shafts of irony, parody and intellectual
spite; but it does have a manliness and a ring of solid genuine
conviction which might remind us of the retort of the Pedant to the
young nobles who so wittily, yet cruelly, ridicule him (presenting
Judas in the show of the Nine Worthies in *Love's Labour's Lost*) :

> This is not generous, not gentle, not humble.
>
> (*V*. ii. 629)

If Dekker has no skill in Comical Satyre, he has a positive talent for
creating situation comedy, straghtforward and broad, with the
minimum of dependence on verbal richness and subtlety. This is
characteristic of Elizabethan Popular comedy, and Dekker's method of
discomfiting Horace is that of the troops' concert: slapstick imitation. His norm of conduct is sturdy enough to measure Horace by:
the self-important, over-severe and *soi-disant* intellectual pose which
Dekker guys deserves such treatment, and the guying is not spiteful.
Thus, when Horace reveals his cowardice, thinking he has been
wounded by Tucca, Dekker is quick to sweeten the atmosphere with
a sunny enough jest: he does not lash his victim:

HORACE   Gentlemen, I am blacke and blewe the breadth of a groate.
TUCCA   Breadth of a groate? there's a teston, hide thy infirmities
>   (*IV*, iii. 145–146)

Perhaps Dekker instinctively grasps that more of Jonson's genius
goes into Tucca than into Asper or Horace. He divines the quarrel in
Jonson's art, and insists on the vital resources of traditional comedy
and its generous spirit, which can sustain and enrich Jonson's art.
If this is implicit, Dekker's explicit gesture is to hold out his hand
in manly friendship, an action as good-hearted as it is yeomanlike,
and, in the end, just and prophetic:

CRISPINUS   We come like your Phisitions, to purge
              Your sicke and daungerous minde of her disease.
DEMETRIUS   In troth we doe, out of our loves we come,
              And not revenge,
>   (*I*, ii, 247–250)

In contrast to Dekker, John Marston was not the man for gesture as
directly unambivalent as this, and such healthy, confident affirma-
tions find no real place in his art. In this sense it is perhaps

paradoxical that the didactic mode suited him so well. Yet the new
Jonsonian form, with its series of episodes loosely articulated by
satire's informing style and purpose, appealed to Marston as a way of
exploring those fluctuations of mood and personality ('personality is
an unbroken series of successful gestures', wrote Scott Fitzgerald)
which quickened his imagination and so often darkened his art with
images of madness and pain. In Marston's Comical Satyres the self-
sufficient episodes absorb the major creative energies; but though
there is a close general imitation of Jonson, with many episodes
(*exempla*) displaying and ridiculing absurd and fantastic behaviour,
there is a distinctive fresh contribution. In *Antonio and Mellida*, *What
You Will*, *The Fawn* and *The Malcontent* parody is often actually an informing principle; apparently serious episodes of distress or fury are
juxtaposed to parodies which disorder and undermine the spectator's
response. Marston, unlike Jonson, excludes none of his characters
from satiric analysis, and with an almost obsessive alertness displays
their capacity for evasion, hypocrisy and self-deception. In fact it is
not only the dramatist who uses parody to display such evasions; the
characters themselves use it consciously and continuously in social
contact and as a ready device in schemes. Of course these comedies
are frequently good humoured, and sometimes very funny indeed,
but it is a rare scene where the witty dialogue and comic situation is
not disrupted by violent images and disordered feeling. As Arnold
Davenport has argued, the non-dramatic and dramatic satires of
Marston, in their intensity and originality, may anticipate and in
some ways even initiate the dominant mood and preoccupations of
Jacobean drama. In the context of City Comedy Marston's importance lies in the exhibition of more profound and subtle ambiguities
of motive and personality through the medium of inherited kinds of
intrigue comedy and Comical Satyre. The Court and city settings
offer, at certain moments, images of the inner anxiety and psychological confusion of the characters; they become, in a sense,
emblems of their human condition.

In relation to the development of City Comedy, the first of his
Comical Satyres which is rewarding to study is *Antonio and Mellida*;
from there we can chart the development and experimentation which
finds a climax in his first masterpiece, *The Malcontent*.

Antonio and Mellida begins with an induction which introduces the
boy players to the audience and shows them playing now the part of

a boy actor, now of a dramatic character; the transitions are sudden, comic, and serve to blur our certainty of response; the emotions seem powerful, they arrest us — and then the pose is cast aside negligently:

ALBERTO   Ha, ha; one whose foppish nature might seem to create only for wise men's recreation, and like a juiceless bark, to preserve the sap of more strenuous spirits. A servile hound that loves the scent of forerunning fashion; like an empty hollow vault still giving an echo to wit, greedily champing what any other well-valued judgement had beforehand chew'd.

FOROBOSCO Ha, ha, ha; tolerably good; good, faith, sweet wag.

ALBERTO   Umph; why 'tolerably good; good, faith, sweet wag'? Go, go; you flatter me.

FOROBOSCO Right; I but dispose my speech to the habit of my part.[3]

The uncertainty of tone is most marked in the heroic rhetoric, where the extreme effects seem to suggest painful states of disturbance, but often modulate into deliberate bathos or turn into self-conscious *bravura*, adorned with well-wrought quotations. There is a curiously unsettled, restless activity in the diction and imagery:

> Antonio's lost;
> He cannot find himself, not seize himself.
> Alas, this that you see is not Antonio;
> His spirit hovers in Piero's court,
> Hurling about his agile faculties
> To apprehend the sight of Mellida.
> But poor, poor soul, wanting apt instruments
> To speak or see, stands dumb and blind, sad spirit,
> Roll'd up in gloomy clouds as black as air
> Through which the rusty coach of night is drawn.
>
> (IV, i. 2–11)

The effect of the induction is to alert us to the separation between the actors and their *roles* and to suggest the fragmentation of the personalities in the play, so that our response to the wild behaviour of Antonio in Act IV may easily be ambivalent — now moved by the quality of his grief, now alerted to the farcical posturing, the swooning, and the stylisation of the action, framed as it is by the farcical confusion of Piero's search for his daughter:

---

[3] *Antonio & Mellida* ed. G. K. Hunter (London 1965). Ind. 33–43

Pursue, pursue, fly, run post, scud away!
[*Feliche sings*, '*And was not good King Solomon*']
Fly, call, run, row, ride, cry, shout, hurry, haste;
Haste, hurry, shout, cry, ride, row, run, call, fly;
Backward and forward, every way about.

(III, ii. 261–264)

and the detached critical comments of the page on the duet in Italian which ends the sequence: 'I think confusion of Babel is fall'n upon these lovers'. G. K. Hunter's criticism of this part of the play valuably relates this dramatic style to that of opera, and sees the juxtapositions of apostrophes of love poetry and base vernacular in terms of counterpoint. The use of 'in suspension' episodes in the Jonsonian mode of Comical Satyre provides Marston with the form for his original and distinctive drama. The play is less sure and controlled than Jonson's, more completely at the mercy of fluctuating and erratic, though alarmingly violent surges of feeling which, in turn, ebb to uncover disgust and ridicule:

O that the stomach of this queasy age
Digests or brooks such raw unseasoned gobs
And vomits not them forth! O slavish sots!
'Servant,' quoth you? Foh! If a dog should crave
And beg her service, he should have it straight.

(II, i. 87–91)

This piece of invective, for example, bursts from the Presenter-Satirist Feliche after he has observed the antics of a rout of fools whose affectations closely resemble those of fools in Jonsonian Comical Satyre; Forobosco, in particular, who is described in the induction as 'the very periwig to cover the bald pate of brainless gentility', vies with Balurdo ('a fool, a noddy, a dizzard') in precious speech, while Feliche provides the audience with a critical commentary: the exemplary manner is apparent:

BALURDO . . . my leg is not altogether unpropitiously shap'd. There's a word: 'unpropitiously'. I think I shall speak 'unpropitiously' as well as any courtier in Italy.

FOROBOSCO So help me your sweet bounty, you have the most graceful presence, applausive elocuty, amazing volubility, polish'd adornation, delicious affability —

FELICHE Whop! Fut, how he tickles yon trout under the gills! You shall see him take him by and by with groping flattery.

FOROBOSCO — that ever ravish'd the ear of wonder. By your sweet self . . .
              I'll do you as much right in all kind offices —
FELICHE   — of a kind parasite.
FOROBOSCO — as any of my mean fortunes shall be able to.
BALURDO   As I am a true Christian now, thou hast won the spurs.
FELICHE   — for flattery.
              O how I hate that same Egyptian louse,
              A rotten maggot that lives by stinking filth
              Of tainted spirits. Vengeance to such dogs
              That sprout by gnawing senseless carrion!
                                        (II, i. 101–109, 115–124)

Marston's Presenter is himself a prey to extreme, perhaps obsessive
feelings; he is not so much a normal character, against whom the
fools are to be measured, as a wild opponent of their kind of obsession. The satirist is obsessive in pursuit of an extreme, is yet
another Humour character; the expression of extremes becomes a
principle of Marstonian dramatic form and the essential concern of
the comedies: their didactic purposes and their concluding re-
establishment of order and sanity become almost perfunctory.

The dominant influence of Jonson is most clearly manifest in
Marston's What You Will[4] and The Fawn,[5] where the form is modelled
on Comical Satyre, the pose of fearless, self-righteous and learned
satiric poet is imitated, and many episodes follow Jonsonian originals
in every detail. When, in a typical instance, the satiric Presenter
Quadratus is faced by the waterfly Lampatho admiring the affected,
absurdly dress-conscious fop Laverdure, the whole phrasing echoes
Cynthia's Revels I, iv, where Amorphus meets Asotus, while Quadratus
imitates Buffone's simile in Every Man Out Of His Humour III, vi:
Laverdure is dressing when Quadratus and Lampatho and Simplicius
(two fools) are announced:

LAVERDURE Mor du garzone: set my richest Gloves, Garters, Hatts, just in the
              way of their eyes, so let them in, observe mee with all dutious
              respect, let them in.
              [Enter Quadratus, Lampatho, Simplicius]
QUADRATUS Phoebus, Phoebe, Sunne, Moone, and seaven Starres make thee the
              dilling of Fortune, my sweet Laverdure, my rich French bloud,
              ha yee deere rogue, hast any pudding Tobacco?

---

  [4] What You Will ed. H. Harvey Wood (London 1938).
  [5] The Fawn ed. G. A. Smith (London 1965).

LAMPATHO   Good morrow Sinior.

SIMPLICIUS   Mounsieur Laverdure, do you see that Gentleman? hee goes but in
            black Sattin as you see, but by Hellicon hee hath a cloth of Tissue
            wit . . . Sinior Lampatho, heer is a French Gentleman Mounsieur
            Laverdure, a Traveller, a beloved of heaven, courts your
            acquaintance.

LAMPATHO   Sir I protest I not onely take distinct notice of your deere
            rarities of exterior presence, but also I protest I . . . very
            passionately doate on your inward adornments and habilities
            of spirit, . . .

QUADRATUS   Is not this rare now: now by Gorgons head,
            I gape and am struck stiffe in wonderment,
            At sight of these strange beasts.

                                        (What You Will II, i)

Marston's faithful imitation of Jonsonian Comical Satyre produces
many episodes of tedious triviality and futility, and threatens the
play with inertia when ill-advised scenes such as the grammar
lesson (II, ii) or the act of the pages (III, ii) are developed. The
sprawling Humour episodes certainly offer fashionable entertainment to the Coterie audience, but Marston's true energies go into the
Italianate comic intrigue which more vitally embodies his satiric
attitude to the characters. Whenever the intrigue plot takes over from
the sub-Jonsonian Humours, Marston's dramatic manner is re-
vitalised, his characters begin to devise trickery, their minds work
vigorously, they are exuberant:

RANDOLPHO   Now what a gigglet is this Celia?
ANDREA   To match so suddaine, so unworthely?
RANDOLPHO   Why she might have —
ANDREA   Who might not Celia have?
            The passionate inamord Jacomo.
JACOMO   The passionate inamord Jacomo.

                                        (I, i)

The device is for Francisco to impersonate the supposedly dead
Albano; both of them suffer from a very severe stutter, though
Francisco can produce a feigned stutter on request, as when he
adopts the role of Albano in III, i :

JACOMO   Me thinkes now, in the common sense of fashion,
            Thou shouldst grow proud . . .

FRANCISCO   Where is the strumpet? where's the hot vain'd *French?*
            Lives not *Albano?* Hath *Celia* so forgot
            Albano's love, that she must forthwith wed,
            A runne-about, a skipping *French-man* —
JACOMO   Now you must grow in heate and stut.
FRANCISCO   An odde phantasma! a beggar! a Sir! a who who who *what you*
            will! a straggling go go go gunds, f f f f fut —
ANDREA   Passing like him, passing like him

The audience can judge the performance for themselves, for in a
moment the 'real' Albano enters (he is not dead after all) and he
delivers a straight version of Francisco's parody lament on incon-
stancy: there is a strength of feeling in Albano's speech which is at
moments disturbing, especially in this equivocal context:

> the soul of man is rotten
> Even to the core; no sound affection.
> Our love is hollow-vaulted, stands on proppes
> Of circumstance, profit or ambitious hopes.
> The other tissue Gowne or Chaine of pearle
> Makes my coy minx to nussell twixt the breastes
> Of her lull'd husband, tother Carkanet
> Deflowres that Ladies bed
>
>   (III, i)

The audience's response is completely dislocated when Albano's
passionate declaration dissolves into irresistibly comic stuttering,
though Albano is actually gripped by agony and hysteria. Albano's
suffering and physical impediment are cruelly mocked, and the
sequence charts the disintegration of his personality, his collapse
into insanity, drowned in images of frightening incoherence:
Francisco's parody does in a sense prepare us for the Humour
demonstration, but it does not prepare us for the violence and
extremity of Albano's distress. Marston unexpectedly shifts the
range and tone from gaiety to menace, and the confusions of intrigue become at times a disturbing metaphor of insanity and nervous
collapse, as when Albano is mistaken for his impersonator (and told
to report to Jacomo that the disguise does not convince!) Marston's
dialogue suggests in its rhythms the extreme agitation of Albano:

ALBANO   *Jesu, Jesu,* what intends this? ha?
SIMPLICIUS O God Sir, you lye as open to my understanding as a Curtizan,
            I know you as well —

ALBANO   Some body knowes me yet, praise heaven somebody knowes
              me yet.
SIMPLICIUS   Why looke you Sir, . . . you are *Francisco Soranza* the Perfumer, I
              maugre *Sinior Satten,* I.
ALBANO   Do not tempt my patience, go to, doe not

in a few more moments Albano has broken down into stuttering
again and the cruel ridicule reaches its powerful climax.

What You Will is remarkable for the complex interweaving of
comic and satiric style, the variety of effects achieved through parody
and the uniquely Marstonian modulation of moods — from witty
gaiety to sombre menace, astringent, gleeful sadism, then back to
brittle mockery, often within a five minute sequence. The scourging
of stuttering Albano culminates in a sequence where Francisco
parodies him to his face, tauntingly, provokingly, up to a note of
extreme, refined agony. The comic vision is disquietingly close to the
tragic; Humours become insanity; and Marston's experimental
projection of the dramatic potentialities of satire reaches towards a
new mode of drama beyond the scope of comedy — but only
tentatively, here.

I wish to discuss *The Fawn* before *The Malcontent* although it seems
fairly certain that it was written later, because in this chapter we are
concerned with Marston's contribution to the genre, and so ought to
concentrate on the greater play, which I leave until last. In any case
The Fawn displays the influence on Marston of both Ben Jonson and,
I think, Thomas Middleton, and is a more conventional performance
in terms of the genre. Marston probably used the Disguised Duke plot
because Middleton successfully adapted it to satiric comedy in *The
Phoenix.* There the disguised son of the duke takes the role of Presenter
and Vice, by turns a detached, critical observer and an agent of
'lazzi' and satiric *exempla.* The plot allows for in-suspension episodes,
for the articulation of the Horatian satiric social survey, and for a
didactic conclusion when the duke unmasks and distributes judgement. It may be that Shakespeare's *Henry IV* initiated the convention,
but *The Phoenix* is a more recognisably satiric play.

Duke Hercules, Marston's Presenter, has an extraordinary gift for
acting the fawning flatterer, sardonic wit, and machiavellian courtier,
and he moves so easily in corrupt company that a kind of implicit
ambivalence in our attitude to him grows as the play proceeds.
There is a moment when Hercules pauses to address the audience in

his true role after his son has declared his motives towards Dulcimel.
Tiberio asserts his innocence in a disquieting speech full of possible
ambiguities:

> TIBERIO. . . . 'Tis past my knowledge, and I prithee, Fawn,
> If thou observ'st I do I know not what,
> Make me to know it, for by the dear light
> I ha' not found a thought that way. I apt for love?
> Let lazy idleness fill'd full of wine
> Heated with meats, high fed with lustful ease,
> Go dote on colour. As for me, why, death o' sense,
> I court the lady?
>
> (II, i. 538–545)

Tiberio's speech itself enacts, imaginatively, the rousing of those very
appetites and instincts, those quickened physical rhythms, which he
claims ignorance of: and he has already heard how his father's
claim to Dulcimel is made despite old age

> though he freeze in August, and his calves
> Are sunk into his toes,
>
> (II, i. 516–517)

Hercules has before this heard the corrupt courtiers maliciously
reporting that Tiberio

> said his father had the hipgout, the strangury, the fistula in ano, and a
> most unabideable breath; no teeth, less eyes, great fingers, little legs,
> an eternal flux, and an everlasting cough of the lungs.
>
> (I, ii. 190–193)

The thought must strike Hercules that neither the courtiers who tell
him this nor his son are deceived by his disguise, and all are combining to mock him savagely. He is moreoever shocked by over-
hearing plots and witnessing the unrelieved evil which swarms in
the court and society. He is, for example, ingratiatingly addressed by
the machiavel Herod:

> Dear Faunus, thou art now wriggled into the prince's bosom, and thy
> sweet hand should minister that nectar to him, should make him
> immortal.
>
> (II, i. 98–100)

Hercules-Faunus responds to such company with sardonic, gleeful
gaiety, urging them on to fuller, more inventive evil:

Afore the light of my eyes, I think I shall admire, wonder at you.
What? Ha' ye plots, projects, correspondences, and stratagems?

(104–106)

(we may recall the villain-hero of the contemporary *Tragedy of Hoffman*
and his exultant, partly comic outburst of glee

Trickes, and devices! Longings! well 'tis good:
Ile swim to my desires, through seas of blood

(*V*, ii.)

The courtiers themselves refer to Hercules-Faunus more than once as a
snake, thus uncannily divining his skill in disguise and temptation.
When he joins them to encourage and elicit their swarming plots and
corruption the following dialogue takes place:

HEROD   [*to Hercules who enters freshly suited*]
             Blessed and long lasting be thy carnation ribbon, O man of
             more than wit, much more than virtue, of fortune! Faunus, wilt
             eat any of a young spring sallet?
HERCULES   Where did the herbs grow, my gallant, where did they grow?
HEROD   Hard by in the city here.
HERCULES   No, I'll none. I'll eat no city herbs, no city roots, for here in
             the city a man shall have his excrements in his teeth again
             within four and twenty hours. I love no city sallets. Hast any
             canary?
NYMPHADORO How the poor snake wriggles with this sudden warmth.

(II, i. 30–40)

Hercules-Faunus moreover has a kind of satiric *sprezzatura* (to debase a
fine concept) which is unnervingly similar to the corrupt wit of
these courtiers; when they gather round a lady to compliment her,
Hercules offers this sardonic comment:

O, this is the fair lady with the foul teeth. Nature's hand shook when
she was in making, for the red that should have spread her cheeks,
nature let fall upon her nose; the white of her skin slipp'd into her eyes,
and the gray of her eyes leapt before his time into her hair; and the
yellowness of her hair fell without providence into her teeth.

(III, i. 75–80)

As this speech reveals, the play continually disrupts witty, conventionally inconsequential scenes with moments of savage cruelty or
horrible, repellent images. There is a strangely modern concern to
turn farce into sickening cruelty, to show the eruption of foul

thoughts, images, even actual pus through smooth, attractive surfaces.[6] There is really no brief for this in the medical imagery of Elizabethan verse satire, and in *The Fawn* the force of nervous energy released in cruelty to satirised and ridiculed characters is memorably disquieting, beyond the range of dramatic comedy. The chief butt of these attacks is Don Zuccone, who unlike the villainous courtiers of, say, *The Revenger's Tragedy* (who are similarly punished in sadistic stichomythia) simply does not seem to deserve it. Hercules himself is the agent of these attacks which even hurt Zuccone physically: Marston's unique feeling for the physical impact of words is noticeable so often in images which are themselves graphically clear, sharply focussed, but convey a feeling of confused, sickening movement, as in Antonio's famous speech

> the keen lightning shot
> Through the black bowels of the quaking air.
> Straight chops a wave, and in his slifter'd paunch
> Down falls our ship, and there he breaks his neck,
> Which in an instant up was belk'd again
> (*Antonio & Mellida* I, i. 216–220)

— this use of words to make a physical effect on the hearer is central to Hercules' cruel attacks on Zuccone:

HERCULES	. . . Hark ye, you'll tell nobody?
ZUCCONE	Not.
HERCULES	As you are noble?
ZUCCONE	As I am honest.
HERCULES	Your lady wife is apparently with child.
ZUCCONE	With child?
HERCULES	With child.
ZUCCONE	Fool!
HERCULES	My Don.
ZUCCONE	With child! By the pleasure of generation, I proclaim I lay not with her this — give us patience, give us patience —
HERCULES	Why? My lord, 'tis nothing to wear a forker.
ZUCCONE	Heaven and earth! . . . O Zuccone, spit white, spit thy gall out.

(II, i. 251–263, 286)

Later in the play a further cruel attack on Zuccone occurs, recalling

---

[6] I have discussed the comparable concern of Cyril Tourneur in my edition of *The Revenger's Tragedy* (London 1967) and suggested how the play is related to Comical Satyre.

the treatment of Albano in *What You Will*, and looking forward to
frequent occasions in mature City Comedy:

HERCULES	And now, lastly, done that for her . . . to be rid from such an unworthy —
HEROD	Senseless —
NYMPH	Injurious —
HERCULES	Malicious —
HEROD	Suspicious —
NYMPH	Misshaped —
HERCULES	Ill-languag'd —
HEROD	Unworthy —
NYMPH	Ridiculous —
HERCULES	Jealous —
HEROD	Arch coxcomb as thou art! [*Exeunt Nymphadoro and Herod*]
ZUCCONE	O, I am sick, my blood has the cramp, my stomach o'erturns.

(IV, i. 429–442)

Jonson may have initiated this kind of comic technique, but Marston
stamped it indelibly with his own unique power.

The play, like *What You Will* and *Antonio and Mellida*, is assured
dramatic comedy. It is intelligently shaped to expose the characters
to a satiric view which continuously probes with subtle though disquieting perception to their concealed ambivalent drives. *The Fawn*
has a more purposeful, assured and sinewy dramatic articulation —
the shaping hand is ever-present — and this is the result I believe of
the influence of Middleton, as well as Marston's own maturity as a
playwright. There is a key moment, to which I referred at the beginning of this discussion of *The Fawn*, where Hercules expresses his
profound sense of disquiet, his feeling of inner confusion, his
bewildered response to the folly and corrupt swirl of insanity and
depravity which the play brings alive. The Presenter's own response
to the play perhaps represents Marston's essential creation in Comical
Satyre: the state of unbalanced, disordered isolation in a world of
menacing, but also trivial and comic confusion:

> HERCULES Amaz'd, even lost in wond'ring, I rest full
> Of covetous expectation. I am left
> As on a rock, from whence I may discern
> The giddy sea of humour flow beneath,
> Upon whose back the vainer bubbles float
> And forthwith break.

(II, i. 548–553)

In *The Malcontent*, rather distinctly a separate achievement, Marston's success springs essentially from a rich organic coherence of theme, mode and dramatic form, rather than from the very incoherence of the comic action as in the early *What You Will* or *Antonio and Mellida*. The satiric impulse is the dynamic of the action and finds complete and satisfied expression since Duke Altofront is simultaneously Malevole, and his *role* as malcontent becomes a dramatic metaphor, so wittily yet seriously does it reveal the pervasive presence of disguise and lies in society.

The mask, not the face, is the true emblem of this world, and only with a mask can Malevole detect and reveal the other masks. The intrigues and 'lazzi' become the equivalent in dramatic action of masks; reversal at the conclusion of episodes closely corresponds to the iconographic and thematic reversal when finally Malevole unmasks to become Altofront, villain is metamorphosed into hero. Altofront's use of disguise is the ironic inverse of the devil's, whose work

> will but skin and film the ulcerous place
> Whilst rank corruption mining all within
> Infects unseen.
>
> (*Hamlet* III, iv. 147–149)

The Malcontent illustrates the characteristics of Comical Satyre clearly and fully, however. A casual opening is contrived with prophetically harsh discords from within and Prepasso's jesting insult to the audience: 'This room is ill-scented.' The arrival of Pietro and train locates the discords in Malevole's chamber, and a brief tirade from him, in terms reminiscent of Thersites, provides Pietro with an occasion for offering the audience a Theophrastian character sketch in Senecan style:

> His highest delight is to procure others' vexation, and therein he thinks
> he truly serves heaven; for 'tis his position, whosoever in this earth can
> be contented is a slave and damn'd;
>
> (I, ii. 20–23)[7]

and no sooner is this done than we are invited to observe this phenomenon in person:

---

[7] *The Malcontent* ed. M. L. Wine (London 1965).

PIETRO See, he comes. Now shall you hear the extremity of a malcontent:

The satirical and witty exchanges which follow raise, and play with, conventional subjects of Complaint and Satire, given life only by the rough diction and violent imagery:

> And how does my little Ferrard? Ah, ye lecherous animal! — my little ferret, he goes sucking up and down the palace into every hen's nest, like a weasel — and to what dost thou addict thy time to now more than to those antique painted drabs . . . Flattery, Pride, and Venery? . . . And how dost my old muckhill, overspread with fresh snow?
>
> (I, iii. 20–26, 34–35)

Malevole, however, has the vigour and high spirits of the Interlude Vice too, and in telling Pietro how there is reason for fearing cuckoldom, Malevole's encouragement seems ambiguous, he exults at Pietro's furious shame, even intensifies it so as to ridicule and punish Pietro (as Zuccone was ridiculed in *The Fawn*):

MALEVOLE A cuckold! To be made a thing that's hoodwink'd . . . the last must know it. Pistols and poniards! Pistols and poniards!
PIETRO Death and damnation!
MALEVOLE Lightning and thunder!
PIETRO Vengeance and torture!
MALEVOLE *Catzo*!

> (I, iii. 94, 98–103)

Indeed Malevole does not stop there, driving Pietro into a frenzy with his suggestions: the dialogue admirably conveys Pietro's mounting hysteria

MALEVOLE . . . clasps his own seed.
PIETRO Hideous imagination!
MALEVOLE Adultery! Why, next to the sin of simony, 'tis the most horrid transgression under the cope of salvation.
PIETRO Next to simony?
MALEVOLE Ay, next to simony, in which our men in next age shall not sin.
PIETRO Not sin? Why?
MALEVOLE Because (thanks to some churchmen) our age will leave them nothing to sin with. But adultery . . . I would dam him . . . I would not trust heaven with my vengeance anything.
PIETRO Anything, anything, Malevole!

> (I, iii. 134–144, 146–149)

As we might expect after this *bravura* performance, Malevole sheds his

disguise and shifts his role to Altofront and his speech to dignified
verse, giving us the sober lofty and judicial criterion against which
the fools and villains are to be measured, voicing the blameless
sentiments of the conventional virtuous man admiring another such :

MALEVOLE   O Celso, constant lord,
                     Thou to whose faith I only rest discovered,
                     Thou, one of full ten millions of men,
                     That lovest virtue only for itself,

(I, iv. 2–5)

Thus Marston faithful to the form of Comical Satyre, seems about to
close the first movement of the play, in which exposition is combined
with the initiation of intrigues by the Presenter-Vice, the voicing of
satiric commonplaces and the completion of one sequence punishing
and ridiculing Pietro. But as it closes it is interrupted by the wholly
unexpected arrival of Bilioso, a humour character and courtier, so that
a satiric *exemplum* inevitably follows. Now, at least, the scene seems
about to conclude, but then Mendoza the 'heavy villain' enters, and
so Malevole subjects him to a violent tirade strongly reminiscent of
Thersites' railing at Ajax, such another mongrel beef-witted lord.
This concluded to Malevole's satisfaction, and the casualness of the
incidents sufficiently emphasised to the audience, Marston ends the
scene at last.

The intrigue now gets under way in a swiftly succeeding cluster of
incidents, and the atmosphere of corruption deepens. It is intensified
rather than dissipated by the bathos of Pietro's attempt to revenge
himself on Mendoza :

PIETRO   . . . Say thy prayers.
MENDOZA   I ha' forgot 'em.
PIETRO   Thou shalt die!
MENDOZA   So shalt thou.

(I, vii. 2–3)

There is an undertone of menace in such farce as this; Pietro's
ineffectual vacillation deepens the disquieting uncertainty already
evoked by the disease imagery, by the nihilistic attitude of the
satirist Malevole, and by the very absence of coherent, causally
connected main plot.

The tough sardonic wittiness of Malevole, recalling Hamlet and
Donne — in The Apparition for example — curbs the tragic potential

of the action and continuously guides the meditations on disease, sin and death towards comic shallows. When Mendoza hears of Pietro's death he affects gravity:

> We, full of hearty tears . . .
> Cannot so lightly overjump his death
> As leave his woes revengeless.
>
> (IV, iii. 53, 57–58)

and despite the fact that Malevole is the supposed agent of this death and that the murder was supposedly horrible, and despite the full, serious moral implications in the main theme of the play, the dialogue is high-spirited, witty, fully comic:

MALEVOLE Now, you egregious devil! Ha, ye murdering politician! How dost, duke? How dost look now? Brave duke, i'faith!
MENDOZA How did you kill him?
MALEVOLE Slatted his brains out, then sous'd him in the briny sea.
MENDOZA Brain'd him, and drown'd him too? . . . I'll hoist ye; ye shall mount.
MALEVOLE To the gallows, say ye? . . . 'dieu, adieu, duke.

> (IV, iii. 67–71, 78–79, 85–86)

We are allowed the thrill of the murder of Ferneze, but he does not die, on the contrary he lives to provide a shock for Mendoza at the conclusion. Marston does indeed give us the thrill of tragi-comedy, 'the danger not the death', but no sooner is the deed done than Malevole appears, his witty detachment distancing and parodying the frightful:

MALEVOLE God arrest thee!
MENDOZA At whose suit?
MALEVOLE At the devil's. Ah, you treacherous damnable monster! How dost?

. . .

They say there's one dead here, prick'd for the pride of the flesh.

. . .

FERNEZE [*wounded*] O! A surgeon!
MALEVOLE Hark! lust cries for a surgeon. — What news from Limbo? How doth the grand cuckold, Lucifer?

> (II, v. 104–107, 114–115, 140–142)

The ridicule of death and tragic passion once completed, Malevole takes off his mask and in his *role* (real self?) of Altofront offers to

Celso a moral judgement on the whole satiric *exemplum* which, we
now see, has exposed the evil Machiavellian nature of Mendoza.
Tourneur took particular note of this rhythm (deriving of course
from Comical Satyre) when he wrote *The Revenger's Tragedy*. Malevole-
Altofront judges Mendoza by the standards of Complaint, with the
didactic clarity of a Morality drama:

> Celso, didst hear? O heaven, didst hear
> Such devilish mischief? Sufferest thou the world
> Carouse damnation even with greedy swallow,
> And still dost wink, still does they vengeance slumber?
> If now thy brows are clear, when will they thunder?
>
> (III, iii. 124–128)

The sequences in which Maquerelle the bawd appears have the loose
'in-suspension' form familiar from Jonsonian Comical Satyre, and the
dialogue ranges over the conventional preoccupations of Complaint
and Satire: sexual depravity, beauty of the flesh subject to ravaging
disease, the evils of painting the face, the horror of venereal disease.
Here too the wit and the jests serve to distance and curb the effect
of such sombre, disturbing meditations; however much Marston
admired *Hamlet* and the bedchamber scene, his achievement in the
Maquerelle scenes was original. Malevole's wit, tautened by inner
pressures, shapes and patterns the crowds of intensely physical
images; the wit seems to protect us from the swarming corruption
he evokes: the tone is critical:

> crabs' guts bak'd, distill'd ox-pith, the pulverised hairs of a lion's
> upper lip, jelly of cock-sparrows, he-monkeys' marrow,
>
> (II, ii. 18–20)

Maquerelle herself is less conscious of the need for distancing such
matters:

> MAQUERELLE Do you know Doctor Plaster-face? By this curd, he is the most
> exquisite in forging of veins, spright'ning of eyes, dyeing of
> hair . . . surfling of breasts . . . that ever made an old lady
> gracious by torchlight;
>
> (II, iv. 27–32)

When Malevole evokes the full sensual thrill of the pleasures of the
palace — so memorably that it served as a major inspiration to
Tourneur — he does so fully ironically, to put fear of cuckoldry in

Bilioso's mind. When Malevole pursues Hamlet's too curious consideration of how the noble dust of Alexander might stop a bung-
hole, his purpose is to awake fear of judgement and righteousness
in Pietro's breast. Thus however powerful and vivid Malevole's
imagination, he uses it self-consciously, with deliberate policy and
detached histrionic skill, to effect the schemes he, as Presenter-Vice,
has devised to expose, correct or destroy folly and evil. Marston's
originality and achievement are seen most clearly when we realise
that the echoes of Hamlet are serious parody: Malevole *acts* Hamlet
because he judges the performance will convince Pietro; it is a most
sophisticated and subtle modulation on the play-within-the-play,
and the guilty creature Pietro does indeed proclaim his malefactions,
'struck so to the soul'. Here is a brief quotation of Malevole's performance: the language has a representative harshness, the diction is
full of clashing consonants reminiscent of Complaint invective:

> Think this: this earth is the only grave and Golgotha wherein all things
> that live must rot; 'tis but the draught wherein the heavenly bodies
> discharge their corruption; the very muck hill on which the sublunary
> orbs cast their excrements. Man is the slime of this dung pit, and princes
> are the governors of these men; for, for our souls, they are as free as
> emperors,
>
> (IV, v. 107–113)

Marston's use of the form and conventions of Comical Satyre extends
inevitably to characterisation, and the gallery of fools, fawning
courtiers, bawds and Machiavels is drawn with stylised, graphic but
limited sharpness in the convention of Humour Comedy and satiric
caricature. Even Malevole, despite his high spirits, his vitality,
wittiness and intelligence, and his preoccupation with disease, sin
and death, is too much engaged by the demands of action in his role
as deviser of intrigue to reveal a full, rich character. Indeed Malevole
is so frequently acting or parodying other parts — including those of
Hamlet and Thersites from other plays altogether — that the audience
will have little time to enquire what his true identity is, unless they
feel unreasonably dissatisfied with the conventional — and rather
dull — duke Altofront.

The *Malcontent* is the fruit of Marston's experiments in his medleys,
and in *Antonio & Mellida*, *Antonio's Revenge*, *What You Will*. It seems
possible that the firmer shaping purpose in Marston's dramatic style
is due to the influence of Middleton's *The Phoenix* and the maturing of

Comical Satyre. Yet Marston's work is more original and valuable than such an account suggests. I have tried to show how the formative elements are transmuted into a unity of high intelligence, subtlety and power; Marston's use of the mask as a central symbol is a climax to his early experiments in the dramatic meanings of parody; in The Malcontent the satiric exposure and correction of vice and folly is absorbed into the poetic unity, and comic parody becomes a dramatic language to explore the perturbations of the mind and heart. Marston is no less shocking, funny, witty and disturbing here than in his other Comical Satyres, but he achieves a sustained, if necessarily precarious, coherence of didactic-satiric purpose, farcical and frightening intrigue, and frequently exuberant comedy. Marston's rich, and often ornate imagery, and continually varied rhythms are the more new and original for their very closeness to Donne and Shakespeare of the period of Hamlet. His language is not derivative, his art is that of the bee, not the spider, and his influence on the development of City Comedy is profound.

POPULAR DIDACTIC ART: Justice in the Stocks. Flettner's woodcut of 1525, reproduced by courtesy of the British Museum and Dr T. W. Craik.

MEDIEVAL SATIRIC ART: *The Dance of Death*. These four scenes reveal a direct relationshp between emblem and the stagecraft of didactic drama. The skeleton acts as Presenter-Satirist, detached critic and also exposer and ridiculer of folly and vice. The scenes satirise the aspirations of the astrologer and the avaricious man, the vain lady and her escort, and card players in a tavern—a representative selection of types in satiric poetry and satiric comedy. Holbein's emblems reveal something of the visual didactic tradition inherited by the playwrights of City Comedy.

The illustrations are from Holbein's *grosser Totentanz*. It is interesting to note that a similar role of Presenter is performed by the figure of folly, clad in cap and bells, in Holbein's woodcut illustrations to the *Praise of Folly* by Erasmus. The basic relevance of Erasmus' book does not perhaps need to be stressed in the present context.

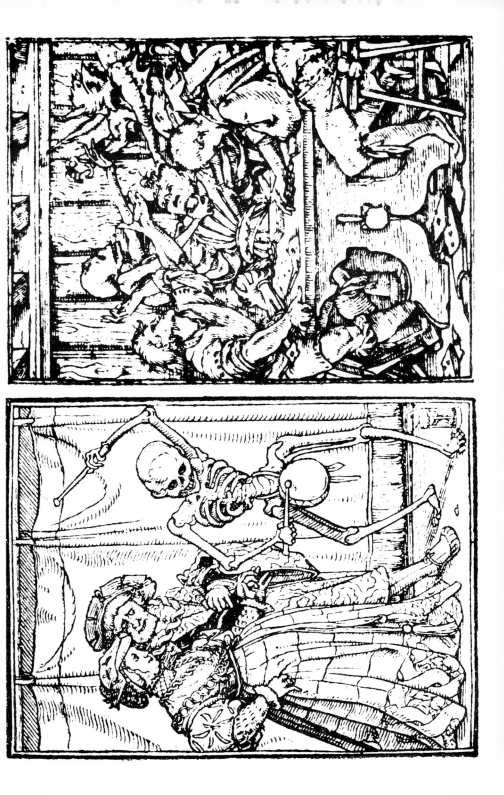

THE TRADITION OF ITALIAN POPULAR COMEDY: *A Scene from a Commedia dell'Arte Performance.* This illustration suggests how a good performance of *The Dutch Courtezan* or *A Trick to Catch the Old One* might have been originally staged, for it shows the characteristic elements which Jonson, Marston and Middleton adapted from Italian comedy and absorbed into the *genre* City Comedy. We see Harlequin stealing a kiss from the courtezan despite the attempts of the jealous old Pantaleone to frustrate him. The Zanni holds her up to accept Harlequin's kiss while simultaneously the tavern host pours wine down his throat.

Pantaleone is visually humiliated by the fact that Harlequin towers over him while kissing the courtezan. The stilts are a kind of image for the witty and ingenious devices of City Comedy tricksters.

Woodcut from the Recueil Froissard reproduced by courtesy of Professor Allardyce Nicoll from his Masks, Mimes and Miracles (London 1931) p. 264.

6 Middleton and the Establishment of a Form

IN THIS CHAPTER I want to trace the development of the *genre* in the comedies of Middleton up to the early climax in his *Michaelmas Term* and Marston's *Dutch Courtezan* and Jonson's *Volpone*: that is to say, from 1602 to 1605. It was after the comedies of Middleton and Marston that the repertory playwrights Dekker, Day, Barry, Field and the rest tried their hands at City Comedy, and their conventionalised work in turn provoked the parody *Eastward Ho*.

Middleton's *The Phoenix* of 1602 has a Presenter who comments on the folly and evil which is displayed, and the play ends with a judgement scene: the links with Jonsonian Comical Satyre are clear. However, the play also looks forward to Marston's *Fawn* in its plot and in its satiric attack on moral turpitude rather than social folly; so, as the *genre* develops, the echoes of Thomas Nashe diminish, and the harsh accent of Complaint grows louder.

In the Humour plays of Jonson set piece rhetorical statements indicated the criteria by which art, conduct or language were to be judged. In *The Phoenix*,[1] serious and uncompromising verse statements about morality precede or succeed prose sequences in which the folly or depravity is seen in action; but some of the follies lashed by Middleton — the sale of a virtuous wife, the murderous

---

[1] *The Phoenix* ed. the Rev. A. Dyce in *The Works of Middleton* (London 1840). All references to Middleton's plays are from this edition.

duplicity of a councellor — are more serious than those characteristic of Jonsonian Comical Satyre. From the outset the plays of Middleton have affinities with Marstonian Comical Satyre, but in contrast Middleton's dramatic method is shaped by a dominant driving purpose. His is not an art which delights in the creation of sequences 'in suspension'; Middleton succumbs to no fatal Cleopatras. This perhaps explains his choice of the Disguised Duke plot, since it must provide a more rigid causal frame for the *exempla*. Furthermore the elements of a Middletonian scene are co-ordinated in a way which inevitably and firmly presents the didactic lesson, and the purposeful control induces the admirable economy of satiric statement, the speed of action, and the sharp clarity of language, which go to sustain the excellence of his art.

Even in this first play the qualities of Middleton's mature dramatic art are discernible. The wit in the dialogue makes a sharp and neat effect, characteristically through implication. Justice Falso's openness to bribery is indicated urbanely:

1. SUITOR   I protest, sir, and this gentleman can say as much, it lies upon
             my half undoing.
JUSTICE   I cannot see yet that it should be so, — I see not a cross (coin)
             yet. [*aside*]
                                                                              (I, vi)

and here Falso hears of his brother's death:

FURTIVO ... made your worship his full and whole executor, bequeathing
             his daughter, and with her all his wealth, only to your dis-
             position.
JUSTICE   Did he make such a godly end, sayest thou?
                                                                              (I, vi)

'Godly' illustrates Middleton's manner of weighting a word with implication; more significant, perhaps, is the fact that Falso retains his vitality and his comic attractiveness even while Middleton ridicules him; Falso may be corrupt, but like the later villains of Middletonian comedy, he has splendid gusto, undeniable vigour:

[*Reading the will*] If she marry by your consent, choice, and liking, make her
dowry five thousand crowns: hum, five thousand crowns? therefore by my
consent she shall ne'er marry;
                                                                              (I, vi)

The wife sale is introduced by some dialogue in which the Presenter and his assistant discuss their plan, and the didactic purpose is clarified in the concluding moments of the *exemplum* where Phoenix has a verse set piece praising

> Reverend and honourable Matrimony,
> Mother of lawful sweets,

(II, ii)

We might think that the didactic point had been plainly enough made in the *exemplum*: indeed there Middleton's manner strongly reminds us of Brecht in its ironic shape:

FIDELIO   [*Reading the bill of sale*] In and to *Madonna Castiza, my most virtuous, modest, loving, and obedient wife* —

CAPTAIN   By my troth, my lord, and so she is. — Three, four, five, six, seven [*counting*] . . .

FIDELIO   *In primis, the beauties of her mind, chastity, temperance, and, above all, patience*—

CAPTAIN   You have bought a jewel, i'faith my lord — Nine and thirty. forty. [*counting*]

(II, ii)

the Captain observes in a line of striking savagery that his wife is

> as lovely a pennyworth, my lord, as e'er you bought in your life.

Middleton has contrived a situation where this seems superficially reasonable, even positive; it is the implications which make it plain that the Captain's attitude and behaviour are literally monstrous, and that Middleton is satirising the presuppositions of commerce, that everything has its price and can be bought and sold; the same implications swarm in Volpone's words

> I wound no earth with plow-shares; fat no beasts
> To feed the shambles; have no mills for yron,
> Oyle, corne, or men, to grinde 'hem into powder.

(I, i) (my italics)

Middleton chooses to hammer home the lesson by subjecting the Captain to a ridiculing sequence in the manner of Marstonian Comical Satyre

PHOENIX   . . . 'twas a most filthy, loathsome part —

FIDELIO   A base, unnatural deed— [*they discover themselves and lay hands on the Capt*]

CAPTAIN   Slave, and fool — Ha, who? O! —

PHOENIX   Thou hateful villain! thou should'st choose to sink,
           to keep thy baseness shrouded.
FIDELIO   Ugly wretch!

                                          (The Phoenix II, ii)

The mood of The Phoenix is not however darkly menacing on the
whole; the play is too controlled and too witty for that; and the
sequences satirising law and lawyers, which comprise a large segment
of the play, are plotted with the insistent complexity of farce; the
climax of the discomfiture of Tangle the lawyer, interminably
carrying on his own suits with money gained through ill counsel to
other litigants, comes in the familiar manner of Comical Satyre; the
tension breaks, he is lashed with words:

1. SUITOR   A judgment, a judgment!
TANGLE   What, what, what?
1. SUITOR   Overthrown, overthrown, overthrown!
TANGLE Ha? — ah, ah! — [enter 2. SUITOR]
2. SUITOR   News, news, news!
TANGLE   The devil, the devil, the devil!
2. SUITOR   Twice Tangle's overthrown, twice Tangle's overthrown!

                                                          (IV, i)

His discomfiture is farcical, ridiculous, but light hearted, even though
there are dark shadows behind his mad babble:

> I shall rot in fifteen jails: make dice of my bones ... quickly dip your
> quills in my blood, off with my skin,

these shadows lengthen and darken in Michaelmas Term — here the
speed of farce keeps them dancing.

The Presenter's role of commentator on follies and administer
of punishment derives immediately from Jonson's Comical Satyre
and the verse set pieces recall those similarly presented in the last of
Jonson's early comedies, Poetaster. Much of the satire in The Phoenix is
carried in Theophrastus-like epigrammatic character sketches and
there are City Comedy commonplaces parodied later in Eastward Ho:

> Sword and Buckler was called a good conscience, but . . . that was too
> manly a fight, too sound a weapon for these our days. 'Slid, we are
> scarce able to lift up a buckler now, our arms are so bound to the
> pox; one good bang upon a buckler would make most of our gentle-
> men fly a'pieces . . . our lawyers . . . quickly despatch your — money.[2]

---

[2] II, iii. cf. Eastward Ho V, i. 34–43.

and, more succinct,

> I cry ye mercy, sir; I call you gentleman still; I forget you're but a
> knight;

(II, iii)

The Jonsonian form is insisted on in the final purgation sequence,
imitated from *Poetaster*; here legal jargon is spewed up by Tangle

QUETO   ... Now burst out,
            Thou filthy stream of trouble, spite and doubt!
TANGLE   O, an extent, a proclamation, a summons, a recognisance, a
            tachment ...
QUIETO   You're quieter, I hope, by so much dregs.

(V, i)

Where Jonson is imitated, he is adapted to the Middletonian manner
even at this early stage.

The play has several complex trickery devices of Italian origin;
one of these sequences is worth noting for its dexterity, its wit and
its polish, showing (again at an early stage) a characteristic excellence
of Middleton's comic art. The 'lazzo' is that in which Phoenix enters
the Jeweller's house and is mistaken for the knight, lover of the
Jeweller's wife. Phoenix jars the doorbell by mistake, the maid
pushes him inside (it is dark) and he wittily manages the affair:

PHOENIX   Fair room, villainous face, and worse woman! I ha' learnt
            something by a glimpse a' th' candle. [*aside*]

The wife then delivers a piece of Complaint which has been directly
inverted from its conventional form; it is a piece of urbane invention
usually associated with Restoration rather than Jacobean Comedy:

> How do you think I am able to maintain you? Though I be a jeweller's
> wife, jewels are like women, they rise and fall ... Why, there's Metreza
> Auriola keeps her love with half the cost that I am at:

(IV, ii)

this urbanity (consisting in the taking for granted of immorality,
duplicity and corruption) is naturally best conveyed through
implication, in the most casual and matter-of-fact kind of dialogue;
(as in that remarkable comedy of Machiavelli, so often related to
English Restoration Comedy, *Mandragola*.) In the present case the
matter-of-factness is expressed by the maid who repulses the real

knight on his arrival; the knight asks that she tell her mistress 'her Pleasure's here'; the maid retorts

> Her pleasure? my mistress scorns to be without her pleasure at this time of night. Is she so void of friends, think you?
>
> (IV, iii)

In *The Phoenix*, then, we can see the formal influences of satire, the Interlude, and estates morality plays. The Presenter contrives or comments on a series of *exempla* satirising a corrupt judge, a grasping lawyer, a greedy Captain, an adulterous citizen's wife and a profligate knight. Two major satiric sequences are balanced by the fast moving 'lazzi' involving three Coney-catchers, and elsewhere the wife, the officers and the knight. Matter from Coney-catching pamphlets and Commedia dell'Arte repertory convention is adapted to the style of Comical Satyre, though already Middleton's purposeful and firm method of articulation makes a more direct and urgently driven comedy.

In *A Mad World My Masters*, as in *The Phoenix*, Middleton sets several verse pieces upholding conventional morality, at strategic points, emphasising the moral condemnation implicit in his direction of the action. These sober didactic passages give substance to a comedy which might seem dominated otherwise by the farcical plotting of Follywit. There is in any case more vigorous life and freshness in Follywit's deceptions of his grandfather Sir Bounteous than in the ironies of Harebrain's duping at the hands of the courtesan and Penitent Brothel. There is no moral force behind the tricking of Sir Bounteous, and the open cheerfulness points to a link with Coney-catching pamphlets. In the concluding sequence of the play there is a similar reluctance to press the darker implications of Follywit's marriage to a scheming whore (a conventional plot of the Commedia dell'Arte anyway) and Middleton is at pains to reproduce the sunny inconsequential atmosphere of a game of wit:

> FOLLYWIT Is't come about? tricks are repaid, I see.

Middleton has lightened the dark potential of earlier sequences, III, ii for example, which is typically Marstonian:

> An itching scab, that is your harlot; a sore scab, your usurer; a running scab, your promoter; a broad scab, your intelligencer;

Wit is evident in the verbal detail of dialogue, and in the epigram-

matic 'characters'. The wittiness there echoes the witty design which
Middleton builds up step by step in the sequences of deception;
complication calls attention to the dramatist's virtuosity. An
example may illustrate this clearly. A matter-of-fact conversation
between mother and daughter, it emerges, is in fact also a conversation between a whore and her bawd; the mother reminds the
daughter

> I have sold thy maidenhead
> To make up a dowry for thy marriage[3]

The blandness deepens the effectiveness; but Middleton has only just
begun. Harebrain now proceeds to congratulate the whore on her
mother's virtue and carriage (he knows nothing) and the whore
replies

> Sh'as always carried it well in those places, sir; — witness three
> bastards apiece. [aside]
>
> (I, ii)

Harebrain asks her to speak to his wife, to

> read to her the horrible punishments for itching wantonness, the
> pains allotted for adultery . . . rip up the life of a courtesan,

Naturally the whore remarks in an aside that to do so would be to

> speak ill of mine own function.

Middleton redoubles the irony. The whore informs Harebrain that
his wife believes that every sin is damned. At this Harebrain himself is
scandalised; according to his own logic, a logic which can be found
in Swift's satire The Abolishing of Christianity, to believe all sins are
damned is really sinful:

> There's a diabolical opinion indeed! then you may think that usury
> were damned; you're a fine merchant, i'faith! or bribery; you know
> the law well! or sloth; would some of the clergy heard you, i'faith; or
> pride; you come at court! or gluttony; you're not worthy to dine at an
> alderman's table!
>
> (I, ii)

---

[3] A Mad World My Masters I, i. Compare the general tone of the later A
Chaste Maid in Cheapside.

The use of 'diabolical' there may be compared to Swift's use of 'grievous prejudices' in the following passage:

> It is likewise proposed, as a great Advantage to the Publick, that if we once discard the System of the Gospel, all Religion will, of Course, be banished for ever; and consequently along with it, those grievous Prejudices of Education; which, under the Names of Virtue, Conscience, Honour, Justice, and the like, are so apt to disturb the Peace of human Minds; and the Notions whereof are so hard to be eradicated by right Reason, or Free-thinking, sometimes during the whole Course of our Lives.[4]

In Middleton the complexities and redoubled ironies of situation and language are not merely entertaining, but expose the fluctuating presence of meaning and value behind words, gestures and attitudes. In Middleton's final masterpiece *The Changeling* we have a famous example of this in Beatrice-Joanna's retort to De Flores, when he confronts her with her guilt for the murder of Piracquo:

> Why, 'tis impossible thou canst be so wicked,
> Or shelter such a cunning cruelty,
> To make his death the murderer of my honour!
> Thy language is so bold and vicious,
> I cannot see which way I can forgive it
> With any modesty.
>
> (III, iv)

Tourneur's *The Revenger's Tragedy* makes satiric comedy from the correlation between politic pretended belief in virtue and honesty, and the use of paint to make pocky faces appear smooth and healthy. Similarly in *The White Devil* Webster makes astringent comedy from Francisco de Medici's mockery of moral earnestness:

> Tush for justice!
> What harms it justice?[5]

Returning to *A Mad World My Masters*, we might now observe the effect in the following exchange when Harebrain thanks the whore for corrupting his wife (though he does not know it)

---

[4] Swift, 'An ARGUMENT *against abolishing* CHRISTIANITY' in *Bickerstaff Papers* ed. Herbert Davis (Oxford 1957).

[5] Webster, *The White Devil* V, iii. cf Hobbes: 'words are the counters of wise men but the money of fools' and see the essay on Webster by J. R. Mulryne in *Jacobean Theatre* ed. J. R. Brown and Bernard Harris (London 1960).

HAREBRAIN Here, wear this ruby for thy pains and counsel.
WHORE   It is not so much worth, sir; I am a very ill counsellor, truly.

                                    (*A Mad World* I, ii)

Similarly, when Follywit discusses himself with his grandfather
(Follywit is disguised) he tells his grandfather he will befriend
Follywit

>   I'll reserve a place for him nearest to my secrets.

                                    (II, i)

When Harebrain has been deceived by the whore, whom he believes
(erroneously) to have overheard talking to his wife, he is pleased.
In fact the whore has mimicked a conversation while Harebrain's
wife was in the act of adultery. Harebrain subsequently recommends
his wife to repeat the visit; she drily replies

>   Be not so fierce, your will shall be obey'd.

                                    (III, ii)

When Follywit proposes marriage to the whore (Sir Bounteous's
mistress) her mother observes

>   I know your grandsire well; she knows him better.

                                    (IV, v)

There follows the clearest example a moment later:

FOLLYWIT he (Bounteous) keeps a quean at this present.
MOTHER   Fie!
FOLLYWIT Do not tell my wife on't.
MOTHER   That were needless i'faith.

In the trial scene in *Volpone* the decisive argument is based on precisely this technique of contriving a situation where the flat truth has
the effect of a lie; Volpone, feigning sickness, is brought in on a
couch to the court; Voltore presents him to the court wholly
accurately and truthfully, and he is acquitted:

>   See here, grave fathers, here's the ravisher,
>   The rider on mens wives, the great impostor,
>   The grand voluptuary! do you not think,
>   These limbes should affect *venery*? . . .
>   Perhaps, he doth dissemble?

                              (*Volpone* IV, vi. 23–26, 29)

In *A Mad World My Masters* Middleton relies on situation and implica-
H

tion for his satiric effect; the decorum of such fast-moving, complex Italianate comic style inhibits the fuller development of character and the more subtle penetration of experience; the play is not by any means a major achievement, but it is of interest, like *The Phoenix* and *Your Five Gallants*, for what it reveals of Middleton's apprenticeship, and for the early treatment of themes which dominate his two important comedies and his later play *Women Beware Women*, in many ways so close to City Comedy.

The latter part of *A Mad World My Masters* is noticeably more inconsequential, light-hearted and trivial. Middleton drains away the force of the bad characters, particularly the whore, so that the final scene can be festive in mood and the play satisfactorily symmetrical in design. In this respect it may be compared to Marston's *The Fawn*. Both plays treat themes which are handled more powerfully in subsequent comedies.

Middleton's *Your Five Gallants* is ostentatiously conventional in conception, for its characters derive clearly from the Interlude tradition and there is some of the naive and adolescent energy of the older style in Middleton's play. The five young protagonists are placed in a series of exemplary situations, and there are 'lazzi' deriving from Italian popular comedy. The Italian air in the ingenious and fast-moving trickery is reinforced by the solid, traditional, Northern, moral preoccupations of dramatic satire.[1] The clarity with which the components of City Comedy declare themselves in this play is remarkable.

The satiric aims of Middleton are more sharply and seriously realised here than in *A Mad World My Masters*. There are several confessions made by characters which give the flavour of moral tract familiar from Coney-catching pamphlets. Primero the bawd gallant confesses proudly that

---

[1] It might be worth noting that the significance, in the history of City Comedy, of such plays as *A Looking Glass for London and England* or *The Three Ladies of London*, lies in their very simple form for a dramatic survey of social types, though we should remember of course that there is a literary influence — from Complaint tradition if not satiric poetry — on such plays themselves. They are wooden, without the subtlety of insight and dramatic life to be found both in Elizabethan satiric poetry and City Comedy. Mr Dessen happily does not over-emphasise the influence of such plays on Jonson, in his article in *Renaissance Drama VII* (1964).

> Many over-cheated gulls have fatted
> Me with the bottom of their patrimonies,
> E'en to the last sop, gaped while I fed 'em,
> Who now live by that art that first undid 'em.[6]

More elaborately and memorably Pursenet the pocket gallant reflects on the ironically regular, orderly, commercial-style pattern of criminal civil war:

> Does my boy pick and I steal to enrich myself, to keep her, to maintain him? why, this is the right sequence of the world. A lord maintains her, she maintains a knight, he maintains a whore, she maintains a captain. So in like manner the pocket keeps my boy, he keeps me, I keep her, she keeps him; it runs like quicksilver from one to another.
>
> (III, ii)

A chain of pearl, too, runs like quicksilver from one to another. It appears in successive trickery sequences, acting as a kind of leitmotiv. Its recurrence suggests to the audience the underlying repetitive, mechanical nature of seemingly varied criminal schemes.

One remarkable and influential convention in City Comedy shaped by Middleton is the lyrical outburst of the villain of the piece, full of eloquent high-spirited vitality yet presented with implicit irony. In the present play the broker gallant rhapsodises:

> Here's a diamond that sometimes graced the finger of a countess; here sits a ruby that ne'er lins blushing for the party that pawned it; here a sapphire. O providence and fortune!
>
> (I, i)

This recalls Falso in The Phoenix:

> I have been a youth myself: I ha' seen the day I could have told money out of other men's purses, — mass, so I can do now, — ... I remember now betimes in a morning, I would have peeped through the green boughs, and have had the party presently, and then to ride away finely in fear: twas e'en venery to me, i'faith, the pleasantest course of life!
>
> (III, i)

and looks forward to Quomodo's vision of his ill-gotten gains in Michaelmas Term:

> O that sweet, neat, comely, proper, delicate parcel of land! like a fine gentlewoman i' th' waist, not so great as pretty, pretty; the trees in

---

[6] Your Five Gallants I, i.

summer whistling, the silver waters by the banks harmoniously gliding . . . Thus we that seldom get lands honestly, must leave our heirs to inherit our knavery:

(II, iii)

and beyond that to Old Hoard in *A Trick to Catch the Old One*:

What a sweet blessing hast thou, master Hoard, above a multitude! wilt thou never be thankful? . . . not only a wife large in posessions, but spacious in content; she's rich, she's young, she's fair, she's wise:

(IV, iv)

It is Middleton's achievement here to admit the full human attractiveness of these characters; though they may act criminally they are still intelligent. If you prick them they bleed, but they are also very likely to stab you in return. Materialists fascinated Middleton, and though he satirises them persistently, the effect can be disturbingly ambiguous, as in *A Chaste Maid In Cheapside*. Of course the ironic design has been called Calvinistic in its determined purpose: the recurrence of situations in which a lie has the appearance or effect of truth, and vice versa, produces a dramatic atmosphere in which finally the deceiver deceives himself, confounded by the fact that

nothing is
But what is not.

In Jacobean tragedy the mannered complexity of plot based on peripeteiea creates an atmosphere in which every event seems to close the net on villainy even while the villains are triumphant; and while there are no deaths in comedy, it is this use of peripeteiea (of which Middleton is the Jacobean master) which strengthens the attack on the usurer-villains. Nevertheless in these comedies one senses the ever present question: is it possibly sheer luck that they are caught out, in life as in dramatic comedy? We recall that the seducer in Machiavelli's *Mandragola* succeeds in seducing the wife and beginning the affair, and then — the play ends! There is no retribution because he is successful, and no divine justice can interfere. Such a fearlessly empirical approach was too disturbing, perhaps, for the English Jacobeans; at least it must *seem* that morality triumphed.

Your *Five Gallants* betrays readily, as I have already remarked, its formal origins in Comical Satyre. Fitzgrave has the role of Presenter, and early on (I, ii) resolves

> cunningly I'll wind myself
> Into their bosoms. I've bethought a shape,
> Some credulous scholar, easily infected
> With fashion, time and humour . . .
>   I'll see
> Whether their lives from touch of blame sit free.

Soon, in the brothel, he offers commentary on the action:

> None that shall see their cunning will believe it
>   (II, i)

he discovers that he has been robbed, and informs the audience in an aside; thus isolating himself from the other characters, he waits behind when they depart and tells us

> My pocket pick'd? this was no brothelhouse!
> A music school? damnation has fine shapes:
> . . . I will find these secret mischiefs out.
>   (II, ii)

Later in III, iv he plots his progress for our better understanding

> I have found three of your gallants

and by IV, v he is able to announce

> The broker-gallant and the cheating-gallant:
> Now I have found 'em all,

Meanwhile he has enjoyed Pursenet's pale imitation of Falstaff lying about the Gadshill robbery and soon afterwards suffers Goldstone's foppish humour (recalling *Every Man Of His Humour*).[7] It is Fitzgrave who administers punishment to the vices, and though the over-schematic device of the masque seems laboured, the fact that the gallants are made to admit their sins and suffer correction in a ritualistic manner sufficiently recalls Jonsonian Comical Satyre. Fitzgrave's glee in his role of punisher is notable: it is like Vindice's:

> 'Twas I fram'd your device, do you see? 'twas I:
> The whole assembly has took notice of it.
> That you are a gallant cheater,
> So much the pawning of my cloak contains; [to *Goldstone*]
> You a base thief, think of Coombe Park; [to *Pursenet*] . . .[8]

---

[7] Ibid IV, v. cf. *Every Man Out Of His Humour* IV, vi. 72–118.
[8] *Your Five Gallants* V, ii cf. *The Revenger's Tragedy* III, v. 164–165.

and in the flyting match at the end of Act IV the accent of Marstonian
invective splutters

PURSENET   Why should you be so violent to strip naked
             Another's reputation to the world,
             Knowing your own so leprous? . . .
TAILBY   . . . a filthy-slimy-lousy-nittical broker, pricked up in pawns
             from the hat-band to the shoe-string . . . his lice must needs be
             mongrels:

as Pursenet echoes the first principle of Jonsonian Comical Satyre, to

        strip the ragged follies of the time
        Naked, as at their birth.

Here, of course, the action is driven forward with firm purpose: it is
a fast moving, deftly plotted comedy, the wit leaps nimbly over the
darker streams of disquiet, pain and evil, directing us to them by
implication. Middleton's comedies are not densely sown with
lustrous, dark images; the language is bare of the elaborate rhythmic
patterns, the over-wrought figurative language of Marston's comedies.
Middleton's syntax has precision, clarity, order: these are the
characteristics of his playmaking, here are the affinities with Brecht.

At this point I propose to break the study of Middleton's successive
Coterie comedies and to consider Marston's contribution of 1604,
The Dutch Courtezan. I do this because Marston's play plainly benefits
from the work of Middleton we have just been considering, while
Middleton's own comedy Michaelmas Term is better seen in comparison
with a play of Jonson, written by 1605; — Volpone. The development
of the genre indeed owes more to these two plays of Jonson and
Middleton than to The Dutch Courtezan.

Essentially The Dutch Courtezan differs from Marston's earlier comedies
in its reliance on a strong main plot, that of the whore Franceschina's
attempted murder of Freevill. The series of 'lazzi' performed by
Cockledemoy therefore form, in effect, a sub-plot. This strong main
plot is in itself notable for the forcefulness with which it articulates
Marston's dark satiric preoccupations — there is a new sinew and
purpose in his direction of the action. The fact that Franceschina is
probably his best drawn dramatic character indicates Marston's
intense engagement with the main action. Of course the 'lazzi' are not
directly related to the main plot, but the variety and excellence of

these trickery sequences similarly recall the dramatic method of
Middleton: they are well plotted, fast moving, direct, and as the
National Theatre Company recently demonstrated, very funny.

Marston's strong main plot is in itself a didactic *exemplum*, a moral
tale. This change from the pattern of early Comical Satyre is further
marked by the satire, which here is less a matter of displaying
foolishness and foppishness than of penetrating psychological study
of evil and sexuality in the characters. The world of *The Dutch
Courtezan* is one turbulent with violence and evil: the play is only by
the narrowest of margins satiric comedy rather than tragedy; a
detached sardonic spirit informs the writing, and its sinew and
muscle ripple the dialogue:

> But employ your money upon women, and, a thousand to nothing,
> some one of them will bestow that on you which shall stick by you as
> long as you live. They are no ingrateful persons; they will give quid for
> quo: do you protest, they'll swear; do you rise, they'll fall; do you fall,
> they'll rise; do you give them the French crown, they'll give you the
> French — [9]

Marston displays intelligent strategy in delaying the entrance of
Franceschina; it is preceded by the introduction of the two male
protagonists Freevill and Malheureux and of the stock clichés about
prostitution. When Franceschina appears, a creature of vital spirits,
flesh and blood, the clichés from Complaint are set in a new, less
reassuring perspective. Freevill, it becomes clear, is a hypocrite who
evades his own nature by twisting arguments:

> ... dost thou not somewhat excuse my sometimes incontinency with
> her enforcive beauties? Speak!
>
> (I, ii. 93–95)

Malheureux attempts to conceal his sudden powerful excitement
with the subject, and Freevill emphasises the ambiguity of the situation and the hypocrisy underlying conventional attitudes to
prostitution:

> Whore? Fie, whore! You may call her a courtesan, a cockatrice, or (as
> that worthy spirit of an eternal happiness said) a suppositary. But
> whore! Fie! 'tis not in fashion to call things by their right names. Is
> a great merchant a cuckold, you must say he is one of the livery ...

[9] *The Dutch Courtezan* ed. M. L. Wine (London 1965) I, i. 111–117.

is a gallant pocky, you must say he has the court scab. Come, she's
your mistress, or so.

(ibid. 97–103)

The intelligently handled theme of the play — the ambiguous nature
of sexual desire and its tortured relationship with public morality —
is fully integrated in the history of Franceschina. She is discarded
because she is only a whore, and Marston's art is sure in depicting
the situation; Franceschina is in a fury when her ex-lover, now her
enemy, appears; the menace implied in her change of tone is
memorably violent:

FRANCESCHINA . . . ick sall have the rogue troat cut . . . Now legion of devil
              seize him! De gran' pest, St Anthony's fire, and de hot
              Neapolitan poc rot him!
              [Enter Freevill and Malheureux]
FREEVILL   Franceschina!
FRANCESCHINA O mine seet, dear'st, kindest, mine loving! O mine
              tousand, ten tousand, delicated, petty seetart!

(II, ii. 41–48)

There is no doubt about the depth of the shock suffered by this
'mere' whore.

Marston undermines the verse set pieces upholding virtue and
right conduct. They are ostensibly meant as didactic pointers against
which the exempla of temptation by the lusts of the flesh are to be
measured and understood; but though the form of The Dutch
Courtezan is didactic in the manner of City Comedy, and though the
whore is outwitted and punished in the conclusion, Franceschina is
too profoundly human to function as a mere embodied Morality
Vice: she introduces disturbing distinctions into the ostensible
black-versus-white conflict. It is worth illustrating this further.

Franceschina forms the idea of using Malheureux to destroy the
lover who has rejected her out of considerations of respectability and
legality. The dialogue admirably suggests by implication the hate-
love passion of Franceschina, imaged in her oath:

FRANCESCHINA Yes, yes, but ick do not love dis same Freevill.
MALHEUREUX   Well?
FRANCESCHINA Nay, I do hate him.
MALHEUREUX   So?
FRANCESCHINA By this kiss, I hate him!

(II, ii. 142–146)

the dialogue at the climax to this temptation scene is rhythmically ordered to heighten the emotional crescendo:

FRANCESCHINA Oh, let me forget it; it makes us both despair.
MALHEUREUX Dear soul, what vow?
FRANCESCHINA Hah! Good morrow, gentle sir; endeavour to forget me as I must be enforced to forget all men. Sweet mind, rest in you!
MALHEUREUX Stay, let not my desire burst me. Oh, my impatient heat endures no resistance, no protraction! There is no being for me but your sudden enjoying.
FRANCESCHINA I do not love Freevill.
MALHEUREUX But what vow? what vow?
FRANCESCHINA So long as Freevill lives, I must not love.
MALHEUREUX Then he —
FRANCESCHINA Must —
MALHEUREUX Die!

(II, ii. 155–167)

There is a difficulty in Marston's conception of Freevill and Malheureux which arises from the City Comedy form of the play. Ostensibly they are the applauded upholders of morality who present and comment on the *exemplum* that whores, being Godless, are in every way vicious and dangerous predators in the commonwealth. Yet the set pieces on the evil of prostitution sound oddly forced on the lips of these two gallants, and Malheureux is a doubly uncertain character, mouthing pious platitudes such as

To kill my friend! Oh, 'tis to kill myself.

after he has shown himself to be wholly at the mercy of selfish desires and voracious lust. It is possible to argue that Marston has sacrificed consistency of character to the demands of comic form; this play, like The Fawn, must end cheerfully, so Franceschina must be ridiculed, the young gallants must triumph and light-heartedness must attend the conclusion. Yet it seems that the most satisfactory account of the play — as with Marston's Comical Satyres — is that which attends to Marston's creative use of parody as an informing dramatic principle. The inconsistency between the predictable formality of the plot and the ambiguous nature of the pseudo-conventional characters becomes a symbol of Marston's real dramatic subject: the dual nature of personality, the dominance of mask and parody in life, the absurdity of narrow formulations of experience symbolised by the convention of the happy ending and the moral conflict of black-versus-white.

I think that the intensity and depth of Marston's conception of Franceschina is masterly, and that Marston subordinates the didactic form of City Comedy to a more subtle and penetrating demonstration of the ambivalence and menacing dangers lurking in the darkness of the heart. The 'lazzi' provide a comic but at the same time a cruel counterpoint to the violent schemes of the courtesan and the heartless schemes of the gallants. Freevill may win, like Cockledemoy, but there is no moral approbation implicit in that victory, and both of them really merit the hanging which poor Mulligrub so nearly suffers. The accidental comedy of the latter's pardon is an apt comment on the total disorder and injustice of the London in which *The Dutch Courtezan* is set.

It is a peculiarly Marstonian talent to take a comedy so deep into the waters of tragedy. It is Freevill who is the helmsman, and at the end he becomes a witty malcontent; he is even gleeful:

> Well, I am great
> With expectation to what devilish end
> This woman of foul soul will drive her plots:

At her final disgrace Franceschina is given no opportunity to attack the gallants or defend herself — and thereby to wreck an ending which seems deliberately smug. In her final appearances Franceschina displays memorable vitality, a passionate naked power rarely equalled by women in Jacobean drama. Marston's psychological study of jealous hate is perhaps unique in its concentrated power to shock us:

> Vill you? Vill you mak-a her run mad? Here, take dis ring; say me
> scorn to wear anyting dat was hers or his. I pridee torment her.
>
> (*V*, i. 92–94)

I have tried to show how Marston uses the conventions of form, style and character familiar in City Comedy, but at the same time how they are parodied and undermined to offer satiric questioning of conventional moral attitudes and simplistic, self-protecting formulations of sexuality.

In *Michaelmas Term* as in *Volpone* and *The Revenger's Tragedy* there is a dominant masterful design: plot is paramount. There is a unity of

tone in the three plays — a tough sardonic detached wittiness — and
this gives the plays a common dramatic style. The clarity and sureness of the action, the symmetry of plot, tend to stylise action and at
times to distance the shocking or horrible: it is through this
distancing that Jonson's and Middleton's plays retain the decorum
of comedy, and that Tourneur's evades the full dimensions of
tragedy.

The plays all deal with violent and rapacious urban societies and
all begin by setting forth the violent dynamism of the society in
which their villains thrive. It is a society composed of actively
scheming, intelligently criminal agents. Quomodo sets before us the
commercial Machiavel whom we have met before in Marlowe's
merchant of Malta, Barabas:

> give me the man
> Who out of recreation culls advantage,
> Dives into seasons, never walks but thinks,
> Ne rides but plots:[10]

while in *Volpone* Mosca delivers the most memorable hubristic
soliloquy in City Comedy about the skill of the trickster and the
joys of witty duplicity:

> But your fine, elegant rascall, that can rise,
> And stoope (almost together) like an arrow;
> Shoot through the aire, as nimbly as a starre;
> Turne short, as doth a swallow; and be here,
> And there, and here, and yonder, all at once;
> Present to any humour, all occasion;
> And change a visor, swifter, then a thought!
> This is the creature, had the art borne with him;
>
> (III, i. 23–30)

When Vindice's schemes are about to burst into success he cries out
exultantly

> Oh sweet, delectable, rare, happy, ravishing!

This is the exuberance of Mosca

> Successe hath made me wanton. I could skip
> Out of my skin, now, like a subtill snake,
>
> (III, i. 5–6)

---

[10] *Michaelmas Term* I, ii. The fuller history of such characters is given in
Bernard Spivack's *Shakespeare and the Allegory of Evil* (Oxford 1958).

and the glee of Quomodo:

> Now, my sweet Shortyard; now the hungry fish begins to nibble;
> one end of the worm is in his mouth, i'faith.
>
> (II, iii)

All three plays end in double *peripeteia* which ridicule and outwit the
villains at last; but certainly Volpone and Quomodo seem unlucky,
the dramatists force their defeat through plotting, while Vindice's
reversal from success to judgement and execution is a witty jest as
well as a moral condemnation, and Vindice strides off with un-
ruffled elegance and unmarred facility for conceits. The reversal
scenes are contrived with comic art, though the savage passions and
deeds of the characters belong to the darker profundity of tragedy
in their *uncontrolled* intensity.

Although *The Revenger's Tragedy* alternates between moods and styles
of tragedy and satiric comedy, the formal elements of the *genre* are
readily detectable there, as also in *Volpone* and *Michaelmas Term*, and
this seems worth discussion. All three plays have didactic *exempla*
shaped with the most astringent satiric keenness, all three contain
set pieces setting forth the critical conclusions to be deduced from
the *exempla*; all three contain conventional Humour characters and
fools, and these are displayed by Presenters; the plays all articulate
satire on general themes traditional to non-dramatic satire, such as
social decay and greed, and its repercussions on the members of the
commonwealth: thus we find in *Michaelmas Term*

> Woe worth th'infected cause that makes me visit
> This man-devouring city! where I spent
> My unshapen youth, to be my ages curse,
> And surfeited away my name and state
> In swinish riots,
>
> (II, ii)

and in *Volpone*

> VOLPONE I turne no moneys, in the publike banke;
>   Nor usure private — MOSCA No, sir, nor devoure
> Soft prodigals. You shall ha' some will swallow
> A melting heire, as glibly, as your *Dutch*
> Will pills of butter, and ne're purge for't;

> Teare forth the fathers of poore families
> Out of their beds, and coffin them, alive,
> In some kind, clasping prison,
>
> (I, i. 39–46)

In *The Revenger's Tragedy* conventional Complaint can be epigrammatic:

> Oh she was able to ha' made a userer's son
> Melt all his patrimony in a kiss,
>
> (I, i. 26–27)

or it can become transformed, ironically, into a kind of apostrophe to evil:

> Faith if the truth were known I was begot
> After some gluttons dinner — some stirring dish . . .
> When base male bawds kept sentinel at stair-head,
> Was I stol'n softly —
>
> (I, ii. 178–179, 186–187)

or it can be meditative, discursive:

> Some that were maids
> E'n at sunset are now perhaps i' the toll-book;
> This woman in immodest thin apparel
> Lets in her friend by water, here a dame
> Cunning, nails leater hinges to a door
> To avoid proclamation.
> Now cuckolds are a-coining, apace, apace, apace, apace!
>
> (II, ii. 137–143)

These three plays share an ethical framework and an inherited tradition of articulating such didactic themes.

The main plot itself has the didactic force of an *exemplum*. Here it may be more pertinent to show how the form of the shorter episodes belongs to the satiric-didactic convention of City Comedy.

The Revenger's Tragedy offers the most obvious links with Morality drama, for Vindice is the Presenter from the first scene of the play, and has this role too in tempting his mother and sister (II, i), in serving Lussurioso in disguise, and in the famous sequences in the summer house (III, v) and at the conclusion (V, iii). In these sequences Vindice is an agent, but his aim is to expose and cruelly punish and ridicule folly and evil. The ridicule is urbane, though taut, when Vindice pretends to share Lussurioso's glee at the anticipated seduction of Vindice's own sister (an episode which has debts to Marston's *Malcontent* and *Fawn*):

LUSSURIOSO   We may laugh at that simple age within him —
VINDICE   Ha! Ha! Ha!
LUSSURIOSO   Himself being made the subtle instrument
             To wind up a good fellow
VINDICE   That's I my lord.
LUSSURIOSO   That's thou.
             To entice and work his sister.
VINDICE   A pure novice!
LUSSURIOSO   'Twas finely managed.
VINDICE   Gallantly carried: a pretty-perfumed villain!
                                        (I, iii. 138–145)

The memorable ridicule sequences have the farcical ebullient energy of *Poetaster* except that the crimes are murder, rape, and incest, not verbal eccentricity, and the punishment is stabbing or poisoning, and verbal torture in the style created by Marston:

DUKE   Oh Hippolito — call treason! [*sinking down, poisoned*]
HIPPOLITO   Yes my good lord. Treason, treason, treason! [*Stamping on him*]
DUKE   Then I'm betrayed.
VINDICE   Alas poor lecher: in the hands of knaves
             A slavish duke is baser than his slaves.
                                        (III, v. 154–158)

In *Volpone* the plot is so conceived that Volpone and Mosca can torment their victims with elaborate and exquisitely wrought devices; the early sequence in which Corbaccio visits Volpone is full of admirably sharp ironies:

MOSCA   A freezing numnesse stiffens all his joynts,
             And makes the colour of his flesh like lead.
CORBACCIO   'Tis good.
                                        (I, iv. 43–44)

Here the effect is doubled by the fact that the audience knows that Volpone is fully awake and listening to Corbaccio, that he is delighting in Mosca's device, while there is metaphoric truth in Mosca's grotesque portrait of his master. The ambiguity of Mosca's motives in viciously ridiculing his patron emerge in the next sequence with

Corvino: unsuspicious of Mosca, Volpone comments on the Corbaccio *exemplum*, himself returning the savage ridicule:

> VOLPONE Nay, here was one,
> Is now gone home, that wishes to live longer!
> Feeles not his gout, nor palsie, faines himselfe
> Yonger, by scores of yeeres, flatters his age,
> With confident belying it,
>
> (I, iv. 151–155)

In the next sequence Mosca encourages Corvino to express all the hate in his bowels: both yell insults at the supposedly deaf and dying Volpone:

> MOSCA Those filthy eyes of yours, that flow with slime,
> Like two frog-pits; and those same hanging cheeks,
> Cover'd with hide, in stead of skin: (nay, helpe, sir)
> That looke like frozen dish-clouts, set on end.
> CORVINO Or, like an old smok'd wall, on which the raine
> Ran downe in streakes.
> MOSCA Excellent, sir, speake out;
>
> (I, v. 57–62)

Volpone compliments Mosca, on Corvino's exit, tells him

> Thou hast today out-gone thy selfe.

Looking over the gold and jewellery he has been brought, and recalling the deceptions practiced by Mosca, he declares

> Why, this is better then rob churches, yet;
> Or fat, by eating (once a mon'th) a man.
>
> (ibid. 91–92)

The display of the folly in Sir Politique Would-Be and the talkative Lady Would-Be is in the manner of Comical Satyre; we are on familiar ground of Comical Satyre when we find that Sir Politique despises Homer and Classical precepts, and Jonson's implied criticism is plain. Sir Politique has, he says, not come abroad to pursue

> That idle, antique, stale, grey-headed project
> Of knowing mens minds, and manners, with ULYSSES:
>
> (II, i. 9–10)

Instead his mind is full of absurd, trivial or obstinately perverse distortions of ideas from politics, scientific experiment, capital investment in industry, astrology, portents. He has heard that a professional clown was a spy and received intelligence

> (For all parts of the world) in cabages;
> And those dispens'd, againe, to'Ambassadors,
> In oranges, musk melons . . .

His language is as affected as the clumsy contrived styles in *Cynthia's Revels*: and the demonstration of his fatuously trivial mind is clear and harsh: here Peregrine reads from Politique's diary:

> I went, and bought two tooth-pickes, whereof one
> I burst, immediatly, in a discourse
> With a *dutch* merchant, 'bout *ragion del stato* . . .
> I cheapen'd sprats: and at St*MARKES*, I urin'd.
> 'Faith, these are politique notes!
> <div align="right">(<i>IV</i>, i, 139–141, 144–145)</div>

This English pair of fools are the more sharply etched by being set, as travellers abroad, in Venice; Jonson has etched out the permanent lineaments of the vain fool abroad; his ironic method here is brutally direct:

> POLITIQUE Within the first weeke, of my landing here,
> All tooke me for a citizen of *Venice*:
> I knew the formes, so well —
> PEREGRINE And nothing else.
> <div align="right">(<i>IV</i>, i. 37–39)</div>

Volpone's attempt to seduce Celia is an admirable parody of materialist rhapsodies, and owes something to *Tamburlaine*; it is the main purpose of Jonson to show through satiric exaggeration the perverse and disgusting detachment of Volpone from natural and vital enjoyments; having chosen to adore and merely possess gold, brighter than the life-giving sun, holier than God, far transcending

> All stile of joy, in children, parents, friends,
> Or any other waking dreame on earth

Volpone can only find stimulation in such precious absurdities as this:

> Thy bathes shall be the juyce of july-flowers,
> Spirit of roses, and of violets,

> The milke of unicornes, and panthers breath
> Gather'd in bagges, and mixt with cretan wines.[11]

Jonson's imagination is touched by Volpone's sheer fantasy, just as he is stimulated by the incredible lengths of absurdity to which plodding, crazed Sir Politique carries his projects; in satirising their almost Marlovian fantasies, Jonson is half seduced himself. Similarly, the intelligence and the intensity of savagery in Volpone sufficiently dominate the play to necessitate an error of judgement by Mosca to bring about his fall. Mosca does not realise that rather than be outwitted and ridiculed, Volpone by nature would prefer to destroy everything he can, along with himself; for he has what Hobbes defined as

> a perpetual and restless desire for power after power that ceaseth only in death.

The suspicion that Volpone is merely unlucky to fall is not without justification.

Michaelmas Term, though like *Volpone* having a powerful villain who is the Presenter and sardonic commentator on some of the main episodes, works more through implication than Jonson's play; though it seems clear that Quomodo's creation owes something to Volpone. The darker, violent atmosphere of London in *Michaelmas Term* seems to derive from the impact made on Middleton by *Volpone*, yet it is an individual creation. Middleton's usurer has common blood with Volpone, but he lacks his fantastic imagination and his intelligence; he lacks, too, a parasite with the sublime art of Mosca.

Michaelmas Term has for a main plot a modernised, urbanised version of *Everyman*. The young innocent abroad is conventional and Middleton clearly indicates the kind of play we can expect in the opening scene; the conventional situation itself is perfunctorily sketched, it is the urgent activity in the language, the compression of statement, which urges us that the play will be alive. Soon enough Quomodo appears, with his two parasites: his vitality, his energy, and his greed surge in the dialogue, full of active verbs:

QUOMODO . . . I have seen what I desire.
SHORTYARD A woman?

---

[11] III, vii. 213–216, cf. Sir Epicure Mammon's fantasies in *The Alchemist*.

I

QUOMODO Pooh, a woman! yet beneath her,
        That which she often treads on, yet commands her;
        Land, fair neat land.
SHORTYARD What is the mark you shoot at?
QUOMODO Why, the fairest to cleave the heir in twain,
        I mean his title; to murder his estate,
        Stifle his right in some detested prison:
        There are means and ways enow to hook in gentry,
        Besides our deadly enmity, which thus stands,
        They're busy 'bout our wives, we 'bout their lands.

It is Quomodo's affinity with Volpone which we note here, (even if
we disregard the parallel with the opening scene of Jonson's play)
and a moment later Quomodo scents his prey:

I have inquired his haunt — stay, — hah!
ay that 'tis, that's he, that's he! . . .
Observe, take surely note of him . . . Keep foot by foot with him, out-
dare his expenses, flatter, dice and brothel to him . . . drink drunk with
him, creep into bed to him, kiss him, and undo him, my sweet
spirit.

                                        (I, i)

The urgent, excited activity of Quomodo's mind here rushes ahead
of the moment and sees the whole scheme acted out; his hungry
imagination devours the land. The process of destroying Easy
('execution' is the term used by Quomodo's wife) begins with
Quomodo's rhapsody in praise of land, comparable to the lyrical
outbursts of earlier villains of Middleton (see my discussion of
Your Five Gallants). Quomodo's lyricism is strikingly at odds with his
sharp brutality, and there is indeed irony in his desire for land,
repository of traditional healthy order and stability. Quomodo's
attempt to buy, or worse steal, his way into such an order is parallel
to Old Hoard's grotesquely commercial and cynical rhapsody in
praise of his new wife and her inheritance: Middleton's ironic
method is the same in both instances:

What a sweet blessing hast thou, master Hoard, above a multitude!
wilt thou never be thankful? . . . she's rich, she's young, she's fair,
she's wise: when I wake, I think of her lands — that revives me;
when I go to bed, I dream of her beauty — and that's enough for me:
                (*A Trick to Catch the Old One* IV, iv)

The use of ironic juxtaposition is a further sign of Middleton's shaping didactic purpose. A scene between a plain honest mother and her vicious, materialistic son makes a firm didactic point about the dehumanisation by urban evil of the prodigal Lethe:

MOTHER	I'll wait upon your worship.
LETHE	Two pole off at least.
MOTHER	I am a clean old woman an't like your worship.
LETHE	It goes not by cleanness here good woman; if you were fouler, so you were braver, you might come nearer.

(Mich. Term I, i)

This *exemplum* is counterpointed by that of the Country Wench, who is ostensibly tempted but, being in fact totally corrupt, allows herself to be persuaded by Hellgill's 'rhetoric':

HELLGILL	thou art fair and fresh;
	The gilded flies will light upon thy flesh.

as the country boy is contrasted to the country girl, so the evil Quomodo is set against a good countryman, the girl's father, who himself began as a city prodigal. In the episode where Easy is overcome (IV, i), Quomodo's wife has an entrance exactly as Quomodo executes the *coup de grace* and remarks that it is

not only vild, but in it tyrannous,

earlier (III, iv) she had watched Quomodo from the gallery as he pursued his deception of Easy; the physical situation suggesting moral disapproval, inviting the audience's condemnation of Quomodo. Middleton emphasises the patterned symmetry of his play by giving Quomodo's wife to Easy in the conclusion, thus diagrammatically and emblematically clarifying the action's didactic meaning.

The art of Middleton in this play is at its best in the sequences where Quomodo and his assistants weave their web about Easy. Here the urbanity, the teamwork and polished technique by which Easy is persuaded into borrowing from Quomodo bring the play into the plane of high comedy; Quomodo, affecting ignorance of Easy's identity, and Shortyard (his assistant) the reassuring friend to Easy, admirably cast the net:

SHORTYARD Must the second party, that enters into bond only for fashion's
          sake, needs be a citizen? what say you to this gentleman for one?
          [pointing to EASY]
QUOMODO Alas, sir! you know he's a mere stranger to me: . . . he may
          inn here to-night, and ride away tomorrow: . . .
EASY   I hope you will not disparage me so: 'tis well known I have
          three hundred pound a-year in Essex . . .
QUOMODO Well, master Blastfield, because I will not disgrace the gentle-
          man, I'm content

Middleton here brilliantly breaks the mood for a moment, giving a
sudden insight into the strain under which the deceivers are working:

EASY   No sir, now you would, you shall not.
QUOMODO Cuds me, I'm undone! he's gone again. [aside]
SHORTYARD The net's broke.

                                                              (II, iii)

but the second episode is successful, these schemers are full of
inventiveness, they recover straight away, and Easy is won over by
the invitation to ridicule Quomodo — an opportunity which his
parasites, like Mosca, take delightedly: here the mock ridicule is,
however, a prelude to the real ridiculing of Quomodo in Act V, for
Middleton takes more revenge on his villain than did Jonson on
Volpone:

SHORTYARD Master Easy, mark my words: if it stood not upon the eternal
          loss of thy credit against supper —
EASY   Mass, that's true.
SHORTYARD The pawning of thy horse for his own victuals —
EASY   Right, i'faith.
SHORTYARD And thy utter dissolution amongst gentlemen for ever —
EASY   Pox on't!
SHORTYARD Quomodo should hang, rot, stink —
QUOMODO Sweet boy, i'faith! [aside]
SHORTYARD Drop, damn.
QUOMODO Excellent Shortyard! [aside]
EASY   I forgot all this . . . How does master Quomodo? is the bond
          ready?

                                                              (II, iii)

Here the style is Middleton's, though the inspiration seems clearly
to have been *Volpone*. Indeed, the final trick by which Quomodo is
outwitted, the signed document cancelling Easy's debts, is used in

precisely the same way as Volpone's signed will giving all to Mosca; and both Volpone and Quomodo feign death and thus call down their own undoing through their failure to guard against the obvious results. It is significant that Jonson's art in plotting gave scope for the unmasking and ridiculing of the disappointed suitors, while Middleton's more straightforward and singleminded comedy ends only with the ridiculing of Quomodo and his evil agents and the restoration to wealth and safety of Easy and Thomasine: Everyman successfully evades the snares of the devil, though it is the devil who has all the vigour, intelligence, diversity, all the lustful enjoyment in his gains and the manipulation of circumstances, in accordance with Nick Machiavel's methods; for Quomodo, like Volpone, like Barabas, as Machiavel notes,

> smiles to see how full his bags are cramb'd;
> Which mony was not got without my meanes.[12]

---

[12] Machiavel's Induction to The Jew of Malta ed. C. F. T. Brooke (Oxford 1910). Marlowe could well be regarded as the first playwright of City Comedy if we take the catastrophe of The Jew to be comic; but on this see G. K. Hunter's article on the play in the Journal of the Warburg and Courtauld Institutes 1964.

7 Conventional Plays 1604-1607

In the study of art no less than in the study of man, the mysteries of success are frequently best revealed through an investigation of failures. Only a pathology of representation will give us some insight into mechanisms which enabled the masters to handle this instrument with such assurance.

E. H. GOMBRICH.

THE FORM AND STYLE of the genre attains a certain maturity between 1604 and 1606, as we have seen in the discussion of The Dutch Courtezan, Volpone and Michaelmas Term. It is a sign of the growing maturity, and also of the popular success of the plays, that in these years a number of lesser repertory playwrights and 'dressers of plays' produced hurried imitations and adaptations of the new genre, working with their cruder methods of conventional play-making. These playwrights made no innovations, they adapted the most striking and novel elements in the work of talented writers but did not generate fresh life: their imitation was that of 'a Creature, that swallowes, what it takes in, crude, raw, or indigested'.

However that such writers were attracted to the genre at all suggests that it might not have been as unpopular and financially unrewarding as Professor Harbage claimed in Shakespeare and the Rival Traditions.[1]

---

[1] I am indebted to Professor L. C. Knights who pointed out to me that Jonson's lines to Fletcher on The Faithful Shepherdess indicate that at least by that time, 1608, the Blackfriars audience was not exclusive in price or social rank but included

> . . . Gamester, Captaine, Knight, Knight's man,
> Lady or Pusil, that weares maske, or fan,
> Velvet, or Taffata cap, rank'd in the darke
> With the shops Foreman, or some such brave sparke,
> That may judge for his six-pence

The recent boom in satire that followed the success of the revue *Beyond the Fringe* supported a weekly magazine, two long-running television shows and various other more or less imitative satiric ventures; it also attracted perhaps the most experienced Popular comedian in the country, Mr Frankie Howerd, whose absorption of the flavour of university style comedy was so successful; it is interesting to note that his complaint about the modern university wits' success recalls the Jacobean Popular writers' half-serious irritation that, in Mr Howerd's words, 'you have to have a degree these days to be filthy in public'.

In this chapter I shall be concerned with a selection of conventional plays which sought to please the audience for City Comedy in the Coterie theatres. In these plays it is notable that weakness is due to the playwright's failure to understand that satire is in fact dialectical: it always presents the audience with an argument; too often these conventional plays offer a straightforward comedy of love intrigue or of double deception, and flavour this form, not that of the *genre*, with satiric allusions or characters imitated and conventionalised from City Comedy. Yet an examination of a few such plays should reveal how a conventional playwright went to work in writing for the *genre*'s enthusiasts, what elements he thought it best to emphasise, what struck him as typical. It should be easy to gauge the influence of the three major dramatists on their imitators, and to show which conventions were vital.

The collaboration of Dekker and Webster in 1604, which produced *Westward Ho* and its successor *Northward Ho*, directly provoked the three parodists who based the main action of *Eastward Ho* on the farcical river journey by London types. *Westward Ho* and *Northward Ho* were perhaps understandably provoking to Jonson and Marston, for the latter's style may be found in every scene —

> for beauty covets rich apparell, choyce dyet, excellent Physicke, no German Clock nor Mathematicall Ingin whatsoever requires so much reparation as a womans face,[2]

(I, i. 76–79)

and Jonson's sharply visualised epigrammatic descriptions, and his satiric set pieces on absurd 'humorous' characters, are faithfully

---

[2] *Westward Ho* I, i. ed. F. T. Bowers in *The Dramatic Works of Thomas Dekker*.

reproduced as soon as the play has begun, to reassure the audience
that it is the real thing, true City Comedy: here Justiniano presents
us with a cuckold in a manner reminiscent of Jonson's Musco:

> His cloak shrouding his face, as if he were a Neopolitan that had lost
> his beard in Aprill, and if he walk through the street, or any other
> narrow road (as tis rare to meete a Cuckold) hee duckes at the pent-
> houses, like an Antient that dares not flourish at the oath taking of the
> *Pretor*, for feare of the signe-posts?
>
> (I, i. 156–161)

Unfortunately, Dekker's intelligence does not manifest itself and give
point and meaning to the scene described: there is *no* satiric point, in
fact.

It might be illuminating to begin with a short consideration of
plot and articulation in the two plays. *Westward Ho* has the character
Justiniano who believes himself cuckolded and determines to watch
his friends being deceived in like manner; there is a superficial
similarity to the Disguised-Duke plot, and Justiniano seems at first
likely to be the play's Presenter and Vice in one:

> . . . I resolve to take some shape upon me, and to live disguised heere
> in the Citty; they say for one Cuckolde to knowe that his friend is in
> the like head-ake, and to give him counsell, is as if there were two
> partners . . . Have amongst you Citty dames? You that are indeede the
> fittest, and most proper persons for a Comedy,
>
> (I, i. 220–223, 225–226)

In fact, however, Justiniano is only occasionally a detached commentator, and then his comments are brief and perfunctory, for
example

> O the quick apprehension of women, the'ile groape out a mans
> meaning presently,

after he has persuaded the wives to take a boat from Blackfriars
(III, iii. 95–96), and his set piece comment when trying to persuade
the wives to meet some young men at a wine house:

> why, even now, at holding up of this finger, and before the turning
> downe of this, some are murdring, some lying with their maides, some
> picking of pockets, some cutting purses, . . . some wives are Cuckolding
> some Husbands.
>
> (II, i. 186–190)

lacks any vital relevance to the sequence in which it is spoken, though lively enough in itself. Justiniano does contrive trickery episodes, but they are not *exempla* and they develop a causal plot which is a straightforward 'story', not organised to make a strong didactic point. The play moves forward in a Popular, literal-minded style. In one scene we see Justiniano persuading the wives to go to a wine house. In a subsequent scene they arrive there, and decide to go somewhere else. The play ends, in fact, when all the characters arrive at the same place together for the first time. Certainly the husbands are deceived by the wives, but the simple *peripeteia* has no satiric-didactic force beyond exposing citizens to ridicule as gulls and their wives as adulterous, selfish and grossly comic. We are directed by the writers to *what happens*, not to the implications, not to the satiric theme that the play articulates, for there is no satiric theme.

The play has a straightforward Popular comic action — a strong emphasis on what happens. Soliloquy is used to inform the audience of a character's proposed line of action:

> Wel my husband is gon to arrest *Monopoly*. I have dealt with a Sargeant privatly, to intreate him, pretending that he is my Aunts Son, by this meanes shal I see my young gallant that in this has plaid his part.
>
> (III, i. 38–41)

There are two sequences in rather poor blank verse dealing with an attempt at seduction and an exposure and correction of this sinfulness; the Popular sensationalism is evident in the use of the corpse which only seems dead and rises once the reversal is effected; it seems as though the playwrights felt that a play wholly in prose, with no lofty main plot upholding the high style of love comedy, was too great a departure for them; hence the somewhat weak rhetoric of the penitent villain, vowing platonic love:

> Mine owne shame strikes me dumb: henceforth the booke
> Ile read shall be thy mind, and not thy looke.
>
> (IV, ii. 165–166)

Justiniano rounds the play off in a mood of cheerful inconsequence:

> all is but a merriment, all but a May-game.
>
> (V, iv. 278)

Northward Ho similarly has an action involving a journey from London for the purpose of seduction and adultery, and there is a formal blank verse episode in which the virtuous wife rejects the suit of a corrupt lecher in Popular romantic comedy style. Once again the merchant who suspects himself of being a cuckold — his name here is Maybery — contrives various trickery episodes to gull those who would deceive him, and once again the method of articulation, like the plot, is Popular in its concern with mere mechanical causation:

MAYBERY   ... hee railes upon her, wills me to take her in the Act ... hee's pulling on his bootes, and will ride along with us; lets muster as many as wee can.

BELLAMONT   It wilbe excellent sport, to see him and his owne wife meete in *Ware*, wilt not?[3]

The play is superior to its predecessor in its symmetry of design, the surer control and the ingenuity of the 'lazzi' and the firmer direction of dialogue. There is a notable superiority in the opening scene of *Northward Ho*.

Here is no longwinded elaboration of motive and situation; instead two men are, as it were, interrupted in the middle of a conversation, what we need to know is conveyed in implication, the cliché is cut short impatiently, the action is directly under way. Soon the two set to work arousing the suspicions of Maybery about his wife, and the curt suddenness of the exchange seems strikingly life-like:

GREENSHIELD In the passage of our loves ... she bestowed upon me this ringe which she protested was her husbands gift.

MAYBERY   The poesie, the poesie — O my heart, that ring good infaith?

GREENSHIELD Not many nights comming to her and being familiar with her —

MAYBERY   Kissing and so forth.

GREENSHIELD I sir.

MAYBERY   And talking to her feelingly.

GREENSHIELD Pox on't, I lay with her.

MAYBERY   Good infaith, you are of a good complexion.

GREENSHIELD Lying with her as I say: and rising some-what early from her in the morning, I lost this ring in her bed.

MAYBERY   In my wives bed.

(I, i. 88–103)

The weight of this is carried by implication, a fact acknowledged by

---

[3] *Northward Ho* IV, i. 268–274 ed. Bowers.

the two men who note that Maybery has given no outward sign of emotion, and so resolved to

> with-draw, and give him leave to rave a little.

This economy of effect, this sureness and control reminiscent of Middleton, is to be observed when Doll wrings fifty pounds out of Allom by pretence at passionate anger:

DOLL   Oh I shal burst, if I cut not my lace: I'me so vext! my father
           hee's ridde to Court one way . . . one of his men (like a roague
           as he is) is rid another . . . and here was a scrivener but even
           now . . .
ALLUM   How much is the bond?
CHARTLEY   O rare little villaine.
DOLL   My father could take up, upon the barenesse of his word five
           hundred pound . . .
ALLUM   What is the debt?
DOLL   But hee scornes to bee — and I scorne to bee —
ALLUM   Pree thee sweete Mistris *Dorothy* vex not, how much is it?
                                   (II, i. 135–137, 140, 143–149)

Similarly direct and purposeful is the scene where Maybery tests out Greensheild's story (II, ii. 35–58) and the gulling of Greenshield in III, ii has the firmly shaped form of an *exemplum*. These scattered signs of the influence of Middleton relate the play directly to his early comedy, but the play remains largely similar to *Westward Ho* in its simple causal plot and articulation derived largely from the journeying of the characters from one street to another. Both plays articulate complex plots and the audience is directed simply to the intrigue and the cleverness with which it is worked out: of course neither play has an intrigue of sufficient intelligence or witty design to reward the audience's closest attention.

Dekker and Webster have attempted in other ways to write within the genre. It is in these areas that the main interest of the two plays lies. The conventional playwright tends to flavour his plot with the genre's style of dialogue, references, and settings; these he regards as the plainest distinctive elements of the genre. John Day's Induction to the *Isle of Gulls* clearly sets out this approach:

> ist any thing Criticall? Are Lawyers fees, and Cittizens wives laid open in
> it: I love to heare vice anotomised, & abuse let blood in the maister

vaine, is there any great mans life characterd int? . . . and there be not
Wormewood water and Copperes int, Ile not like it[4]

in *Northward Ho* and *Westward Ho*, heeding the demands of this
imaginary City Comedy spectator, the playwrights have flavoured
their plot with satiric set pieces, with many metaphors and similes
drawn from stock themes of the satirists; there are characters drawn
as typical London types and presented as, of course, scurrilous and
prone to bawdy jesting, thieving, deception and adultery. Great
attention is paid at the beginning of the play to catching the style of
bitter, Marstonian satiric prose, to the emphasis on the City and the
fact that the characters are citizens, and to the detailed setting of the
scenes in specific streets and taverns of London as in the Coney-
Catching pamphlets. It is indicative that so little of the method of
satiric comedy is understood by Dekker and Webster that their
trickery episodes suggest derivation from Jest Books, the source of
so many episodes in Coney-Catching pamphlets, rather than Jonson,
because of their exclusion of moral and didactic considerations which
are the primary impetus of satiric drama. We may recall that detailed
setting of Coney-Catching episodes in specific parts of London was
similarly intended to give sensational interest to otherwise very
commonplace material. Both in the insistence on the 'City' setting
and on the geography of London we may see a similar purpose to
that of the pamphleteers.

Hence, in *Westward Ho*, there is an insistent use of the prefix 'City',
often where it has no force of meaning: we find 'Citizens wives',
'City Mercers and goldsmiths', 'City bawds', 'a good Citty wit', 'high
wit from the Citty', 'O the pollicy of women, and Tradesmen',
'Jealousie hath undone many a Cittizen', 'Citty dames . . . proper
persons for a comedy', 'you have few Cittizens speake well of their
wives behind their backs'. In *Northward Ho* similarly 'our young sonnes
and heires in the Citty', 'custome of the Citty', 'Cittizens Proverbe',
'you do many devises for Cittizens wives: I care not greatly because I
have a Citty Laundresse already, if I get a Citty Poet too', 'neare a
Gentleman of them all shall gull a Citizen' — such references
frequently have no other function than to insist that the play is set
in the city of London.

The playwrights adopt the same technique with names of streets

---

[4] John Day, *The Ile of Gulls* (London 1606) sig A2ᵛ.

and areas of London; hence the conventional references to proceed-
ing up Holborn towards Tyburn, 'the Brokers in long lane' (Northward
Ho) 'the middle Ile in *Pawles*' (*Westward Ho*), and other references to
Bucklersbury, the Exchange, Bedlam, Fleet Street, the Counter, St
Martins, the Stillyard, Blackwall, Limehouse, Brentford, Ham,
Bridewell, Shoreditch, Woodstreet, Ludgate, Grays Inn, Westminster,
Croyden, Charing Cross, Putney, Queenhithe, Lambeth, Coalharbour,
Pudding Lane, Cheapside, Wapping, Moorfields, Highgate Hill,
Cuckoldshaven, Enfield, Ware, Bishopsgate, Guildhall, Lumbard
Street, St Clements; though most of these occur in both plays, it is
nevertheless an impressive list, and a technique which the writers of
Eastward Ho took note of when they came to compose their parody.

It is typical of these two plays that imitation of Marstonian invective should be given to a whore who, though she is supposedly
colleague to the Dutch Courtezan, is in fact sister to Shakespeare's
Doll Tearsheet, created in 1597 for the Popular stage:

> the rotten toothd rascall, will for sixe pence fetch any whore to his
> maisters customers: and is every one that swims in a Taffatie gowne
> Lettis for your lippes? uds life, this is rare, that Gentlewomen and
> Drawers, must suck at one Spiggot: . . . I'me as melancholy now as
> Fleet-streete in a long vacation.
>
> (Northward Ho I, ii. 43–46, 51)

Nor is it wholly surprising that the Captain whose 'humour' is
roaring turns out to be cousin to Fluellen of Shakespeare's *Henry V*,
while the Dutchman Hans van Belch is treated with the good humour
that Hans the shoemaker receives in that Popular comedy set in
London four years earlier, the *Shoemakers' Holiday*. Certainly the many
references to satiric themes and the jests about sex have their effect
in creating an atmosphere similar to that in a Marstonian City
Comedy; and since this was perhaps the aim of the collaborators, it
may be inappropriate to dwell long on the more serious weaknesses
of the two plays.

The two relevant plays by Day reveal further evidence of this
indecorous mixing of styles and character types, for Day, like Dekker,
was by training a Popular repertory playwright. Day had a marked
allegiance to those early Shakespearean comedies which had been
published, his habitual method of dramatic composition was
Popular, and in composing his Coterie work he flavoured his plays

with intensive imitation of the satiric and bitter passages in three
successful or notorious comedies which had most recently appeared:
Westward Ho, *Northward Ho*, and the later *Eastward Ho*. Though many of
these echoes are from the best written of the three plays, and the
most plainly satiric — indeed its political satire led to the prosecu-
of the authors — even that play, *Eastward Ho*, is dense with satiric
references which had become conventional to the *genre* by late 1604.
Dekker and Webster helped to make such references characteristic
by constantly reiterating them in carelessly uninventive form; in
every scene of these three plays John Day could have found satiric
'flavouring' for his own work. Thus a rapid glance through *Northward
Ho* and *Westward Ho* notes the following conventionally 'satiric'
lines:

> she hath red in the Italian Courtyer,
> $\qquad\qquad\qquad$ (*Westward Ho*, I, i, 13)
> I spake to her, as Clients do to Lawiers without money
> (to no purpose)
> $\qquad\qquad\qquad$ (*ibid*. II, ii. 17–18)

wee (whores) are not currant till wee passe from one man to
another. (*Northward Ho* I, ii. 83)

sold one Maiden-head ten severall times, (*ibid*. I, iii. 11–12)

three Taylors go to the making up of a man, (II, i. 9)

like a usurer, that will use a man with all kindness . . . and after-wards
take the extremitie of the forfature; (II, ii. 168–170)

Like your Cittizen, I never thinke of my debts, when I am a
horseback. (V, i. 45–46)

There is probably another major source for Day's City comedies,
though its influence in Jacobean drama is so widespread that it can
perhaps be assumed automatically: it is Shakespeare's *Henry IV* and
— to some extent — *Henry V*. What is striking about those plays in
relation to City Comedy is the close accuracy with which they
rendered the London scenes of low life, the trickery episodes
presented by the disguised Prince Hal and his servant Poins, and the
strong feeling for the London locality. The episodes in which Hal
tricks Falstaff and talks with low life characters, and the episode
in which Falstaff tricks Mistress Quickly into allowing him to
continue living off her, find echoes in the tavern and bawdyhouse

episodes in *Westward Ho* and *Northward Ho*. Such figures as Pistol and Fluellen persist in the imagination of repertory playwrights, not only Dekker but typically Day and the author of the conventional Middle-tonian comedy *The Puritan Widow*, with its Corporal Oath and Captain Idle. In *The Isle of Gulls* those jests which do not derive from Coterie comedy are in the style of Shakespearean comedies which had been published — *Love's Labour's Lost* and *A Midsummer Night's Dream*, for example — and, inevitably, *Henry IV*.

Day is able to imitate Popular romantic comedy because his Coterie work is still in form and in its articulation regular, causally plotted drama with a romantic main plot and low life sub plot; though it has satiric *exempla* too. In *Law Tricks* Day certainly does his best to embitter the action with elements of Italianate, Marstonian evil and corruption; indeed he contrives to include poisoning, attempted adultery, seduction for financial profit, disguises and dissolute prodigality in a plot which already has a Disguised-Duke outline, with duke Fernese observing all, and judging at the end. The distinction to be made between Day's handling of the Disguised-Duke plot and Marston's is the lack of conviction, of intensity, in Day's articulation of evil characters; Lurdo may be ostensibly a Machiavel and a Malcontent, but he seems to be engaged rather in a charade than a real attempt at seduction of Emilia, who in any case is playing a game with him:

EMILIA   Ile in your presence sit uppon his knee,
           Exchanging kisses; If you speake to me
           Ile pout in scorn . . .
LURDO   Square to my humour fit.
EMILIA   I was a Beggar borne . . .
           Traded in lust and gainefull brothelrie.
LURDO   The fitter for my turne.[5]

The couplets divided among the two bantering characters emphasise Day's lack of serious purpose and feeling for the satiric mode.

Law Tricks, like the *Isle of Gulls*, follows the pattern established by Dekker and Webster of heavy satiric flavouring at the beginning of the play. Hence the exchange between the cynical Malcontent Lurdo and Polymetes:

---

[5] John Day, *Law Tricks* III, i. in *The Works of John Day* ed. A. H. Bullen (London 1881).

LURDO   Prince, be a Lawyer.
POLYMETES   Of all Land-monsters some that beare that name
            Might well be sparde, whose vultur Avarice
            Devoures men living: they of all the rest
            Deale most with Angells and yet prove least blest.
                                                        (I, i)

Soon Lurdo is explaining how a brace or two of dead wives enrich
a skilful widower, and his Italian deviousness in plotting arouses the
ironic admiration of Emilia:

LURDO   A private doore
            a secret vault and twentie odde tricks more . . .
EMILIA   My Lord, your Law-plot's most judiciall.
                                                        (II, i)

The equivalent cynical courtier-malcontent in the *Isle of Gulls* is
Dametas, and before his appearance the audience is provided with
several epigrammatic descriptions of him which proclaim their
derivation from City Comedy:

HIPPOLITA   Why your quotidian, *Dametas* the Court surfet, hee that dwells
            in your eye, like a disease in your blood . . .
VIOLETTA   fie upon him, he becomes the great chamber worse then a
            Gentleman-usher with wry legges.
HIPPOLITA   He is the most mishapen sute of gentility that ever the Court
            wore.
                                                        (Sig A4ʳ)

It is clear that this dialogue is influenced by Comical Satyre's ridicule
of mannerisms; but the two princesses Violetta and Hippolita
have a different parentage, from early Shakespearean comedy; when
they fall to mildly scurrilous broad jests, the first echo is of *Midsummer Night's Dream* III, ii; when they go to the chase whole passages
echo IV, i of the same play, while the main plot's characters are taken
from the noble lovers of Sir Philip Sidney's Romance *The Arcadia*, and
at key moments betray their (indecorously) respectable and high
minded lineage, as in the courtly formality of the game of bowls:

VIOLETTA   By the faith a me, well led,
LISANDER   Would I might lead you,
VIOLETTA   Whither?
LISANDER   To my bed.
VIOLETTA   I am sure you would not?

LISANDER   By this aire I would.
VIOLETTA   I hope you would not hurt me, and you should.
LISANDER   I'de love you sweet.
VIOLETTA   Sowre, so I heard you say.
LISANDER   Accept it then.
VIOLETTA   Of what acquaintance pray?

                             (Sig E1^r and E1^v)

This kind of dialogue had not been in fashion since *As You Like It*, and as far as fashion was concerned was about as old as old Hieronymo by 1606. Day's taste for delicate gaiety is shown in his frequent use of such words as 'game' and 'comedy', and 'sceane of mirth': the *Isle of Gulls* has plenty of satiric dialogue, but the plot itself subdues the violent or savage elements which we are led to expect from the early exchanges:

> I tell thee knave I could hang thee by my pattent, if it were granted once, Ile tell thee how it runnes, It allowes mee 24 knaves, 6 Knights, 10 fooles, 13 fellons, and 14 traytors by the yeere, take em howe, why, when, and where I please . . .
> such Court-spyders, that weave their webbes of flatterie in the eares of greatnesse, if they can once entangle them in their quaint trecherie, they poysen em

                             (Sig B2^r, B2^v)

Day introduces a second politician (in the Machiavellian sense) in the latter part of the *Isle of Gulls* when the straightforward comic action is becoming too overtly unsatiric. This Machiavel, Manasses, offers biographical data in the form of a Theophrastian character:

> My great Graundfather was a Rat-catcher, my Grandsier a Hangman, my Father a Promooter, and my selfe an Informer.

                             (Sig E4^v)

this echoes *Westward Ho* III, ii. 5–10; when he describes his criminal activities, he echoes *Your Five Gallants* III, ii and *Eastward Ho* II, ii. 11–16; when Manasses brings in the two messengers who describe the abuses and discontent in the kingdom since the duke has abandoned it, the passages which most plainly refer to contemporary Jacobean discontents and James's habitual impatience with government, when it conflicted with country sports, have actually been lifted almost *verbatim* from Sidney's *Arcadia*. In this sense we can say that the *Isle of Gulls* is a genuine, if sporadic, contemporary political satire, although

K

even here the satire consists largely in allusions, not in the dramatisation of the satiric-didactic view of the playwright. Thus the duke seems to have no interesting or even general personal similarity to James I, Dametas is a merely conventional dramatic figure, the rival princes even if dressed as English and Scots still offer little witty criticism of either; stripped of Scots costume, they lose their identity. They are in fact conventionalised figures based on the young nobles in *Love's Labour's Lost*, and acting out elements in the plot of Sidney's *Arcadia*; as the conclusion of the *Isle of Gulls* shows, the play is of an Italianate form, and it ends when all the trickery episodes are complete, the last episode involving the winning of the two princesses by one pair of princes with the blessing of the duke (or king, as the speech prefixes call him once or twice in the 1606 quarto).

Since the *Isle of Gulls* was designed by Day partly to 'cash-in' on the notoriety gained by the Blackfriars comedy of the preceding year, *Eastward Ho*, he made sure that the vital element — satire of James I, his court and his new knights — should be prominent. Hence Dametas' remark, in retort to the captain's claim to the rank of gentleman

> Why so I hope are wee sir, and of the best and last edition, of the Dukes owne making.
>
> (Sig B2^r)

Hence, too, the frequent and often unnecessary references to 'policy' and the corruption of the court. This is the technique once more of flavouring a straightforward play with fashionable matter. In *Law Tricks* Day is aiming at the Middletonian kind of City Comedy with its extensive and accurate setting among lawyers, merchants and financiers with much turning on the decision in court and the signing of mortgages, bonds, and so forth. In *Law Tricks* therefore we find many references to law and legal terms, though the plot of the play contains no legal matter whatsoever. There are numerous uses of 'law' as a prefix with little gain in meaning:

LURDO   A secret vault and twentie odde tricks more . . .
EMILIA   My Lord your Law-plot's most judicial (p. 29)

WIN   She intends to make a Gull of the Prince
         (And an absolute Goose of you)

LURDO   Still good in Law: ile fetch him ore of all,
               Get all, pursse all,   (p. 36)

LURDO   Neither the Law nor I
               Know any reason why Horatio —
               But mum, Law-tricks!   (p. 18)

Similarly, Day uses legal terms either gratuitously or incorrectly:

>   Ile have a trick
> By way of Habeas Corpus to remove
> This talking Gossip   (p. 46)

> I made thee and the rest away by a bill of Conveyance at his back
> (p. 66)

> Our smooth conveyance   (p. 68)

> But *nuda veritate*, in bare truth,
> And *bona fide*, without circumstance,
> *Splendente sole*, the bare sun nere saw
> A wench more capable of wit and law.   (p. 78)

In both plays he reveals his allegiance to the Elizabethan popular theatre; the low prose invective, like the low life characters, could well be found in his own *Blind Beggar of Betnal Green* (1600?) or in one of Dekker's Popular comedies; here is Emilia in *Law Tricks*

> As for you Sisley bumtrinckets Ile have a bout with you at the Single
> Stackado   (p. 82)

and here Mopsa in the *Isle of Gulls*:

> goe fetch Raph our horskeeper, let him that got the calf keep the
> cow in a knaves name and he wil,
>
>   (Sig H1ᵛ)

If Day's *Isle of Gulls* is more firmly a City Comedy in those places — of which there are many — where it directly echoes *Westward Ho, Eastward Ho*, the *Dutch Courtezan, Your Five Gallants, Volpone, Every Man In His Humour* and the rest, it did bring down the wrath of the authorities, who committed sundry of the actors to Bridewell because of its political satire. Thus, obliquely, Day earns his place among the playwrights in the genre.

Barry's *Ram Alley* is in some respects the most successful of the conventional plays; this may be because it faithfully imitates

Middletonian comedy. The main plot has certain recognisable similarities to *A Mad World My Masters* and *A Trick to Catch the Old One*, and there are certain echoes in the dialogue, for example in the gleeful soliloquy of the lawyer Throat which recall those of Quomodo or Old Hoard:

> My fate looks big! methinks I see already
> Nineteen gold chains, seventeen great beards, and ten
> Reverend bald heads, proclaim my way before me.
> My coach shall now go prancing through Cheapside ...
> I now in pomp will ride, for 'tis most fit,
> He should have state, that riseth by his wit.[6]

Again, when early on we are given a satiric character sketch of Throat, the firm syntax of the verse and the economy of statement proclaim the stylistic influence of Middleton:

> Thus: in Ram Alley lies a fellow, by name
> Throat: one that professeth law, but indeed
> Has neither law nor conscience; a fellow
> That never saw the bar, but when his life
> Was call'd in question for a cosenage.
> The rogue is rich; to him go you,
>
> (I, i)

The purposeful dialogue directs our attention to the plotting, which is complex but also witty, and provides some excellent surprise *peripeteiea* and disguise deceptions in the Middletonian manner; when Oliver appears to wed his widow and William ridicules him, the dialogue recalls Middleton with some precision and the form is that of a Comical Satyre sequence:

OLIVER   Good morrow, bride, fresh as the month of May,
         I come to kiss thee on thy wedding day.
WILLIAM Saving your tale sir ...
         The truth is, I have laid my knife aboard.
         The widow, sir, is wedded.
OLIVER   Ha!
WILLIAM Bedded.
OLIVER   Ha!   (V, i)

Throat the lawyer, like Old Hoard the miser in *A Trick to Catch the Old*

---

[6] Ludovic Barry, *Ram Alley* III, i. in *Dodsley* 4th ed. (London 1874–76) reprinted New York 1964.

One, marries a whore under the impression she is respectable and rich; Throat's ridiculous entry of the house he believes he owns in Act IV is admirable situation comedy emerging wittily out of the main deception plot, while such sequences as that in which the whore twists her way out of the clutches of a serjeant are given densely local colour and technical accuracy in the manner of Middleton:

SERJEANT   I have an action
        At suit of Mistress Smell-smock, your quondam bawd:
        The sum is eight good pound for six weeks' board,
        And five weeks' loan for a red taffeta gown,
        Bound with a silver lace.
WHORE   I do protest,
        By all the honesty 'twixt thee and me,
        I got her in that gown in six weeks' space
        Four pound, and fourteen pence given by a clerk
        Of an inn-of-chancery that night I came
        Out of her house;   (IV, i)

The fast moving and well controlled plotting, and the sinewy economy of the dialogue suggest that Barry imitated Middleton — the play was probably written after *A Trick to Catch the Old One*, the play with which it seems to have the closest similarity — but of course it lacks that assurance, that clarity and order of Middleton's dramatic articulation and its dialogue is without the vigour, the subtlety or the variety of its model. There is the constant use of conventional satiric allusions as in the work of Dekker and Webster or Day, and the obtrusive flattery of the inns-of-court students and their prowess with the ladies. The characters are not given full vigorous independence, even Boutcher the chief trickster and Throat the villain lack such individuality as would free them from their Middletonian parents. But the play has formal characteristics of the genre.

There is another significant source for the play — Jonson's *Volpone*. The first appearance of Throat is when he emerges from his study, as the directions read

        books and bags of money on a table
                    (I, i)

He then delivers a rhapsody to gold and its source in legal affairs

which is obviously based on Volpone's hymn to gold in Act I of that
play: the rhythm of the opening lines is unmistakably similar:

> Chaste Phoebe, *splende*; there's that left yet,
> Next to my book, *claro micante auro*.
> Ay, *that's the soul of law*; that's it, that's it, (my italic)
> For which the buckram bag must trudge all weathers

There is the direct echo of Volpone's

> Haile the worlds soule, and mine.

Ram Alley has certain formal characteristics of City Comedy; the
disguised and detached commentator and satirist appears in the
person of Constantia, who offers didactic comment at the conclusion
of a scene early on:

> Pandarism! why, 'tis grown a liberal science
>   (I, i)

In a later sequence, possibly echoing the scene in *Volpone* where
Volpone is abused for

> Those filthy eyes of yours, that flow with slime
>   (I, v)

William abuses his father to Taffeta, whom he desires; his father is in
hiding and overhears everything. William's ridicule is in the
tradition of satiric comedy, extending over personal appearance and
sexual inadequacy; Taffeta replies by ridiculing William's clothes in
the style of Comical Satyre.

> His breeches must be plaited, as if he had
> Some thirty pockets, when one poor half-penny purse
> Will carry all his treasure; his knees all points
>   (IV, i)

The father explodes with rage, rushes out and abuses William
in his turn. Similarly, a sequence in which the bragging captain is
ridiculed, actually is crueller and more deliberate than the beating
of Pistol with the leek in *Henry V*; were it not for Barry's obvious
debt to Shakespeare's play-scrap mouther, in creating Captain Face,
we might be led to compare it with the exposure of Tucca's cowardice
in *Poetaster* IV, vii. It is a sign of Barry's derivative method that he
should choose the easiest and most obvious model of a stage
braggart to lash in the manner of Jonson or Marston, just as he
chooses the most hackneyed of all tragedies, the *Spanish Tragedy*, to

parody in the manner of early Marston, derisively, but unimaginatively, unwittily.

Barry's play contains elements chosen from the best plays in City Comedy; they are well integrated into his firm and intelligent plot, and the atmosphere is successfully flavoured with the stock allusions and jests from City Comedy, and has effective sequences set in prison, in the suburbs, in the lawyer's house. The London scene is frequently referred to by naming particular streets and areas, as in *Westward Ho*, *Northward Ho* and, for that matter, as in Middleton's City Comedy. Barry seems to have modelled his play on the latest and freshest of Middleton's plays performed at the rival Paul's Boys' Theatre; in this he shows his efficiency as a conventional repertory writer, always ready to adapt to the latest successful fashion. His play is for the most part too lighthearted, like Day's; the episodes lack the serious implications and the satiric purpose of Jonson or Middleton; but in those where he has imitated the form of the satiric sequence characteristic of City Comedy, his achievement is higher than that of Dekker and Webster, Day, or such less relevant writers as Armin, Field, or Machin. The moral of this is obvious. Form is paramount, and shapes style.

I have chosen to deal only with the more interesting conventional plays here, in order to attempt to show the characteristics of these plays, to indicate how they were made, and what the conventional writers thought most remarkable and successful in the genre. It may also reveal something of the quality of the best plays in the genre, if we set beside them the work of writers whom Jonson dismissed as 'rogues'.

Yet it is an indication of the sustaining richness reposing in the genre's conventions that Barry's wholly undistinguished conventional play should be so manifestly actable and effective. Here we may note an analogy with the history of the Coney-catching pamphlet, another 'kind' in which wholly conventional methods of composition produced lively, firm and enduringly attractive popular literature. Barry's play is effective because he so fully grasped and used the conventions, not at all because he was more original than Day or Dekker.

Now that the study of the first phase of City Comedy is complete, it may be worthwhile to review the question of the relationship of the *genre* to the Jacobean background. I have been concerned to stress the formal and conventional elements in the realism of the plays and to demonstrate that the important plays engage serious and enduring moral issues. Where details of Law and financial transactions are used in the plays, we may say that almost invariably their importance is minor. Economic policy and academic discussion of legal problems certainly receive even less attention in the major plays of the *genre* than we might have expected, given the strong element of Inns of Court students, lawyers, and gentry, in the Jacobean audiences. Similarly, the political satire in the early plays of Marston derives largely from satiric tradition, and subsequent political satire in City Comedy is, arguably, more notable for its frequency than for its subtlety of insight. This may well be due, of course, to the dominance of convention and tradition in the drama of the age. We are told that Jonson took the spectacularly successful financier Thomas Sutton for his model in creating the character Volpone; and yet it is not easy directly to relate the action of *Volpone,* or its hero-villain, the embodiment of avarice and perversion in a grand dramatic caricature, to the career of Sutton or other such figures (Pallavicino for example) which we find in the analyses of modern historians. All this is perhaps obvious enough; but my point is that the case of *Volpone* is typical, not unique. Volpone perhaps has more in common with Marlowe's Barabas than with any real Jacobean financier, and in the present study I have traced, similarly, the clear dramatic lineage of subsequent usurers in City Comedy. It is evident that had Jonson wished to record with close fidelity the complexities and subtle technicalities of Jacobean business life — and his dramatic theory does not encourage one to think he did — the stage conditions and dramatic conventions afforded little encouragement. On the contrary, the formative elements of City Comedy encouraged the stylisation of character and setting in accordance with the requirements of the satiric-didactic schema, emphasising the patterns of underlying moral conflict and the presence of evil in the seemingly indifferent and haphazard circumstances of everyday city life. It is paradoxical that even those lesser playwrights whose serious satiric purposes might be questioned and who might have been, therefore, expected to provide more detailed, realistic accounts of city life, in fact produced plays more clearly stylised and conventional than those of Middleton or Marston. In this sense the conventional plays, like the Coney-Catching pamphlets, testify to the basically critical element in the realism of City Comedy. If we attend, not to the particular details of Jacobean life represented in the plays, but rather to the main areas of emphasis, we may find truly important — though tentative — insights into the age.

We have seen how the plays are set more and more frequently in London itself: a crowded, confusing maze of streets, business houses and brothels, law courts, prisons and inns. These settings are evidently meant to interest an audience for whom they are familiar in daily life. The distinctive emphasis on London may reflect the city's growing selfconsciousness, and we might recall that the rise of the London 'season' has been traced to this period,[7] while the city continued to grow as a social centre for the gentry, many of whom sent their sons to the Inns of Court, if not Oxford or Cambridge, to acquire some general education and social poise rather than academic or professional qualifications. The playwrights of City Comedy were clearly aware of these students and ex-students as an element in their audience (the playwrights themselves had close connections with the Inns of Court) and it might be argued that these circumstances *explain away* City Comedy's increasing interest in dishonest and ruthless moneylenders and lawyers, in a city which is itself presented as largely corrupt and hostile, governed by impersonal (and inhuman) laws of chance and the money market.

Clearly there is some force in the argument that it became rather the fashion to scourge the vices of the city. However, such an explanation takes insufficient account of the playwrights' increasingly ambivalent attitude towards the skilful, ruthless materialist who knows how to manipulate capital and the technicalities of the law — and in this sense, of course, Jonson's *Volpone* certainly is a significant comment on the Jacobean background. In the plays the growth of emphasis on the capitalist and lawyer in the city is accompanied by an increasing ambivalence of attitude towards their methods and appetites. In both respects we may consider that City Comedy is a significant reflection of developments in the political and economic life of the age, and certainly may be related to profound sources of conflict and change in early seventeenth century England.

---

[7] See for example F. J. Fisher, 'The Development of London as a Centre of Conspicuous Consumption in the Sixteenth and Seventeenth Centuries' (*Trans.R.Hist.Soc.* 1948).

As for the city of London itself, it is obviously a most significant subject for study in the plays, where the reactions of characters to its size and complexity have, at times, a strikingly modern ring. We saw in the more conventional plays of 1604–1607 how deficient art diluted the atmosphere created in such plays as The Dutch Courtezan or Michaelmas Term, so that the London setting of Westward Ho was not much more convincing than that in a Coney-Catching pamphlet by Greene, and it might be noted that precisely this point is made by the three intelligent collaborative authors of the splendid parody Eastward Ho, who emphasise the crudity of their targets by ironic iteration of hoary clichés in plot and character, and also moral-didactic comment: here for example the prodigal-gallant Quicksilver discourses with mistress Synnedefie:

QUICKSILVER . . . Ile to the Court, another manner of place for maintenance I hope then the silly Cittie . . . I shallbee a Marchaunt for-sooth: trust my estate in a wooden Troughe as hee does? What are these Shippes, but Tennis Balles for the windes to play withall? Tost from one wave to another; Nowe under-line; Nowe over the house; Sometimes Bricke-wal'd against a Rocke, so that the guttes flye out againe; Sometimes strooke under the wide Hazzard, and farewell Mast(er) Marchant.

SYNNEDEFIE Well Francke, well; the Seas you say are uncertaine: But hee that sayles in your Court Seas, shall find 'hem tenne times fuller of hazzard . . . hee that rises hardly, stands firmely: but hee that rises with ease, alas, falles as easily.

QUICKSILVER A pox on you, who taught you this morallitie?

(II, ii. 57–59, 61–71, 88–92)

Inflated burlesque of the details of city life is further displayed in the whole series of conventional situations and parodies of attempts at local colour. The burlesque incorporates some true satiric comment:

TOUCHSTONE Yes, Maister Deputy: I had a small venture with them in the voyage, a Thing, cald a Sonne in Lawe, or so. Officers, you may let 'hem stand . . . One of 'hem was my prentise, M(aister) Quicksilver, here, and when he had 2. yeare to serve, kept his whore, & his hunting Nag, would play his 100. pound at Gresco, or Primero . . . he was a Gentleman, and I a poore Cheapeside Groome. The remedie was, we must part. Since when he hath had the gift of gathering up some small parcels of mine, to the value of 500. pound disperst among my customers, to furnish this his *Virginian* venture; wherein this knight was the chiefe, Sir *Flash*:

(IV, ii. 223–225, 227–230, 234–239)

In this passage an ironic relationship is established between the vaunted exploits of voyagers (Drake is earlier saluted by Sir Petronell Flash in III, iii) and the debased, contemptible and un-heroic background of moneylenders, investors and contacts in the city. Such contemporary satire in *Eastward Ho* is certainly shrewd, but it should be noticed that it is expressed through an ironic burlesque of dramatic 'realism', through a deliberate self-conscious parody of conventional, City Comedy, 'London' characters and settings. By calling attention to their parody of crude dramatic realism Jonson Chapman and Marston direct us to the real satiric concerns — both literary and social — which underlie the whole play, and reveal perhaps unexpectedly sophisticated possibilities in critical realism. We are given not literal accuracy of reporting, but intelligent dialectic.

In the main course of City Comedy up to *The Devil Is An Ass* of 1616 the city background is of importance for its continuous contribution to the dramatic atmosphere. There is often an imaginatively creative interplay between the dramatic action and the urban settings. In Marston we first see how the city background can intensify and mirror the bewilderment and suffering of his characters, and in subsequent plays the London backgrounds seem often to reflect, ironically, the intricacies and unpredictable though constant hazards of the city, which is at once familiar yet hostile and impersonal.

8　Middleton and Jonson

'Hang art, madam, and trust to nature for dissembling'
(CONGREVE, *The Old Bachelor* III, i)

MICHAELMAS TERM, I have argued, marks an advance in Middletons art; in that play the dark and savage potential of the action expresses itself with a power more usually found in satiric tragedy. *Michaelmas Term* may be seen to echo the influential *Volpone* of Jonson, and the influence of Marston, too, in dramatising violence, savagery and disease in urban, familiar locations, is equally apparent. The conventional elements are organised into a powerful dramatic whole by the psychological penetration which informs the character drawing and the powerful thematic imagery. The intensity with which *Michaelmas Term* is written, the urgency with which the action is articulated, testify to the inspiration Middleton found in the genre City Comedy at this point of its early maturity.

Comedy with the elaborate, fast moving and complex intrigue deriving from Italian convention demands a decorum in which characterisation is slight: Shakespeare himself obeyed this decorum when he wrote *The Taming of the Shrew*. Middleton, however, modifies what he takes from the Italian tradition; in *Michaelmas Term* and the later *A Trick To Catch The Old One* the fast moving complex Italianate intrigue recurs, but the subtler motivation of character, the sharper insight which informs the writing produces a more satisfying drama — the characteristic elements are re-ordered. Middleton develops character with sharp intelligence, with wit, with truth to nature.

156

It will be recalled that there is a sequence in *Michaelmas Term* (II, iii) in which Quomodo and his creatures play upon Easy the young heir. They work on his insecurity, his vanity, hope, guilt, friendliness and anger so that his emotional struggle finally delivers him, flapping weakly, on the bank. There the dramatic art is of a higher order altogether compared with the 'lazzi' of the early plays. In his last two comedies, *A Trick To Catch The Old One* and *A Chaste Maid In Cheapside*, this higher level of writing is sustained. The major 'lazzi' are prepared for more elaborately because the audience needs to know more of the psychology of the protagonists if they are to appreciate the conflicts. This may be illustrated by an analysis of Middleton's technique in the early sequence where the Host deceives the *senex* Lucre.

At first the Host appears to be a character deriving from the stock figure of Jest Book episode, and indeed he represents himself as such to Lucre with complete success. He is, however, as soon appears, actually a Middletonian wit and Coney-catcher, a more complex character altogether. Witgood the young schemer recalls his past cameraderie with the Host and tells us he has 'rinsed the whoreson's gums in mullsack many a time' in good Jest Book style; but the Host's attitude to their relationship turns out to be less predictable:

WITGOOD Comes my prosperity desiredly to thee?
HOST   Come forfeitures to a usurer, fees to an officer, punks to an host,
        and pigs to a parson desiredly? why, then, la.[1]

The host implies a different motivation in assisting Witgood — for him it is just part of the civil war. Middleton is also insisting that his audience attend to the characters as individuals rather than conventional puppets; the Host's role may be that of Vice for the moment, but the possibilities are manifold, and he may turn on Witgood at any time, like any other predator, bawd, usurer or intelligencer. The dialogue swarms with such implications and the now alerted audience can enjoy the success of the Host's gambit with Lucre. Lucre relies on his prided man-of-the-world's shrewdness in judging the Host to be of 'a good blunt honesty'. The latter builds up this impression, makes Lucre think he is being skilful in eliciting the information:

LUCRE What countryman might this young Witgood be?

---

[1] *A Trick to Catch the Old One* ed. Dyce I, ii.

HOST A Leicestershire gentleman, sir.

LUCRE My nephew, by th' mass, my nephew! I'll fetch out more of this,
i'faith: a simple country fellow, I'll work't out of him. [Aside] —
And is that gentleman, sayst thou, presently to marry her?

(II, i)

In the phrase 'I'll work 't out of him' Middleton focuses the ironic
comedy of the situation; in fact the central interest in the sequence
is this study of character, and the soon doubled irony intensifies the
clarity with which Lucre is exposed as a vain man whose intelligence
succumbs to any appeal to self love, and whose vigour, strength and
appetite drive him deep into folly. The Host contrives a story of
Witgood's wealth which causes Lucre to reverse the scornful
criticism made only moments earlier; the directness of this volte-face
has a didactic clarity; and Lucre's lies in praise of Witgood betray
Lucre's wholly materialistic, obsessive greed:

HOST Since your worship has so much knowledge in him, can you
resolve me, sir, what his living might be? . . .

LUCRE Who, young master Witgood? why, believe it, he has as goodly a
fine living out yonder, — what do you call the place?

HOST Nay, I know not, i'faith.

LUCRE Hum — see, like a beast, if I have not forgot the name — pooh! and
out yonder again, goodly grown woods and fair meadows: pax on't,
I can ne'er hit of that place neither: he? why, he's Witgood of
Witgood Hall; he, an unknown thing!

(II, i)

Here the dialogue carries complete conviction as spoken English,
and at the same time it reveals the submerged thoughts, busily
swarming beneath the surface. At the pause before Lucre's 'why,
believe it' Lucre has thought up the ploy of seeming forgetful about
the property, and at 'pooh' he decides to name Witgood Hall,
judging it necessary to impress the Host. Thus the Host, a detached,
disguised trickster, watches with amusement as Lucre, the duped
would-be trickster exercises his art and reveals his greed. The Host
concludes the demonstration by forcing Lucre to revile and condemn
himself — the wicked uncle — and the satiric-didactic aims of the
sequence are fulfilled:

HOST . . . trust me sir, we heard once he had no lands, but all lay mortgaged
to an uncle he has in town here . . .

LUCRE Why, do you think, i'faith, he was ever so simple to mortgage his
    lands to his uncle? or his uncle so unnatural to take the extremity of
    such a mortgage?

(II, i)

A similar concern with subtler motivation is evident in the scene
where Hoard woos the courtesan under the mistaken impression
that she is wealthy:

COURTESAN Alas, you love not widows but for wealth!
    I promise you I ha' nothing, sir.
HOARD   Well said, widow,
    Well said; thy love is all I seek, before
    These gentlemen.

(III, i)

She points out Hoard's failure to take note of this statement at the
end of the play, emphasising the patterned ironic construction of the
plot based on character; Hoard's greed once aroused, the Courtesan
has little difficulty in provoking him to marry her secretly, thus
closing the last door by which Hoard might discover the truth.
The ridicule is directed with some invention and wit by Middleton;
at the moment where the Courtesan relinquishes Hoard's fictitious
rival, Witgood appears as the detached Commentator:

COURTESAN Is my love so deceiv'd? Before you all
    I do renounce him; on my knees I vow (kneels)
    He ne'er shall marry me.
WITGOOD   [looking in] Heaven knows he never meant it!

(III, i)

The manipulation of the two misers by the Courtesan for Witgood's
benefit is done by shrewd calculation of their psychology and
admirable timing of temptation. Lucre becomes desperate through
repeated rebuffs, finally commits himself:

Widow, believe't, I vow by my best bliss,
Before these gentlemen, I will give in
The mortgage to my nephew instantly . . .
Nay, more; . . . he shall be my heir;

(IV, i)

Hoard rejoices at this scene (which he has eavesdropped) and this
very glee is turned against him by dashing his hopes, then deluding
him into thinking he has found a way out. Full of self-love at this

achievement (as he conceives it) Hoard accepts all Witgood's debts
in return for Witgood's empty declaration of relinquishment of
claim to the Courtesan. Hoard's vanity and greed are emphasised in
several places to prepare for this scene. He declares his idea of love:

> to enrich my state, augment my revenues, and build mine own for-
> tunes.
>
> > (II, ii)

Witgood has recommended Hoard to the Courtesan solely for his
acquisitive success:

> he's rich in money, moveables, and lands; marry him:
>
> > (III, i)

Hoard early on reveals voracity, power and energy on the scale of
Volpone's:

> I'll mar your phrase, o'erturn your flatteries,
> Undo your windings, policies, and plots,
> Fall like a secret and despatchful plague
> On your secured comforts.
>
> > (II, ii)

and at the point of his gulling, Witgood relinquishes the love of the
Courtesan and, much more emphatically, claim to

> any of her manors, manor-houses, parks, groves, meadowgrounds,
> arable lands, barns, stacks, stables, dove-holes, and coney-burrows;
> together with all her cattle, money, plate, jewels, borders, chains,
> bracelets, furnitures, hangings,
>
> > (IV, iv)

This long list of solid material wealth makes an impression of the
very air being darkened by the mass of possessions. The comment on
Hoard's attitude to love and marriage is memorable. This particular
satiric device is used comparably by Jonathan Swift. To quote Swift
may usefully reflect Middleton's satiric purpose:

> And, being no Stranger to the Art of War, I gave him a Description of
> Cannons, Culverins, Muskets, Carabines, Pistols, Bullets, Powder,
> Swords, Bayonets, Sieges, Retreats, Attacks, Undermines, Counter-
> mines, Bombardments, Sea-fights; Ships sunk with a Thousand Men;
> twenty Thousand killed on each Side; dying Groans, Limbs flying in
> the Air: smoak, Noise, Confusion,[2]

---

[2] *Gulliver's Travels* Part IV, chap. V, p. 247, ed. Herbert Davis
(Oxford 1959).

There are formal characteristics of the play which relate it to City
Comedy; more specifically, *A Trick To Catch The Old One* reveals the
influence of Jonson's *Volpone*. Certain sequences are handled in an
overtly stylised, emblematic and schematic manner. The three
creditors may be a pale imitation of Voltore, Corbaccio and Corvino:
Middleton's dramatic style is very mannered here, to emphasise the
absoluteness of their obsessive avarice, and their absurdly predictable
responses:

1 CREDITOR I am glad of this news.
2 CREDITOR So are we, by my faith.
3 CREDITOR Young Witgood will be a gallant again now.
(II, ii)

and when Witgood flatters them their response is comparable:

WITGOOD   I may tell you as my friends.
1, 2 & 3 CREDITORS O, O, O!

This farcical stylisation prepares for the attempts of each creditor in
turn to bribe Witgood privately, which is, again, reminiscent of the
first half of *Volpone*. In addition to the three creditors there are Hoard's
three gentlemen, who repeat the suit of Hoard to the Courtesan, and
having done so they sue for credit with mechanical repetitiveness:

1 GENT I was the first that moved her.
HOARD You were, i'faith.
2 GENT But it was I that took her at the bound.
HOARD Ay, that was you . . .
3 GENT I boasted least, but 'twas I join'd their hands.
(III, iii)

Middleton uses the same style in the sequence where Hoard indulges
his Faustus-like fantasy with the figures of the tailor, barber,
perfumer, falconer and huntsman, treated as possessions, dancing
like puppets to his tune in the Morality Play manner. The sequence
(IV, iv) recalls indeed the less polished manner of Comical Satyre, as
do the ridicule sequences:

MONEYLOVE . . . Witgood is a spendthrift, a dissolute fellow.
HOARD   A very rascal.
MONEYLOVE A midnight surfeiter.
HOARD   The spume of a brothel house.
(II, ii)

L

Later, Hoard agrees to let Lucre plead with the already married
Courtesan:

COURTESAN You may stand by and smile at his old weakness:
           Let me alone to answer him.
HOARD   Content;
           'Twill be good mirth i'faith. How think you, gentlemen?
LAMPEY   Good gullery! . . .
LUCRE   All spite and malice! . . .
           O master Hoard, your spite has watch'd the hour!
           You're excellent at vengeance, master Hoard.
HOARD   Ha, ha, ha!
LUCRE   I am the fool you laugh at:

                                                    (IV, i)

Hoard is similarly discomfitted:

LIM   In your old age doat on a courtesan!
HOARD   Ha!
KIX   Marry a strumpet!
HOARD   Gentlemen!
O. HOARD   And Witgood's quean!
HOARD   O! Nor lands nor living?
O. HOARD   Living! . . .
HOARD   Out! out! I am cheated; infinitely cozen'd!

                                                    (V, ii)

The Courtesan's repentant octosyllabics at the conclusion actually
echo *Cynthia's Revels* directly, referring us to the lineage of this style —
Comical Satyre.

The clarity of opposed principles, which characterises the ethical
debate in City Comedy, may seem crude when expressed in these
stylised sequences, and in the outcome of the plot where Hoard is
ridiculed and left with a prostitute for a wife; but this 'poetic justice'
is merely the frame for subtle and acute articulation of the action
in the main development; the didactic point is stated with epigrammatic and emblematic simplicity precisely because of the
complexity which its illustration involves.

The psychological acuteness of Middleton's character drawing is
manifest in the villain-miser Hoard. As we have seen, Hoard has an
irrepressible animal vigour and lusty, crude high spirits which are
attractive; when 'winning over' the Courtesan, whom he believes to
be rich, his businessman's cynical sense of humour is undeniably

attractive and truthful: the Courtesan protests that she is poor, can offer nothing but love; Hoard guffaws at what he takes to be her naive scheming and deception:

> Well said, widow,
> Well said; thy love is all I seek.

The same animal appeal informs his famous self-congratulatory outburst 'What a sweet blessing hast thou, master Hoard' which, for all its crude materialist aspiration has an undeniable vigour and broad humour. Of course such *hubris* invites a heavy dousing in ridicule, but for the first time Middleton has given fully convincing life to that stock conventional target of the satirists, the land-grabbing merchant-usurer. It is a mark of Middleton's mature art that the sequence ridicules Hoard's vanity, greed and folly while simultaneously revealing his energy, courage and sheer animal gusto. It is a truthful portrayal which stands up to the weight of irony, ridicule and moral censure without losing life and psychological truth. In the event Hoard emerges as perhaps a more convincing London citizen than the sentimentally presented, Popular, more famous creation of Dekker, Simon Eyre the shoemaker. Hoard has the courage and the stature to stand up to ridicule, to accept defeat and criticism; and having done so, he can find his voice, and his manhood, again:

> So, so, all friends! the wedding-dinner cools:
> Who seem most crafty prove ofttimes most fools.

A Chaste Maid in Cheapside was written for the Popular stage between 1611 and 1613 and it is interesting to note what modifications Middleton makes to the style and form of City Comedy as he had written it previously for Coterie audiences. Hoard, in the preceding play, had by his very aggressive, ruthless materialism, challenged the truth of Dekker's character, the citizen shoemaker who becomes Lord Mayor and in the process grows more and more the naively patriotic, loyal tradesman, rather than the politic, ruthless careerist we might expect. The distinction of a deeper complexity in motive and character and situation by Middleton gives his play an intellectual strength missing in Dekker's. These qualities are manifest in *A Chaste Maid In Cheapside*, though of course it does not take up the subject and form where they were laid down by Middleton five years earlier.

The plot is based on ironic patterns familiar from earlier Middletonian comedy, and 'lazzi' involving the young prodigal, the
cuckold, the rich knight, the country wench, similarly emphasise
the continuity, while at key points the dialogue has the characteristic
savage edge and sinewy vigour. The play's general articulation is,
however, looser, slower moving, more like the sloppy articulation
of the Popular work of Dekker or Day. Similarly, it includes the
ridicule of only one character in a full blooded sadistic manner (Sir
Walter) and the dialogue is marked by the pursuit of obvious,
laboured and unintelligent sexual and vulgar jests in Popular style.
One scene, in fact, has been called one of 'the rankest in all Elizabethan drama'[3] and certainly lacks the wit of Middletonian or
Jonsonian work elsewhere. I think that Middleton's use of the style
and conventions of Popular comedy here can be shown to be
deliberate and purposeful; that the seeming contradiction of the
two styles within the play is not a weakness, and that the author's
purpose does not differ from that in his earlier, tight-knit, urgently
driven Coterie City Comedies.

What Middleton does is to 'place', ironically, the naive predicta-
bility and superficiality of Popular, particularly Dekkeresque,
elements which he uses in the play. We may suggest that the sheer
volume of witless, crude bawdy is Middleton's implied comment on
the taste of Popular theatre audiences, a sardonic rejoinder to the
claim that theirs is just 'good healthy dirt', 'part of life's rich
earthiness':

YELLOWHAMMER Have you the wideness of her finger, sir?
TOUCHWOOD   Yes, sure, I think I have her measure about me:
              Good faith, — 'tis down, I cannot shew it you;
              I must pull too many things out to be certain.
              Let me see — long and slender . . .[4]

There is no contradiction in the presence of Popular and Coterie
styles together in this play. It will be recalled that in chapter VII the
discussion of *Westward Ho* centred round the diffuseness which
resulted from the reliance on Popular conventions of playmaking;
there a series of scenes having no common theme or purpose,
directed towards building up no comprehensive picture or comment
on society, was strung together merely by the common presence of a

[3] M. C. Bradbrook, *The Growth and Structure of Elizabethan Comedy*, p. 172.
[4] *A Chaste Maid in Cheapside* ed. Dyce I, i.

set of City Comedy characters. In Popular comedy the characteristic looseness of articulation derives largely from the playwrights' aim to present episodes purely for their comic potential — anything goes, so long as the audience laughs, and if it does not laugh the clowns will, likely as not, speak more than is set down for them or

> will themselves laugh, to set on some quantity of barren spectators to laugh too, though in the mean time, some necessary question of the play be then to be considered :[5]

In *A Chaste Maid In Cheapside* the dialogue is frequently desultory and loose, catching the inconsequentiality, the hack-work flavour of Popular work, the better to satirise it. An example from early on in the play may illuminate this technique.

The chaste maid herself, at the point where she is about to 'die', delivers a pitiable cry which is sufficiently sloppy and sentimental, the half-suppressed echoes of earlier death speeches from famous Popular plays like *Romeo and Juliet* giving that characteristic *ersatz* flavour (familiar from the Romantic main plot speeches of Dekker in *Satiromastix* or *Westward Ho*):

> O, my heart dies! . . .
> Farewell, life! . . .
> O, bring me death tonight, love-pitying fates;
> Let me not see tomorrow upon the world!
>
> (IV, iii)

This has been preceded by such Popular Jest Book material as the jests of the Cambridge porter (I, i), the misunderstanding of the Stage Welsh with Dekker style 'mistaking of words' (IV, i) and the vulgar and meandering dialogue of the christening party scene (III, ii). When the chaste maid prepares to 'die' she sings a lament of sufficient sweet sentimentality, and her father responds to her death with predictably 'noble' rhetoric:

> YELLOWHAMMER   Take her in,
> Remove her from our sight, our shame and sorrow.
> TOUCHWOOD   Stay, let me help thee, 'tis the last cold kindness
> I can perform for my sweet brother's sake.
>
> (V, ii)

and Touchwood Senior provides a lament in true Popular Act V style:

---

[5] Hamlet's speech to the players.

What nature could there shine, that might redeem
Perfection home to woman, but in her
Was fully glorious? Beauty set in goodness
Speaks what she was;

(V, iv)

Here we have exact and illuminating instances of Middleton's use
of parody to make a strong positive comment on the characters who
speak it. Middleton has not the least intention of presenting such
sentimentality for its own sake. The speeches bear a weight of irony
which is soon enough revealed. Moll's swan song is appreciated by
her mother for its sweetness — her mother is more interested in it
than in the fact that she is apparently dying, and her father remarks
with polite interest 'she plays the swan and sings herself to death'.
The father is planning ahead at the very moment his daughter is
being borne off dead on a bier; what he calls 'our shame and
sorrow' is in fact for him a financial scheme that has failed (she has
not been well married off) so another scheme must be floated;
he sets about planning:

YELLOWHAMMER . . . its our best course, wife . . .
                T'absent ourselves till she be laid in ground.
WIFE   Where shall we spend that time?
YELLOWHAMMER I'll tell thee where, wench:
                Go to some private church, and marry Tim
                To the rich Brecknock gentlewoman.

'Naturally' his wife, bereaved as she is, cheers up instantly at this:

    Mass, a match;
    We'll not lose all at once, somewhat we'll catch.[6]

In the last instance quoted (V, iv) the funeral oration of Touchwood
Senior is echoed by a mourner and then it is exposed as cant by the
rising of the dead from their coffins, itself a parody of the stock
Popular convention.[7]

TOUCHWOOD SNR I cannot think there's anyone amongst you
                In this full fair assembly, maid, man, or wife,
                Whose heart would not have sprung with joy and gladness
                To have seen their marriage day.

---

[6] V, ii. Compare the skilful use, by Marlowe's Jew Barabas, of emotional
lamentation and outburst to gain time for fresh planning in The Jew of Malta
I. 549–607 and III. 158–211.

[7] See M. C. Bradbrook, Themes and Conventions of Elizabethan Tragedy, p. 121 n.

MOURNER   *It would have made a thousand joyful hearts.* (my italics)

TOUCHWOOD SNR Up then apace . . . [*Moll and Y. Touchwood rise out of their coffins*].

(*V*, iv)

In this intelligent sequence we note the impatient distaste for stupid and vulgar sentimentality and dramatic cliché which marks the best satiric comedy from the *Jew of Malta* forward. Indeed this sequence may be compared with that in the *Jew of Malta* where Barabas and Ithamore strangle a friar with a jest on their lips, prop him up on his staff 'as if he were begging of bacon' and look on, mocking his death and his holy robes, both sacrosanct topics elsewhere in Elizabethan drama. In the *Jew of Malta* as in *A Chaste Maid In Cheapside*, it is these conventional taboos, no less than the dramatic characters, which are satirised.

This purpose is in fact central to the play, for Middleton's satire focuses on those characters who, devoid of all religious and moral conviction, uninterested in morality, do not recognise the existence of love between man and woman, father and son, mother and daughter. All human relationships are conceived of in terms of financial contract. This theme finds expression everywhere in the play, even in throw-away jests:

Thieves, thieves! my sister's stol'n! some thief hath got her:
O how miraculously did my father's plate 'scape!
'Twas all left out,

(*IV*, ii)

Tim's attitude to his sister is precisely the same as his attitude to the plate; and her father, Yellowhammer, regards his daughter as a marketable commodity, as I pointed out earlier. It is the financial concern of Touchwood Senior which prevents him fathering a family while it is precisely for financial and property reasons that Kix wishes for children. It is insistence that financial considerations are the sole valid considerations that leads Allwit to submit to the boorish domination of Sir Walter Whorehound, and it is such considerations which drive Allwit to prevent Sir Walter from marrying. One of the neatest ironies in the plot is that Allwit's selfishly acquisitive motives result in a situation where the sexually acquisitive desires of Young Touchwood find satisfaction instead. In the christening party scene the effect is to strip every character and reveal their rapaciously selfish desires, masked as they are by cant about religion, family affection, the joys of birth. The real father, the cuckolder Sir Walter, wears the mask of Godfather (a savagely direct irony) and the titular father is dressed in one of the cuckolder's suits. This scene presents a microcosm of the comic world of Middleton, paying lip service to Christian ideals, but actually closely resembling that presented by the analysis of Thomas Hobbes.

Middleton presents in his mature comedies a moral and critical analysis of City society; his forceful purpose does not, however, deny the fuller human qualities in his villains. He presents with honesty and insight the vigour, the resilience, the human joys and fears and disappointments felt by characters who are condemned and satirised by the plays' design. At the centre of figures such as Quomodo, Lucre, Hoard, Whorehound, Allwit, is their menace, their evil, their corrupting effect on society; but their threat is at once less sensational and more real and persuasive when we see what vitality, courage and intelligence they summon in pursuit of their prey. The purpose of the brilliant lyrical outbursts uttered by these figures is to show that even when they ignore the dictates of humanity and moral law they can still be attractive. Middleton does not over-simplify the kind of life from which the threat springs. Indeed he was, like Jonson, fascinated not only by their animal vitality but also by the sharp clarity with which they cut through convention and dogma to the thing itself. Certainly in the comedies Middleton does not hesitate to show that these figures are anti-pathetic to any Christian ethic; on the other hand it is his acknowledgement of the practical possibility of Allwit's successful existence by pragmatic policy alone which shows that Middleton is turning over the question 'why is this feasible if it is immoral?'; it is out of this quarrel with himself that Middleton makes his art. Middleton's treatment of Allwit is powerfully ironic, the conclusion of the play manifestly condemns Allwit to hell; and yet for Allwit financial and material success and enjoyment continue. He is not punished as even the brilliantly politic Volpone is punished. Allwit, like Face in the *Alchemist* (in date the closest play of Jonson to *A Chaste Maid in Cheapside*) evades punishment because his wit is obviously perfectly adapted to his environment, he wins what he has and can keep it, as long as his wit holds out (to paraphrase Hobbes). Both

Allwit and Face have one rule in life — trust nobody. As Face remarks, with Middletonian irony, when asked where the rogue Face is, and his comrades:

> I thought 'hem honest, as myselfe, sir.

The pervasive irony of these comedies itself implies that nothing and nobody is to be trusted — 'Force, and fraud, are in war the two cardinal virtues', said Hobbes. These are the twin sources of energy in the City Comedy of Thomas Middleton.

The *Alchemist* has Italianate complexity of plot, speed of action, wittily invented situations and intelligent insights into character such as we found in *Volpone* and the comedies of Middleton. The *Alchemist*, however sublime and universal its excellence, here takes its place in the direct continuation of the *genre* after the major contribution of Middleton.

In the opening scene of the play the three tricksters are discovered in conflict; their criticisms of each other, though cast in the terms of low comic invective, turn out to be just and acute in the subsequent action. Subtle claims to have made Face fit 'for more then ordinarie fellowships' when he was, beforehand, among 'broomes, and dust, and watring pots', while Face for his part claims to have raised Subtle from destitution at Pie Corner taking his 'meale of steeme in, from cookes stalls', looking 'piteously costive' with a pinched nose. Doll tries to halt the quarrel by reminding them that they must work together, and her cry immediately points up the continuity from Middletonian comedy to The *Alchemist*, and suggests the atmosphere of the play:

> Gentlemen, what meane you?
> Will you marre all? . . .
> Will you un-doe your selves, with civill warre?
> (I, i. 80–82)

Certainly Face, Subtle and Doll do not recognise what Hobbes was to call 'dominion'. If they do not war with one another it is so that they can war with men at large.

The three tricksters base their schemes on intelligent perception of their victims and manipulation of motive and temperament; their dupes are all greedy, the sin most familiar to the tricksters and therefore the best to control and direct in others. The chief dupe has

the most powerful passion, the strongest fantasies of wish fulfilment
centring on a deep obsession with the Philosopher's Stone. The
stone is the symbol of the absurdity and sterility at the heart of
greed: in itself it is cold, dull, shapeless, unfeeling, dead; and with
this of all things Sir Epicure expects to transform the world into a
fairyland of riches.

It is to be emphasised that the central image of the play has
emblematically direct didacticism. The vital drive of The Alchemist is
towards the exposure and ridicule of greedy fools and their fantasies,
its outcome reveals that in a state of civil war where man is to man
as wolf to wolf, supremacy and security are brief, the way to them
nasty, and the qualities required for their attainment basically
brutish. Intelligence is certainly essential for success; but he who is
politic is also witty.

The play's form reveals the same clarity and direct didactic
purpose inherent in the symbol of the stone. The house deserted
by Face's master is like the dukedom deserted by the disguised duke
in earlier plays, and though Lovewit is only present at the conclusion, his appearance fulfils the function of offering a detached, intelligent and critical view of people and events; Lovewit comments on
the folly of the citizens and gulls exercised and exposed as a result
of his absence. Face has performed the role of Vice, chief deviser of
'lazzi' and exempla which satirise and ridicule Mammon, Ananias and
Tribulation, the would-be gallant Kastril, Drugger the slow-witted
tradesman, Lovewit's citizen-neighbours; and Jonson's survey
includes the tricksters themselves, for Subtle and Doll receive harsh
treatment in the catastrophe, though Face, by his wit and skill,
escapes scot free. Even here, the genre has precedents. Of course it
must not be denied that the dazzling speed of the action and the
complexity of the intrigue are complemented by the exhilarating
fecundity in 'lazzi' of Subtle, Doll and Face. At those moments where
all three are thrown into a crisis which they must survive by instant
action — as, for example, when Mammon arrives in the middle of
Dapper's audience with the Queen of Faery in III, v — we are so
interested in what will happen next, in what plan will be devised,
that we may well assume that the play depends altogether on
surprise, the illusion of spontaneity. A more thorough examination
of the satiric-didactic element, the form of the exempla and the manner
in which characters are satirically presented, does however reveal

how the play actually is based on the form of City Comedy and derives much of its superb comic potential from the conventions of the *genre*. The remainder of this chapter attempts to illustrate this more closely.

The opening scene of the play, as I have already remarked, offers us satiric, epithetical descriptions of the rogues and of their careers; the quarrel elicits these Theophrastus-style 'characters' in an admirably dramatic manner, but we do well to note how typical of City Comedy the satire is:

SUBTLE You were once (time's not long past) the good,
       Honest, plaine, livery-three-pound-thrum . . .
FACE   And your complexion, of the *romane* wash,
       Stuck full of black, and melancholique wormes,
       Like poulder-cornes, shot, at th'*artillerie-yard* . . .
SUBTLE   Cheater.
FACE   Bawd.
SUBTLE   Cow-herd.
FACE   Conjuror.
SUBTLE Cutpurse.
FACE   Witch.
DOLL   O me!
          (I, i. 15–16, 29–31, 106–108)

Doll, who makes them leave off quarrelling and submit to confession and correction, completes the *exemplum* form; its use by Jonson is ironic: the rogues are thus brought back to the strait and narrow path of crime.

The scenes in which the aspirants Mammon, Drugger and the rest call at the house recall closely in form and function the scenes in *Volpone* where Voltore, Corbaccio and Corvino arrive, seeking news of their favour with Volpone and their chances of getting his wealth. Here Dapper's suit to the 'doctor' is taken up by Face with a great show of pessimism, and several attempts to attract the interest of the 'doctor' (Subtle) fail. The denials finally give way to some reluctant interest from Subtle, whose timing is admirable; his final and regretful acceptance of Dapper's money is like Quomodo's technique of getting Easy to sign the bond in *Michaelmas Term*. The skilful gradations of the trickster's gullery, which conclude in Dapper's complete belief in the queen of Faery, present not only a highly comic spectacle but also bring out with sharp clarity the essential

connection between the ordinary and common credulity of Dapper
— superstition in domestic affairs — and superstition in the soaring
fantastic nonsense about fairyland; thus the comic sequence serves
also to bring out the essential kinship of Dapper and Sir Epicure
Mammon, even though the tricksters would never dare to make
quite such open fun of Sir Epicure to his face as they do of Dapper:

FACE   Did you never see
            Her royall *Grace*, yet?
DAPPER   Whom?
FACE   Your aunt of *Faerie*?
                    (I, ii. 148–149)

Just after this exchange Face makes a doubly ironic jest to bring
home to the audience how cool and objective, how politic, such a
rogue as Face needs to be:

> Well then, away. 'Tis but your bestowing
> Some twenty nobles, 'mong her *Graces* servants;
>   (I, ii. 172–173)

The audience is brought back to an awareness of the tricksters'
essential predatoriness, regains its detached critical attitude to all the
characters, loving nobody too freely.

The tricksters have no difficulty at all in eliciting the folly,
fantastic superstition and greed in Drugger and Mammon. Drugger's
speeches are frankly contrived by Jonson to show off his folly; he
and Mammon betray themselves through their comically inappropriate juxtapositions, jumbling mythical with domestic,
magical with banal:

> And I would know, by art, sir, of your worship,
> Which way I should make my dore, by *necromancie*.
> And, where my shelves. And which should be for boxes.
>   (I, iii. 10–12)

This from Drugger may be set beside Mammon's claim

> I have a peece of JASON'S fleece, too,
> Which was no other, then a booke of *alchemie*,
> Writ in large sheepe-skin,
>   (II, i. 89–91)

Subtle and Face ridicule Drugger with the barest Empsonian type of
ambiguity:

FACE   He lets me have good *tabacco*, and he do's not
        Sophisticate it, with sack-lees, or oyle . . .
        Nor buries it, in gravell, under ground . . .
        A neate, spruce-honest-fellow, and no goldsmith . . .
SUBTLE Your chest-nut, or your olive-colour'd face
        Do's never faile: and your long eare doth promise.
        I knew't, by certaine spots too, in his teeth,

>   (I, iii. 23–24, 26, 32, 46–48)

When Subtle ridicules Mammon, it is with the heaviest criticism
used of characters in Jonson — that their actions are in direct
opposition to reason, nature and custom. Mammon's total folly
could not be presented more emphatically than here:

> Me thinkes, I see him, entering ordinaries,
> Dispensing for the poxe; and plaguy-houses,
> Reaching his dose; walking *more-fields* for lepers . . .
> Searching the spittle, to make old bawdes yong;

>   (I, iv. 18–20, 23)

and when Mammon makes his first appearance Surly acts as the
detached, critical commentator on the whole scene. Surly acts as
spokesman for truth, reason, custom: he detects trickery:

MAMMON   In eight, and twentie dayes,
        I'll make an old man, of fourescore, a childe.
SURLY   No doubt, hee's that alreadie.

>   (II, i. 52–54)

Such deflation is very amusing too:

SUBTLE Ha' you set the oile of *Luna* in *kemia*?
FACE   Yes, sir.
SUBTLE   And the *philosophers* vinegar?
FACE   I.
SURLY   We shall have a sallad.

>   (II, iii. 99–101)

Yet Surly's didacticism here is unflinching:

> Rather, then I'll be brai'd, sir, I'll beleeve,
> That *Alchemie* is a pretty kind of game,
> Somewhat like tricks o'the cards, to cheat a man,

>   (II, iii. 179–181)

and when Surly sees Doll he exclaims, much like Fitzgrave at the
'music school' (*Your Five Gallants* II, ii) 'Hart, this is a bawdy-house!

I'll be burnt else' (II, iii. 226). Surly's plan to test the tricksters by
disguising as a Spaniard, unmasking to expose them in full career, is
another instance of the Disguised-Duke plot-form; one such plot is
acted out within another in The Alchemist because Surly's didactic role
actually fails, for the first time in City Comedy.

In the sequence where Subtle, Face and Doll attempt to gull the
'Spaniard' (Surly in his disguise) Jonson provides a supreme instance
of the comic ridicule convention of the genre:

SUBTLE 'Slud, he do's looke too fat to be a Spaniard.
FACE   Perhaps some Fleming, or some Hollander got him
        In D'ALVA'S time . . .
SURLY   Gratia.
SUBTLE He speakes, out of a fortification.
                            (IV, iii. 28–30, 32)

The fact that Surly dislikes ridicule makes him as comic as the
tricksters whom he deceives:

FACE   Cossened, doe you see?
        My worthy Donzel, cossened.
SURLY   Entiendo.
SUBTLE Doe you intend it? So doe we, deare Don.
        Have you brought pistolets? or portagues?
        My solemne Don? Dost thou feele any? [Face feels his pockets] . . .
        You shall be sok'd, and strok'd, and tub'd, and rub'd:
        And scrub'd, and fub'd, deare Don, before you goe.
                            (IV, iii. 39–43, 97–98)

The tricksters have the gleeful boisterousness of their ancestors in
Comical Satyre; and when their target Surly takes off his disguise he
is revealed as the Presenter, explaining, judging, in the convention
of the role:

            Lady, you see into what hands, you are falne;
            Mongst what a nest of villaines! . . .
            I am a gentleman, come here disguis'd,
            Onely to find the knaveries of this Citadell.
                            (IV, vi. 1–2, 8–9)

Surly's satiric ridicule of Face and Subtle is unsparing, his threat of
'a cleane whip' recalls the sternness of Comical Satyre correction, the
severity of Jonson's purpose there.

Surly has thoroughly outwitted the tricksters, has all the evidence needed to expose them. At this moment it seems that nothing can save Face and Subtle; but quick thinking produces a masterstroke, and the entry of Kastril the roaring boy (momentarily everyone had forgotten about him) is perfect because his sole characteristic is given a situation in which it can be useful. Next Drugger appears (the Marx Brothers frequently used this comic effect — cf. the sequence in *A Night At The Opera* where about twenty-eight people on diverse errands all enter the tiny cabin already filled by Groucho's luggage) and he is told that Surly intends to steal the widow; he begins roaring too, and at this climax of noise and struggle Jonson effects one of the most memorable entrances in comic drama with Ananias, who intones his jargon greeting ('Peace to the household') with unintended aptness. Subtle points out to Ananias that Surly is dressed elaborately as a Spaniard; thus defeat is turned into victory, the dominant follies of the gulls are directed full at Surly, who can do nothing against this stream of insane hostility. The tricksters successfully alter and combine the three separate schemes of deception (on Drugger I, iii and II, vi, on Ananias II, v, III, i and III, ii, and on Kastril III, iv and IV, ii) and the new 'lazzo' serves not only to outwit Surly but also to expose the folly of the gulls — it is also an *exemplum*, in fact.

The scene is superbly effective not only because of the close succession of surprises, the sudden entrances of widely contrasting, absurd figures, the violent reversal for Surly, but also because the dupes are all seen together on stage for the first time and they do not realise what they have in common, nor that the tricksters have brought about a climax of ridicule directed towards them while they display their extreme 'Humours':

SURLY	Why, this is madnesse, sir,
	Not valure in you: I must laugh at this.
KASTRIL	It is my humour: you are a Pimpe, and a Trig,
	And an AMADIS *de Gaule*, or a *Don* QUIXOTE.
DRUGGER	Or a Knight o'the *curious cox-combe*. Doe you see?
ANANIAS	Peace to the houshold.
KASTRIL	Ile keepe peace, for no man.
ANANIAS	Casting of dollers is concluded lawfull.
KASTRIL	Is he the Constable?
SUBTLE	Peace, ANANIAS.
FACE	No, sir.

KASTRIL   Then you are an Otter, and a Shad, a Whit,
                 A very Tim.
SURLY   You'll heare me, sir?
KASTRIL   I will not.
ANANIAS   What is the motive?
SUBTLE   Zeale, in the yong gentleman,
                 Against his Spanish slops —
ANANIAS   They are profane,
                 Leud, superstitious, and idolatrous breeches.

                                                    (IV, vii. 37–49)

After this the audience may feel that a little calm will follow, but
almost before the actors have got their breath back Jonson devises a
further shock — Lovewit, Face's master, owner of the house, returns.
The disguised duke has returned to unmask folly, to judge and to
restore order.

   Act V begins with a short sequence exposing the slow wittedness
of the citizen neighbours, which prepares us for Face's brazen
outfacing and ridiculing of their truthful account of events. Face
here proceeds exactly in the manner of Voltore, pleading to the
court in Volpone IV, vi. Face appeals that the events are too absurd
to be credible, and gives weight to this by his new 'disguise' of
sober, dutiful butler (which in fact he actually is, in one sense) and
he directs all the force of the accusations of Surly, Mammon and the
rest back on their own heads, claiming they suffer from absurd
delusions. Lovewit provides the audience with an alternative viewpoint from which the events of the play do indeed appear drunken
fantasies and apparitions. The appeal to the norm enhances Jonson's
achievement, of course, as well as giving richness to the situation;
he is directing us to the completeness of his art. With every turn
Face contrives new traps for his impassioned enemies. The cool
Machiavel wins the approval of the judge himself. The righteous
but wild protests of Kastril and Ananias swamp the more reasonable
analysis of Surly, making their claims seem ridiculous; they complete
their own gullery:

KASTRIL   You will not come then? punque, device, my suster!
ANANIAS   Call her not sister. Shee is a harlot, verily.
KASTRIL   I'll raise the street.
LOVEWIT   Good gentlemen, a word.
ANANIAS   Sathan, avoid, and hinder not our zeale.

LOVEWIT   The world's turn'd Bet'lem.
FACE   These are all broke loose
          Out of S.KATHER'NES, where they use to keepe,
          The better sort of mad-folkes.
                                              (V, iii. 50–56)

Doll and Subtle have meanwhile planned to ditch Face in true
City Comedy Style:

SUBTLE   Soone at night, my DOLLY,
          When we are shipt, and all our goods aboord,
          East-ward for Ratcliffe; we will turne our course
          To Brainford, westward, if thou saist the word:
          And take our leaves of this ore-weaning raskall,
                                              (V, iv. 74–78)

and they look forward to unlocking the trunks of spoil

          And say, this's mine, and thine, and thine, and mine—
                                              (V, iv. 91)

in true Hobbesian fashion. Face has, however, forseen this eventuality,
his self-interest cunning and efficiency being a match for theirs.
Warning them to run for it, Face announces the end of their partner-
ship, significantly, with a legal metaphor; their particular social
contract to protect each other from each other's fear and greed is now
broken:

          here/ Determines the indenture tripartite
          Twixt SUBTLE, DOL and FACE.
                                              (V, iv. 130–132)

Hobbes had conversations with Ben Jonson, it is recorded.

Face the comic Machiavel is perfectly adapted to his environment,
acutely aware of its springs of motivation in greed and fear. Face
triumphs where even Volpone failed. Jonson acknowledges the
practical possibility that a ruthless materialist and opportunist can
go on thriving indefinitely in Jacobean London; men like Face
win the urban civil war.

The play utilises the conventions of City Comedy to present an
analysis of the varying follies to which men are driven by greed.
The three tricksters wield the bait and contrive a series of exempla
exposing the essential ridiculousness, futility and sterility of human
greed. The success of Face is in itself an ironic comment on the total

M

dedication of his urban society to acquisitiveness: Face is the ideal citizen, from one point of view. The first and seemingly conclusive unmasking of the conventional 'Disguised Duke' — in the form of Surly — actually fails for the first time in the history of the genre to bring folly and wrongdoing to order. The old-fashioned morality, as embodied in the plot-convention and the character Surly, can no longer control and dominate the new kind of criminal and Coney-catcher. When the second judge, Lovewit, appears, he can do no more than acknowledge the skill and wit of Face; and though the other fools, hypocrites and maniacs are judged and ridiculed in conventional fashion, Face evades punishment. Jonson himself is conscious that Face's victory is, if not moral, yet convincing.

9 Bartholomew Fair and The Devil Is An Ass: Final Plays

IN Bartholomew Fair Jonson takes a further step in his ironic variation of the convention of the disguised duke, which we examined in the Alchemist. This plot convention embodies the didactic form derived from Morality drama, as we have seen, the duke taking on the role of Presenter and distributing judgement, reward and punishment at the conclusion. In The Alchemist Surly attempted to fulfil this role but was outwitted and ridiculed by Face, and even Face's master Lovewit, the final Presenter, was unable to administer punishment to the brilliant, if criminal, schemer. In Bartholomew Fair there is no doubt who has the role of Presenter of the 'humours' and commentator on the exempla: the Disguised-Duke figure is Justice Overdo. However, Justice Overdo is so far from being capable of control over his society, of shrewd judgement and domination, that he actually suffers ridicule, beating and being thrust into the stocks; and this he deserves more than the rogues and fools who surround him. Here the Presenter and commentator is actually the biggest fool, the worst judge of men, his filling of the role is a sheer parody of it. In fact Jonson here turns the familiar plot inside out, for the play concludes when the Presenter-Judge has himself suffered exposure, ridicule and physical correction of folly.

Although Overdo is a parody of the Presenter, the conventional didactic form of the genre is retained. Bartholomew Fair is constructed

179

loosely, in a manner reminiscent of the Comical Satyres, with a
series of didactic episodes exposing the foolish 'humours' of the
large gallery of characters, concluding in the correction and return
to normality of some and in the statement of the moral lessons to be
drawn from what has passed. This play shows Jonson returning to
the style of his earliest experiments in satiric drama and bringing all
the resources of his mature mastery to bear on a problem he failed to
solve in 1599–1601 : how to write a masterpiece while virtually
dispensing with a strong main plot and one or two major protagonists. It is the consciousness that he was attempting something still
original, experimental and difficult at this mid-Jacobean time that
explains Jonson's insistence, in the ostensibly old-fashioned
Induction, that his play Bartholomew Fair is not to be judged by
Popular Elizabethan criteria, which have 'stood still, these five and
twentie, or thirtie yeeres'. Although the play has a verbal flavour
reminiscent of the first, Elizabethan 'Humour' play, this is deliberate,
a full return to the style of Comical Satyre, the richly physical,
closely observed, satirically pointed epithetical dialogue; and
Jonson has not lost his scorn for the groundlings who cannot judge
his difficult art and their open Popular stages 'as durty as Smithfield,
and as stinking every whit'. Yet it is true that in this, as in Jonson's
other great plays, his facility for Popular comic dialogue and for the
Popular Elizabethan comic manner finds expression and contributes
to the whole. Bartholomew Fair ridicules its characters; but first it
brings them to life.

The play is made up of a succession of 'humour' demonstrations;
but it may be useful at the outset to establish the closeness in style
and mood with the Elizabethan Every Man In His Humour; Jonson's
deliberate return to the comic form of his early days is to be noted
in the sharply visualised physical descriptions, cast in the form of
satiric epithets. Quarlous, for example, ridicules the folly of
Winwife's pursuit of widows. This he thinks unnatural:

> thou must visit 'hem, as thou wouldst doe a Tombe, with a Torch, or
> three hand fulls of Lincke, flaming hot,

> (I, iii. 74–75)

and he predicts that Winwife will soon

> walke as if thou had'st borrow'd legges of a Spinner, and voyce of a
> Cricket.

When the name of the Puritan Zeal-of-the-Land Busy is mentioned, a deflating retort is delivered by Quarlous:

JOHN   Rabbi Busy, Sir, he is more then an Elder, he is a Prophet, Sir.
QUARLOUS   O, I know him! a Baker, is he not?

                                                          (ibid. 116–118)

and this traditional comic device (like that in The Alchemist IV, i. 55–57):

MAMMON   Me thinks you doe resemble
           One o'the Austriack princes.
FACE   Very like,
           Her father was an Irish costar-monger.

is followed up by a Theophrastian character of Busy in the lengthy style of Comical Satyre:

   A notable hypocriticall vermine it is; I know him . . .

                                                          (ibid. 135–148)

In the next scene Waspe gives another such Character of his pupil, while providing a full demonstration of his choleric 'humour' to which we have been directed by John Littlewit:

   . . . if hee apprehend you flout him, once, he will flie at you presently.
   A terrible testie old fellow, and his name is Waspe too.

                                                          (I, iv. 44–46)

Jonson's manner of demonstrating Waspe's 'humour' is bluntly farcical, very close to the manner of Chapman in An Humorous Day's Mirth:

JOHN   Will't please you drinke, Master Waspe?
WASPE Why, I ha' not talk't so long to be drie, Sir, you see no dust or
       cobwebs come out o'my mouth: doe you? you'ld ha' me gone,
       would you?
JOHN   No, but you were in hast e'en now, Mr Numpes.
WASPE What an' I were? so I am still, and yet I will stay too;

                                                          (I. iv. 96–102)

The clear didactic form in which these 'humours' are articulated is emphasised by the comments of Winwife and Quarlous on the departure of Waspe and Cokes:

QUARLOUS Well, this dry-nurse, I say still, is a delicate man.
WINWIFE   And I, am for the Cosset, his charge! Did you ever see a
          fellowes face more accuse him for an Asse?

                                                          (I, v. 48–50)

Once these characters have been introduced (they simply walk on stage, are recognised, introduced and their 'Humours' pointed out and displayed) Jonson brings on Justice Overdo, the Disguised-Duke-Presenter, who in true Elizabethan style (and like the Presenter Fitzgrave in Middleton's *Your Five Gallants*) delivers an expository soliloquy absolutely in accord with the convention. It is here that Jonson's less conventional purpose reveals itself: for Overdo is 'disguised' as a fool, an irony like that of Face being 'disguised' as a rogue. Jonson insists on the irony:

> They may have seene many a foole in the habite of a Justice; but never till now, a Justice in the habit of a foole.
>
> (II, i. 7–9)

Having given sufficient evidence of his absurdity, and of the abuses in the Law, Overdo proclaims his intended course of action, according to the convention, and stepping back at the entry of various denizens of the Fair including the female Falstaff, Ursula the pig-woman, Overdo begins his *role* of Presenter-Commentator, marking in an aside the accusation of Leatherhead that the gingerbread men are made of rotten ingredients. It is barely a minute later that Overdo is commenting on Ursula:

> This Pig-woman doe I know, and I will put her in, for my second enormity, shee hath beene before mee, *Punke*, *Pinnace* and *Bawd*, any time these two and twenty yeeres, upon record i'the *Pie-poudres*.
>
> (II, ii. 71–74)

and soon Overdo is beside himself at the somewhat trivial dishonesty of Ursula's lesson to Nightingale in giving customers short measures. Having witnessed the ludicrous reactions of Overdo to the commonplace conversation of the tradespeople, we fully appreciate the irony of Ursula's greeting to the disguised Justice — 'what new Roarer is this?' — and we are able to conclude that Overdo is no match, either in wit, shrewdness or authority, for those he presumes to censure. Ursula's contemptuous hospitality fits the facts:

> Bring him a sixe peny bottle of Ale; they say, a fooles handsell is lucky.
>
> (ibid. 138–139)

Jonson's mastery of irony asserts itself: the sequence which began with the demonstration of the Fair's denizens has ended with the exposure of Overdo's folly, though the formal structure has not been changed.

In the subsequent scenes Jonson takes care to emphasise with force the direct wrongness of Overdo's judgement; the didacticism is of the simplest kind. The cutpurse appears with the balladsinger; Overdo comments as if he were on the bench, and Jonson follows with fact:

OVERDO   What pitty 'tis, so civill a young man should haunt this
           debaucht company? . . . A proper penman, I see 't in his
           countenance, he has a good Clerks looke with him, and I
           warrant him a quicke hand.
MOONCALF   A very quicke hand, Sir.
EDGEWORTH All the purses, and purchase, I give you to day by conveyance,
           bring hither [aside]]whispered].

                                                        (II, iv. 30–37)

This direct demonstration of Overdo's error may be compared to the way Jonson demonstrates Captain Tucca's cowardice in *Poetaster IV*, vii. 19–26 and Bobadilla's in *Every Man In His Humour IV*, ii. Its traditional lineage may be traced back through Shakespeare's *Henry IV* and the 'lazzi' of Hal and Poins to prove Falstaff's cowardice, but this should not obscure the fact of its admirable didactic effect.

Having demonstrated the inadequacy of Overdo's judgement, Jonson next devises a situation which reveals the pernicious practical results of such stupidity. Overdo is putty in the hands of these Coney-catchers; but it is surely one of the best inventions in the play when the balladsinger and cutpurse use Overdo himself as the unwitting decoy in their theft of Cokes's purse. It is a redoubled irony that Overdo's version of the decoy entertainment should be a Puritan tirade against tobacco, full of the hoariest jargon. As far as Edgworth is concerned, the effect of a Puritan tirade or the ballad of 'The Wind-mill blowne downe by the witches fart' is identical; and Jonson's satiric implication is that they are indeed in every other respect equivalent. The upshot is that Cokes is robbed, Overdo is soundly beaten (boisterous physical correction is administered in *Bartholomew Fair* in the Comical Satyre manner) and Overdo's parody of Puritan cant serves as a fitting satiric introduction to the entry of Zeal-of-the-land Busy. Overdo's sermon has the full broad comic effect of Falstaff's parody of Puritanism: ·

OVERDO Neither doe thou lust after that tawney weede, tabacco.
COKES Brave words!
OVERDO Whose complexion is like the Indians that vents it!
COKES Are they not brave words, Sister?
OVERDO And who can tell, if, before the gathering, and making up thereof, the *Alligarta* hath not piss'd thereon?

(II, vi. 21–27)

In fact Jonson's dialogue smacks strongly of his old Elizabethan manner, there are even close echoes, perhaps deliberate, of the Falstaff sequences in Shakespeare's *Henry IV*, in the satiric descriptions of Ursula — 'a walking Sow of tallow', 'an inspir'd vessell of Kitchin-stuffe', 'quagmire', 'a whole shire of butter', one who as she says herself 'shall e'en melt away . . . I doe water the ground in knots, as I goe'.

A further significant Elizabethan element in *Bartholomew Fair* which might aptly be considered at this point is the dramatisation of Coney-catching pamphlet material and the deliberate rehearsal of the moralistic, naive tone of Robert Greene in poor Overdo. Overdo indeed refers to his 'black book' in which these 'enormities' are to be inscribed; and it was just Greene's style to over-dramatise some minor abuse like Ursula's technique for giving short measures (as I point out in *Appendix A* below). Jonson does, however, also take pains with hitting the humours of the 'Bartholomew-birds' and such episodes as the cutting of Cokes' purses, the tobacco taking, the wandering madman's appearances, are intended to excite the pleasure of recognising familiar localities, create an atmosphere of intimacy, while also displaying London's low life, demonstrating the criminal techniques and the depravity, moral and physical, of petty criminals, prostitutes, fairground booth holders and suchlike. The densely physical, strongly visual language of the low life characters gives conviction to episodes which are, plainly enough, absolutely conventional to the *genre* and had been the stock-in-trade of the pamphleteers before Elizabeth died. If the form of the episodes is conventional, the spirit in which they are presented is in fact closer to pre-Comical Satyre, Popular, Elizabethan, comedy. The strongest link with *Every Man In His Humour* is in the broader Elizabethan generosity of the comedy, the absence of correction by verbal or actual lash: the failure of a man well read in Horace and Cicero, the ridicule of a moralist and the punishment of a tutor contrast with the thunderous and popular defence of the boisterous, quarrelsome puppet play and the unhindered progress of pig-woman, horsecourser-cum-bawd, stupid citizen couple and stupefied blockhead. Whatever revolution in Jonson's attitude to folly is revealed in *Bartholomew Fair*, it is to be noted that the formal characteristics undergo no revolution; and it is this element which I wish to pursue further.

By the time Overdo delivers his conventional soliloquy reporting progress as Presenter-Commentator (III, iii) Quarlous the gentleman and his companion Winwife have also taken up the *role*, in several sequences, of detached critical commentator: for example in the scene where Ursula goes sprawling in the hot fat, where Cokes is robbed of his second purse and where Waspe displays his choler (II, v and III, v). It is when Quarlous gives way to his own choleric 'Humour' and takes a direct part in the game of vapours that we may be sure of his own folly: he is unable to fulfil the demands of balanced, authoritative and just comment in the conventional *role*. Jonson uses this infringement of convention to point out Quarlous' folly, and enforces the lesson that a quarrelsome humour grips most of the people in the Fair (the symbolic overtones of which are by now becoming apparent) with the emblematically clear device of the game of vapours: in the game, as in the Fair itself,

> Every man to oppose the last man that spoke: whether it concern'd him, or no.
>
> (IV, iv. s.d.)

This game recalls the futile games in *Cynthia's Revels* except that here it is directly functional in clarifying the didactic point; and the absurdity of this universal civil aggressiveness, this violent disorder to which everyone is so susceptible, is soon paralleled by the appearance of Troubleall, who has been driven mad by contact with the order of civil justice, and is incapable of any action lest it be unlawful: thus Troubleall represents the other extreme of absurdity from the Roarers; he is the victim of Zeal-of-the-land Busy and Overdo, as Knock-hum and Ursula are their victors; and we judge, as Jonson means us to judge, that it is better to tumble in the stews with all our wits about us than to drift, half-conscious and barely alive, every action first approved by a legal warrant. It is in precisely such absolute terms that ethical debate is characteristically presented in didactic drama, and *Bartholomew Fair*, no less than *Volpone* or *The*

Alchemist, has a very firm, clear and plain didactic base, however complex and crowded its episodes may be. It is only because of the absurdity, the *extreme* folly of Zeal-of-the-land Busy or Overdo, that we find ourselves warmly approving the humanity of Knock-hum, seller of horseflesh by day and human flesh by night, taking pity on the *extremely* pitiful victim of *excessive* legal discipline, Troubleall:

KNOCKHUM   Ha! mad child o'the *Pye-pouldres*, art thou there?
           fill us a fresh kan, *Urs*, wee may drinke together.
TROUBLEALL   I may not drinke without a warrant, Captaine.
KNOCKHUM   S'lood, thou'll not stale without a warrant, shortly. *Whit*,
           give mee pen, inke and paper. I'l draw him a warrant presently.
TROUBLEALL   It must be *Justice Overdoo's*.
KNOCKHUM   I know, man. Fetch the drinke, *Whit*.

                                                       (IV, vi. 2–9)

It is remarkable that though Troubleall is amusing through his constant insane repetitions, he is not ridiculed in the play, because he is a fundamental didactic emblem in himself. The play offers a warmly Elizabethan, magnanimous view of errant humanity; but it does so by ridiculing the opponents of such humanity through conventional techniques of City Comedy, and it does not fail to expose the folly and absurdity of the Fair people in the *exempla*. The main satiric force is directed towards Puritanical attitudes to art and life: the didactic purpose of Jonson is to demonstrate that here, in 1614, these attitudes are more of a threat to the Commonwealth than even the crassest stupidity, fashion-following or pretentiousness which he had ridiculed in the Comical Satyres of 1599–1601. Though this is a more complex attitude than his earlier one, it is no less clear, firm, and emphatic.

The first satiric-didactic climax of the play presents a memorable tableau on stage, the most effective of all kinds of didactic technique; Jonson provides the sophisticated equivalent of Hell Mouth (cf. the prison grate in *Eastward Ho* Act V) with the three pairs of stocks, into which are thrust the three representatives of discipline and authority — Justice Overdo, Prophet Busy, Tutor Waspe. These three are visited by the living symbol of all victims of hateful repression, Troubleall, so that the didactic point is made, primarily, in dumb show. In the second place Jonson emphasises the individuality of the three fools and their strikingly obstinate abnormality by the fact that they pay no attention to each other, on the contrary giving virtuoso demonstrations of their 'Humours'; thus Waspe:

> Sir, you are a welsh Cuckold, and a prating Runt, and no Constable.
>
> (IV, vi. 47–48)

and here Overdo and Busy persevere in their absurdity:

WASPE What are you, Sir?

BUSY One that rejoyceth in his affliction, and sitteth here to prophesie the destruction of *Fayres* and *May-games*, *Wakes*, and *Whitson-ales*, and doth sigh and groane for the reformation, of these abuses.

WASPE And doe you sigh, and groane too, or rejoyce in your affliction?

OVERDO I doe not feele it, I doe not thinke of it, it is a thing without mee. *Adam*, thou art above these battries, these contumelies. *In te manca ruit fortuna*, as thy friend *Horace* saies; thou art one, *Quem neque pauperies, neque mors, neque vincula terrent*. And therefore as another friend of thine saies, (I thinke it be thy friend *Persius*) *Non te quaesiveris extra*.

> (IV, vi. 88–101)

It is evident that nothing can correct these fools; not even a token, *theatrical* cure is presented as it was in the Comical Satyres; but if they cannot be cured, their folly can be further demonstrated, and the double irony of Overdo's cozening by Quarlous makes a masterly 'lazzo'.

In this sequence (V, ii) Overdo has determined to aid his victim Troubleall; but his plan is overheard by Quarlous, who notes that to disguise himself as Troubleall could be useful. We are thus able to witness the admirable irony of Overdo, having grasped that Trouble-all has been wronged, failing to grasp that it is not Troubleall to whom he gives the warrant: Overdo is constitutionally incapable of detecting fraud and doubledealing. However plainly Overdo is instructed, nothing can correct his profound lack of judgement and insight — the two cardinal requirements for his legal duty. The result is that an admirably intelligent 'lazzo' also serves a central didactic purpose in the best tradition of City Comedy. Quarlous's disguise has illuminated the central theme of the play, the ubiquity of folly: Dame Purecraft observes of the real Troubleall

> Mad doe they call him! the world is mad in error, but hee is mad in truth:
>
> (IV, vi. 169–170)

and so she reveals to the fake the criminal hypocrisy of Zeal-of-the-land Busy: a mad confession about a sane pretender to madness to another who looks like a madman, and who remarks that to ignore this offer she makes him would be 'truly mad', and who is then approached by a mad judge who thinks himself sane and gives him, absurdly, an unmerited, unlimited warrant for any kind of insane or illegal action. The world is truly mad! Jonson has set the stage for the final *exemplum*, also a visually meaningful didactic emblem; in fact the puppet show is presented with perhaps the most emphatic didactic technique to be found in the play. As a satiric comment on the characters of the play and their world, the puppet show has the unanswerable appeal of high burlesque; it also has the function of eliciting the antagonism of the chief fools and triggering off the debate which is the climax to the main themes of the play; and the debate concludes, as in *Poetaster*, with a supremely Aristophanic *jeu d'esprit*.

This last sequence is introduced by Overdo's return to his *role* of Commentator, as in the first appearance he made in Act II, i. Overdo is little changed in his attitude, sardonically observing in an aside that Whit's pimping proposition will prove the 'chiefest enormity', determining to follow it for the good of the Commonwealth, and watching with growing disgust the introduction of the puppets. Cokes is drawn towards the show, trailed by a crowd of boys (significantly enough) and the vulgarity and grossness of the puppet-show is emphasised by the forthright comment of Waspe:

> I ha' beene at the *Eagle*, and the blacke *Wolfe*, and the Bull with the five legges, and two pizzles; (hee was a Calfe at *Uxbridge Fayre*, two yeeres agone) And at the *dogges* that daunce the *Morrice*, and the *Hare* o'the *Taber*; and mist him at all these! Sure this must needs be some fine sight, that holds him so,
>
> (*V*, iv. 83–89)

Jonson's affectionate scorn for such low Popular amusements found expression, we recall, in the final Act of *The Alchemist* too:

LOVEWIT   He hung out no banners
               Of a strange Calfe, with five legs, to be seene?
               Or a huge Lobster, with sixe clawes?
NEIGHBOUR 6   No, sir.
NEIGHBOUR 3   We had gone in then, sir.

                                                    (*V*, i. 7–10)

The point had already been made, by the puppet master, in the plot-analysis, working through the crudest method of burlesque deflation and diminution, the crudest infringement of elementary decorum:

> Now do I introduce *Cupid*, having *Metamorphos'd* himselfe into a Drawer, and hee strikes *Hero* in love with a pint of *Sherry*,
>
> (*V*, iii. 126–128)

The deflation works partly, as other critics have noted, by reducing all events to their lowest physical basis; just as Knock-hum sees everybody in terms of horses, bears or whales, as Ursula, the centre of vigorous fertile life in the Fair, is presented in overwhelmingly and exclusively physical terms, so here the Classical story of tragic love is reduced to a matter of drunken lust brought on by crude, sweet liquor.

When the puppet play starts it is immediately evident how very provoking it must seem to a Puritan, and it is also notable that Jonson revives the style of early Elizabethan drama, which he means to defend from Puritan attack.

In *The Devil Is An Ass* Jonson is at even greater pains to call attention to that tradition remembered from his youth. Jonson's lofty, classical, exacting eye does not gloss over its crudeness; but neither does he conceal his deep and affectionate respect. It may be interesting to set side by side parodied lines, first in *Bartholomew Fair*, second in *The Devil Is An Ass*. The preoccupation of Jonson with this older tradition as he wrote these final plays in the *genre* he originated will be considered at greater length below:

> Who chances to come by, but faire *Hero*, in a Sculler;
> And seeing *Leander's* naked legge, and goodly calfe,
> Cast at him, from the boat, a Sheepes eye, and a halfe.
>
> (*V*, iv. 123–125)

Thus from the puppet play; and here is the Vice, Iniquity, in the later play:

> I will teach thee to cheate, Child, to cog, lye, and swagger,
> And ever and anon, to be drawing forth thy dagger:
> To sweare by Gogs-nownes, like a lusty *Juventus*,
> In a cloake to thy heele, and a hat like a pent-house,
>
> (*The Devil is an Ass*. I, i. 48–51)

The naiveté and pedestrian quality these examples share plainly

derive from Tudor drama: it is this whole tradition, from the great
Morality play to the crudest Popular farce, from Hamlet to the Merry
Milkmaids, from The Alchemist to the bull with five legs and the ballad
of (Saint George that O did break the Dragon's Heart,) that Jonson sets
out to defend: and if the ballads are banned, it will be only a matter
of time before The Alchemist is banned too. Jonson, conscious in his
later maturity of the vitality and richness of the tradition within
which he wrote, had the courage and the magnanimity to defend its
whole body.

It is in this way that we may see the debate between Zeal-of-the-
land Busy (and later Overdo) and the puppets, as crucial. The
quarrel is set forth in unambiguous terms; the puppet master claims
to have the warrant of the Master of the Revels; Zeal-of-the-land
retorts that his profession is damnable, idolatrous, satanic. The
puppet master admits

> Sir, I am not well studied in these controversies, between the hypo-
> crites and us.

and in two asides the gentlemen direct our attitude to the events:

BUSY   . . . assist me zeale, fill me, fill me, that is, make me full.
WINWIFE   What a desperate, prophane wretch is this! is there any
          Ignorance, or impudence like his? to call his zeale to fill him
          against a Puppet?
QUARLOUS I know no fitter match, than a Puppet to commit with an
          Hypocrite!

                                                              (V, v. 45–51)

When Busy cannot win by browbeating his opponent, he resorts to
the accusation that male actors impersonate women. The puppet's
retort to this has the shocking, farcical, lewd yet conclusive logic of
Aristophanes; it ridicules Busy in the true-fashion of Comical
Satyre.

And now, when Busy has been confuted and converted, up springs
Overdo and tries once more to assert himself in his role of Disguised-
Duke-Presenter: he had given us warning earlier of his intent to

> reveale my self, wherein cloud-like, I will breake out in raine, and
> haile, lightning, and thunder, upon the head of enormity.
>
>   (V, ii. 4–6)

Now he proposes to stop the puppet show and indeed the whole
play in order to bring those who have erred to account — 'to take

Enormity by the fore head, and brand it' — for his role is completed
— 'I have discover'd enough'. Overdo now launches into a rhetorical
period strongly reminiscent of the woodenly didactic Elizabethan
Interlude-style play *A Looking Glass for London and England*. Overdo
certainly succeeds in assembling the characters and assigning them
their faults and misdeeds, as regularly as any Middletonian Presenter,
as confidently as the Duke in Marston's *What You Will*. At just this
point, however, Overdo suffers a decisive reversal; his own wife,
among the eager audience for the puppets, shows her presence by
vomiting. Quarlous now takes over the role of expositor, distributes
final judgement as he reveals the author of the 'lazzi' to be himself.
This conclusion has the conventional form familiar in City Comedy
from *Every Man In His Humour* forward; furthermore, it recalls the
manner of Middleton in *A Trick To Catch The Old One*. It will be recalled how Hoard had the courage to stand up and acknowledge his
wrongdoing, defeat, and deserved punishment, and in so doing
gained dignity as a human being. It is precisely such a course that
Quarlous recommends to Justice Overdo:

> remember you are but *Adam*, Flesh, and blood! you have your frailty,
> forget your other name of *Overdoo*, and invite us all to supper. There
> you and I will compare our *discoveries*.
>
> (V, vi. 96–99)

and Overdo, like Hoard, finds the courage to be humble, to face his
faults, and set forward again. Jonson rewards him with a quotation
which might stand at the head of any of his satiric comedies:

> *Ad correctionem, non ad destructionem; Ad aedificandum . . .*

It is fitting to break off there: the play is indeed in the highest
fashion edifying, a rich fruit of its *genre*. Jonson's reworking of
Comical Satyre form is superbly successful, his inversion of the
Presenter role is an admirable didactic device (made possible by the
complete familiarity of his audience with the convention) and his
broader, generous attitude to old-fashioned Popular comedy
releases, with unexampled exuberance and richness, his talent in the
great native tradition of Nashe and Shakespeare. In *Bartholomew Fair*
Jonson's curbing wit, classical learning and didactic skills are all
directed towards the defence of that native tradition for the first
time; a superb fusion takes place. *Bartholomew Fair* is the true climax
to Jonson's earlier experiments in Comical Satyre.

The Devil Is An Ass contrasts with Bartholomew Fair by relying on a
firm, fast moving and strongly articulated main action; if the earlier
play is the climax to the experiments in Comical Satyre, then The
Devil Is An Ass is the terminal point in Jacobean City Comedy, the
modified, Italianate form developed by the interrelated experiments
of Middleton, Marston and Jonson. The satiric tone is harsher than
in Bartholomew Fair, and links the play with Jacobean predecessors such
as Volpone, Michaelmas Term and The Alchemist. The intelligence and wit
displayed locally in dialogue and handling of situations show Jonson
at the height of his powers, and his thorough reliance on the conventions of the genre merely serves to emphasise the imagination and
invention with which he creates fresh, living drama. In any event, it
is perhaps to enrich the meaning of the word 'convention' if we
apply it to the line of aspiring wealth seekers, Volpone, Mammon
and Meercraft, and their Middletonian brothers Falso, Quomodo,
Hoard, Yellowhammer.

Jonson begins this last great play with an Induction in Hell, the
purpose of which is to initiate a plot which once more follows the
Disguised-Duke pattern. The role of Presenter and Commentator is
given this time to a devil, whose aim is the exact reverse of the
conventional Presenter: instead of observing, exposing and correcting
folly and vice, the devil's aim is to initiate and spread vice and
iniquity. This ironic inversion of the convention emphasises the fact
that it is a convention; and having openly reminded the audience of
the old Morality play origins of Jacobean satiric City Comedy,
Jonson makes a further satiric point by suggesting that Medieval
Christianity and its drama are old fashioned and neglected, not only
because of atheism and fashion 'nowadays' but because

> they are other things
> That are receiv'd now upon earth, for Vices;
> Stranger, and newer: and chang'd every houre . . .
> And it is fear'd they have a stud o'their owne
> Will put downe ours. Both our breed, and trade
> Will suddenly decay, if we prevent not.
> Unlesse it be a Vice of quality,
> Or fashion, now, they take none from us . . .
> They have their Vices, there, most like to Vertues;
> You cannot know 'hem, apart, by any difference:
> (I, i. 100–102, 108–112, 121–122)

Here Jonson uses the term *Vice* (and *Vertue*) in two senses: both the
abstract concept and the old dramatic character 'in his long coat,
shaking his wooden dagger'. He is therefore also pointing out to the
audience that in the City Comedy *genre* the *Vice* character still treads
the boards, though now dressed like a usurer, miser, like Hoard or
Volpone, while the rest of the conventions, similarly modified, stand
behind these more sophisticated and naturalistic, Jacobean, Morality
plays. In a characteristic witty ambiguity Jonson asserts the traditional
origin of his play while denying it, indicates the vitality of its
characters while simultaneously ridiculing their Popular, vulgar and
old fashioned appeal. He puts Morality play characters on the stage
while stating that it cannot be done (in fact it is a Morality Devil
who states that Iniquity is too old fashioned!) and relates them to
their role in ballads and folk superstition of the Tudor period; thus
the devil's work:

> the laming a poore Cow, or two?
> Entring a Sow, to make her cast her farrow?
> ... sowre the Citizens Creame 'gainst Sunday
> (I, i. 8–9, 19)

becomes as naive and vulgar as the traditional butt for Jonson's
ridicule, Popular taste. This is a marvellously complex illustration of
the lifelong conflict in Jonson's art between his classically educated,
serious, exacting critical mind, his determined reforming zeal and
innovatory achievement in drama, on the one side, and his Elizabethan, Popular inheritance in comic technique, language and mood,
his traditional religious faith, his sympathy with rogues, tavern
roarers, pig-women, Jest Books and Balladry, and their vitality, on
the other side. In *The Devil Is An Ass* we do indeed find, as Jonson
implies, the old conventions in new guise, up-to-date Jacobean
villains who run rings round a character from the old Morality
drama (that is, a naive rustic out of Popular dramatic convention);
but the Morality play conventions persist, it is only that the Prodigal
and the Vices have reversed roles, and Jonson has taken the opportunity to give the conflict the added significance of symbolising his
new drama outshining the crude, unintelligent and uninventive old
convention with which he began. This masterly play presents the
tradition which was the *genre's* origin within the rich, subtle, new
comic form which evolved out of it.

The main theme of the play consists in the outwitting of the gulls

N

Fitzdottrel, Pug the disguised devil, Lady Tailbush, by the Coney-
catchers led by Merecraft and by the sane gentlemen Wittipol and
Manly. The ridicule of Fitzdottrel is a main feature of the first half
of the play, and is carried in sequences exposing innate foolishness
as well as in 'lazzi' devised by the rogues and gentlemen. These wits
combine to outwit Fitzdottrel in Act IV, though their interests clash
in the crisis of the action, where the two prizes, Fitzdottrel's wife
and wealth, bring the persons of the play together, before the eye of
justice, sanity and order. The Presenter, Pug the disguised devil,
having failed to spread vice and having merely been the victim of
more skilful agents of ill will, delivers expository soliloquies in the
conventional form, though their content is undignified. His career
as a Presenter-Vice concludes with the Chief Devil's appearance,
judging his actions, ridiculing his folly, which we have witnessed
in the preceding *exempla*, and taking him away from the City. This
outline indicates the formal relation of the play to the *genre* of City
Comedy; if we begin a closer examination with Meercraft's appearance it should be possible to indicate the fresh invention with which
Jonson invigorates convention.

Meercraft is introduced by one of his creatures and enters accompanied by another (supposed to be a servant from a lady appealing
for Meercraft's services), while directing his self-advertising remarks
to two other creatures. It is only after all these preliminary ploys
(which recall those of Quomodo in *Michaelmas Term*) that Meercraft
deigns to attend to his actual target Fitzdottrel. Even then he hooks
him in obliquely:

MERECRAFT   ... [*to Fitzdottrel*] But you must harken, then.
INGINE   Harken? why Sr, do you doubt his eares? Alas!
            You doe not know Master *Fitz-dottrel*.
FITZDOTTREL He do's not know me indeed. I thank you, *Ingine*,
            For rectifying him.
MERECRAFT   Good! Why, *Ingine*, then [*he turnes to Ingine*]
            I'le tell it you. (I see you ha' credit, here,
            And, that you can keepe counsell, I'll not question.)
            Hee shall but be an undertaker with mee ...
                Hee shall not draw
            A string of's purse. I'll drive his pattent for him.
            We'll take in Citizens, *Commoners*, and *Aldermen*,
            To beare the charge, and blow 'hem off againe,
            Like so many dead flyes, when 'tis carryed.

> The thing is for recovery of drown'd land,
> (II, i. 29–36, 40–45)

Here Jonson refines even on the swift, irresistibly confident decisiveness of the rogues deceiving Mammon in The Alchemist; specifically to be remarked here is the aside to Ingine 'I see you ha' credit, here' — this to his own accomplice! — and the simile which fits the act so perfectly and yet conveys Meercraft's real ruthlessness: 'like so many dead flyes'. What follows is even more admirable. Meercraft's aim is to 'blind with science' of course; and he does so by being absolutely specific about figures and details of engineering; here Jonson's poet's eye for the sharply observed physical detail strengthens his portrayal of a highly intelligent confidence trickster. Jonson's sardonice portrayal of Meercraft's projects works through subtle inflation; the fantasies, like those of Volpone, Mammon, and their ancestor Tamburlaine's, are composed of real material: in the present case Meercraft's project for draining the fens is wholly feasible; the basic logic of the bottle ale project too is sound — and present day industrialists might not laugh at a technique of saving

> in cork,
> In my mere stop'ling, 'bove three thousand pound,
> (II, i. 92–93)

This satire has several layers. In direct dramatic terms, Jonson is emphasising the skill of Meercraft who here brilliantly varies the Mountebank's stock technique. Meercraft's imagination builds up a series of projects so diverse, in such quick succession, that it seems there is a limitless number of opportunities for technology, for industrial development and investment; indeed, Meercraft implies, nothing is impossible, we can make wine from grapes and then make wine again from the grapeskins and then more wine from the pulp; soon enough perhaps we shall make air from a vacuum. Industry, Meercraft tells his prey, is an actual, unromantic, existing Philosopher's Stone. Thus in Meercraft Jonson gives us the alchemist all over again, so that he can satirise a different manifestation of the folly induced by greed.

Meercraft's list of projects is significant in another respect; Meercraft's excited salestalk produces a whole jumble of totally unrelated schemes, so bizarre in their variety and relative sizes as to be absurd, even though each might in itself be reasonable. This,

Jonson implies, is the way man applies the logic of science — in treating dog skins! Further, the achievements of scientific technology which we know of are so close to the impossible that it is just as likely that the logic of science will be used to confute that logic — if the land and sea can be increased or diminished at will, how soon will it be before wine is made from lees, air from vacuum, or as the alchemists dreamed, gold from lead? It is no doubt because of Jonson's own reluctant acknowledgement of the power of modern science that Meercraft's projects are in the main feasible and likely to have immense rewards for investors and revolutionary effects on society (for example, fen drainage, the fully mechanised mass production and bottling of ale, the manufacture and sale of forks). The skilful use of capital in industrial investment surely is the nearest actual substitute man has found for alchemy, we could suggest from our mid-twentieth century viewpoint. But if Jonson conveys the excitement of aspiration, yet he divined the motives of capitalists and industrialists to be vicious and foolish: the satiric form determines his presentation of Jacobean scientific and commercial ventures. Ironic pattern is dominant.

It is a complex irony when Fitzdottrel privately consults the supreme cozener Meercraft and also sees fit to warn Pug the devil to beware of

> old croanes, with wafers,
> To convey letters. Nor no youths, disguis'd
> Like country-wives, with creame, and marrow-puddings.
> Much knavery may be vented in a pudding,
>
> (II, i. 163–166)

Pug's soliloquy, commenting on the naive warnings of Fitzdottrel about 'policy', show the devil even more innocent than the gull; Jonson uses the conventional role of commentator to reflect ironically on the character who fills it, and emphasises Pug's innocent ineptitude in the immediately subsequent sequence. There, all Pug's efforts at Machiavellian seduction are brushed aside by Mistress Fitzdottrel as the obvious play-acting of a hired tempter: she calls out to the imagined husband:

> Come from your standing, doe, a little, spare
> Your selfe, Sir, from your watch, t'applaud your *Squire*
> That so well followes your instructions!
>
> (II, ii. 130–132)

This double irony is a witty reversal of the stock City Comedy sequence in which the trickster demonstrates the evil in a character for the benefit of disguised or concealed, detached witness-commentators. Mistress Fitzdottrel, knowing her husband's enthusiasm for new plays, including Ben Jonson's The Devil Is An Ass (see I, iv. 21) naturally assumes she is involved in a conventional *exemplum*, a vice demonstration from the *genre*. This is perhaps Jonson's most subtle and effective use of the old Comical Satyre fashion for witty infringements of the dramatic illusion.

The irony of Pug's presence in the role of Presenter-Commentator emerges again when the love scene between Wittipol and Mistress Fitzdottrel is interrupted by Fitzdottrel, who then beats his wife. Pug suddenly realises that in hindering the lovesuit he has behaved morally, strictly against his brief from hell. He continues this course by behaving like a country gull, being simultaneously cozened of a ring and taken in by a whore: the conventional episodes of the *genre* make Pug look ridiculous, one after another — Jonson's virtuoso handling of the *genre* is imaginative and sharply enforces the satiric point: Pug's career as Vice actually turns out to be the stock role of gull, the butt of ridicule and 'lazzi'.

As Meercraft moves through the play he comes into contact with a wide range of City life; as in Bartholomew Fair, Jonson is eager to include as much of London as he can, though here his approach is more analytic, and the focus is on the working of industry, courtiers' monopoly distribution, patent medicines, sharking tradesmen and moneylenders, the sale of honours, legal corruption and property swindles. If Bartholomew Fair absorbs the subject matter and style of Comical Satyre, The Devil Is An Ass clearly enough gives a last and a brilliant dramatic life to the main subjects and characters of mature City Comedy, conventional in the plays of Middleton, Marston and Jonson from 1602–1607. Indeed Jonson seems to be recalling the atmosphere of Middletonian comedy in the 'lazzo' of the ring, beginning with the remarkably lean, sinewy dialogue between jeweller Guilthead and his son, a dialogue which is overtly expository, gesturing towards clichés of Middletonian plot such as the cycle of rich tradesmen cozening landed gentry, going to live in the country, seeing his children grow up as gentry, the young prodigals coming to the city 'with their lands on their backs', being cozened of their inheritance by City sharks, Coney-catchers and tradesmen in their

turn; other cliché situations discussed are equally Middletonian in
their insistence on the 'war of every man, against every man';
Guilthead warns his son

> Wee must deale
> With Courtiers, boy, as Courtiers deale with us.
> . . . There,
> Nothing is done at once, but injuries, boy:
>   (III, iii. 4–5, 12–13)

Meercraft shows himself a really skilful businessman, quick thinking,
devious, technically knowledgeable in a way familiar from Middleton's Coney-catching money-sharks:

> I must ha' you doe
> A noble Gentleman, a courtesie, here:
> In a mere toy (some pretty Ring, or Jewell)
> Of fifty, or threescore pound (Make it a hundred,
> And hedge in the last forty, that I owe you,
> And your owne price for the Ring) He's a good man, Sr . . .
>   (III, ii. 2–7)

However when Meercraft is opposed by Everill, a rogue of some
experience, he reveals his kinship with Volpone and Face; indeed
the argument is resolved in just the way of Face and Subtle: it
needs teamwork to win the urban civil war:

> EVERILL   . . . I have, now,
>   A pretty tasque, of it, to hold you in
>   Wi' your Lady Tayle-bush: but the toy will be,
>   How we shall both come off?
> MEERCRAFT   Leave you your doubting.
>   And doe your portion, what's assign'd you: I
>   Never fail'd yet.
>   (III, iii. 220–225)

and Meercraft's final 'lazzo', the attempt to cozen Fitzdottrel of his
estate, is in its detail reminiscent of the deed signing in Volpone and
Michaelmas Term, and in its form conventional to the genre in its middle
period. It might further be remarked that Manly, the upright, un-
waveringly moral gentleman, survives uncozened and unridiculed
here, in sharp contrast to Surly in The Alchemist but exactly like the
approved norm of conduct in City Comedy of the 1602–1607
period; in fact Manly's role is wholly and plainly didactic, his comments are to be relied on and it is he who delivers the judgement

and the moral homily which is to be learned from the *exemplum* provided by the play.

The conclusion similarly recalls the more rigidly didactic form of City Comedy in its middle years, in the hands of Middleton. The final 'lazzo' is disrupted by a popular figure from City Comedy of 1604–1607, the Keeper of one of the London prisons, and the news he brings of the departure of Pug back to hell causes Fitzdottrel to unmask his own feigning and the lies of the lawyer, and Manly steps in to complete the moral judgement; his terms are notably serious, unrelentingly moral; his tone is severe.

> Sir, you belie her. She is chaste, and vertuous,
> And we are honest. I doe know no glory
> A man should hope, by venting his owne follyes,
> $\qquad$ (V, viii. 151–153)

and though the criminals are not directly punished, they are recommended to correction:

> Let 'hem repent 'hem, and be not detected.
> It is not manly to take joy, or pride
> In humane errours
> $\qquad$ (ibid. 168–170)

It is, lastly significant that the Morality play characters conclude their part in Jonson's City Comedy some time before the full play ends: the old comedy, having set the new going, fades in importance until its close is merely a delayed trigger for the real climax and resolution; thus, symbolically, Jonson indicates the origin of City Comedy, and reworks the most popular elements from Middleton, his pupil and rival, in this last rich fruit of the *genre* which began, eighteen years earlier, with *Every Man In His Humour*.

When Jonson completed *The Devil Is An Ass* two decades had passed since he embarked on his experiments in satiric comedy. Here, in his mature mastery, he turned back to the plays he remembered from his youth, perhaps in acknowledgement of their vital influence on his own remarkably original achievement, perhaps too because in them he found once more the richest inspiration. Jonson's overt summoning of the older drama in his last masterpiece gives a striking unity to the *genre* he fathered; so Jonson's

> firmnes makes my circle just,
> And makes me end, where I begunne.

10 Conclusion

IN WRITING THIS BOOK I have not heeded Patrick Cruttwell's warning that it is a hazardous project to mix a work of literary history with a work of literary criticism, but I have been encouraged by the fact that Cruttwell did not heed the warning himself. In the preface to his study *The Shakespearean Moment* he writes that 'links between literature and extra-literary factors are things of great subtlety, to be investigated with appropriate caution' and goes on to observe that 'the whole art consists, on the one hand in keeping your critical perception honest and flexible . . . and on the other hand, in keeping your historical knowledge always under the guidance of the literary view'.[1]

I have had to explore areas of non-literary background, and chapters II and III deal in some detail with those explorations, but it was my purpose there to clear an approach to the plays which might have the virtue of freshness and which certainly did take as starting point and conclusion their dramatic art. If the social, political and economic affairs of the time were relevant to Jacobean satiric drama, I hope I have shown that the connection was more subtle and oblique than we might expect from the argument of Unwin or — to some extent — L. C. Knights who quoted him:

[1] Patrick Cruttwell, *The Shakespearean Moment* (reprinted New York 1960), p. xii.

'a study of the leading characters in *The Devil Is An Ass* . . . would be by far the best introduction to the economic history of the period'.[2]

Drama and Society in the Age of Jonson, perhaps the most influential study of the relationship between the plays and the background, appeared thirty years ago. I have tried to bring certain aspects of that background into closer focus with the aid of up-to-date historical studies, and to offer an alternative account of its broad development; as a consequence, I have found it necessary to reassess the relationship of the plays of Jonson, Marston and Middleton to Jacobean life. I chose certain key aspects of Jacobean social, economic and political life and investigated them in the light of recent historical scholarship. I found it centrally interesting that capitalism could hardly be described as 'nascent' in late Tudor England, since on the contrary it had long played a crucial part in the national economic life and had been vital to the expansion of the medieval wool trade. It seemed to me important to show how the progressive diminution of royal power could be explained in terms of the price rise. This must modify any reading of Jacobean satiric attacks on royal profligacy and degeneracy, and also partly explains the many outbursts against usury and profiteering. Traditional hostility to usury, recorded in medieval Complaint and Sermon literature, continued in the Elizabethan Age also and could hardly have encouraged the formation of a large London money market. It is ironic that such a market could have assisted the Crown in the crucial years of its decline and of the rise of parliamentary opposition and Puritanism. If anything, hostility to usury actually hastened the disintegration of the Tudor ideal of the State.

It seemed necessary, then, to show how the whole mercantile and industrial community depended on capital; nevertheless it seemed necessary to question whether it could have been as a whole as vicious as Volpone, as savage as Barabas or Quomodo, as vulgar and lumpish as the citizens in *Eastward Ho*. It seemed mistaken to suppose that predatory entrepreneurs and favourites were so new a phenomenon that in 1605 or 1606 they really signalised — and were understood as signalising — the disintegration of national order and harmony.

If a Marxist interpretation of the English Revolution is arguable

---

[2] Cit. Knights, *Drama and Society*, p. 178.

still, it must resist the temptation to impose over-rigid and over-simplified patterns on rebelliously confused and contradictory events, especially in the early decades of the seventeenth century. Marxist criticism of the plays must proceed with even more caution, for the literary traditions which the playwrights inherited from Morality and Interlude drama, from religious invective and Classical satire, dominated their approach to their subject matter. The playwrights distorted actuality because neither the moral purposes nor the conventions of their art lent themselves to objective reporting. On the contrary the satirist was concerned to present a hostile and critical analysis of the follies and evils of the times: the 'image of the times' held up by Satire excluded a great deal and reflected distortion not normality. Jonson in his Comical Satyres attended to the critical theory of Sir Philip Sidney, a representative Renaissance Humanist, who wrote that 'Comedy is an imitation of the common errors of our life, which (the poet) representeth in the most ridiculous and scornefull sort that may be, so as it is impossible that any beholder can be content to be such a one'. The didactic purpose of Comedy seemed fundamental to Sidney, and clearly at odds with any documentary accuracy: Art must select, 'for what is it to make folkes gape at a wretched Begger, or a beggerly Clowne; or, against the lawe of hospitality, to jest at straungers, because they speak not English so well as wee doe? *What do we learne?*'.[3]

Though I have emphasised that the *genre* was first and last satiric art not objective reporting, I did not conclude that it had no relation at all to its historical context, and in fact I traced a significant and vital relationship to the main issue in political affairs, the shift in power from Crown to Parliament, merchants and industrialists. The effect of the price rise and the spread of the scientific method was a momentous phenomenon which disturbed the religious and intellectual and psychological life of the nation as well as its economy and government. The essential dynamic of the plays in City Comedy is the conflict between order and authority on the one hand, and intelligently aggressive insubordination on the other. Thus we have Marston's Duke Altofront who is also Malevole the sceptic and criminal, Middleton's Hoard, simultaneously a villain and an attractive comic figure, and his Allwit, implicitly condemned by the

---

[3] Sidney, *The Apologie for Poetrie* ed. Collins (Oxford 1907), pp. 30 and 56.

dramatist's ironic method but escaping the immediate consequences by his skilful policy; and we have Face in The Alchemist being rewarded for his intelligence, Justice Overdo thrown deservedly in the stocks in Bartholomew Fair, and the devil himself dethroned and superseded by the skilled professional villainy of the criminals in The Devil Is An Ass. The ironic inversion is repeated with insistent frequency. As reverence for government and king declines, and the power of lawyers, merchants and M.P's rises, so the emblem of Justice in the Stocks becomes central in City Comedy.

It may be significant that the ironic victories of City Comedy rogues correspond to the growing power and success of merchants and parliamentary opposition in Jacobean England. The comic and satiric potential in materialism, cynicism and frank ruthless 'policy', which City Comedy playwrights exploited so fully, had of course been explored earlier by Christopher Marlowe, and we may recall that T. S. Eliot called Jonson Marlowe's legitimate heir. It may be appropriate to point up this heritage by suggesting that much Jacobean comic spirit is anticipated in the curt retort of Tamburlaine's lieutenant Techelles:

THERIDAMAS Doost thou think that Mahomet will suffer this?
TECHELLES   Tis like he wil, when he cannot let it.[4]

and Techelles's words might have expressed the attitude of the Opposition to James's claim to be king by divine right.

These plays first appeared one after another on the boards of the several Coterie and Popular stages between 1597 and 1616. In the intimate world of Elizabethan theatre, where the playwrights knew each other well enough to write personal parodies such as Jonson's of Marston and Dekker, and Dekker's of Jonson, it is reasonable to suppose that they would have taken an interest in each other's work when it was performed, and that there was a good deal of cross-fertilisation and imitation as well as mere parody. My discussion of the plays traces chronologically the evolution of the form and conventions of the genre, and the result of this is to set some of the best known plays in a fresh context. Most critical studies of Marston's comedies and of Jonson stress their characteristic 'Marstonian' or 'Jonsonian' excellence. However in the present study individual plays are related to the context of the genre as much as

---

[4] Marlowe, The Conquests of Tamburlaine Part I, IV, iv.

to their author's whole *oeuvre*; thus *The Fawn* is related with Middleton's *The Phoenix* to Jonson's Comical Satyres, *Volpone* is seen in the context of Marston and Middleton's early assured comedy, while Middleton's *A Trick to Catch the Old One* is seen as part of the explanation for Jonson's development in style and manner from *Volpone* to *The Alchemist*.[5]

I have emphasised certain dramatic qualities of City Comedy which do not seem to have attracted much attention from critics, though they are superbly manifested in the modern didactic masterpieces of Brecht; I have tried to show how in Middleton's comedies there is a remarkable dramatic energy, richly intelligent handling of character and a sinewy purposefulness which gives compelling power to the action. These plays seem to me strongly suited to a Brechtian style of performance and production, and yet they are almost wholly neglected in our contemporary theatre. In critical work there has been little enthusiasm apart from Professor Bradbrook in *The Growth and Structure of Elizabethan Comedy*. Both Samuel Schoenbaum in his book *Middleton's Tragedies* and N. W. Bawcutt in his edition of *The Changeling* regard Middleton's comedies as preparation for the tragedies, while even in a largely sympathetic account R. B. Parker[6] concludes that they lack achieved coherence in form and purpose, oscillating between 'amoral vitalism and a more than Calvinistically determined scheme of retribution', taking refuge from either extreme in 'grotesquerie'.

L. C. Knights's preference for the comedy of Dekker and Heywood on Popular stages over that of Middleton seems hard to justify on the grounds that 'Middleton has . . . a positive animus against the

---

[5] It seems to me that the importance and critical usefulness of the *genre* in providing perspective for an understanding of the individual work can hardly be overstated. E. H. Gombrich has declared that 'if the history of an art is of any relevance to aesthetics, it is precisely because it will help us in these first rough and ready classifications on which all our subsequent understanding may hinge. Granted that a great work of art is so rich in structure that it remains potent even when misunderstood: if we are really out to receive its "message" we cannot do without all the contextual aids the historian can unearth'. E. H. Gombrich *Meditations on a Hobby Horse* (London 1963), p. 67.

[6] 'Middleton's experiments with comedy and judgement' in *Jacobean Theatre* ed. J. R. Brown and Bernard Harris.

citizens, but he has nothing to set against their standards'.[7] I have argued that Middleton shows a penetrating insight into moral issues and a distinctive, subtle dramatic art already mature in *Michaelmas Term*. In Middleton's tragedies we see a more exclusive, intense and mannered treatment of themes already superbly handled before 1607. I have tried to show how Middleton by working through implication restrains the tragic potential of his comedies. Their strikingly lively, intelligent yet disturbing quality derives from the tension between the satiric-comic form and the tragic themes of savagery, disease and evil. It is in this way that the dramatic manner of Tourneur in *The Revenger's Tragedy* and of Shakespeare in Act III of *Timon of Athens* may be indebted to Middleton's art of comedy. The case of Marston, thanks to Arnold Davenport and G. K. Hunter,[8] needs less defence; but Marston's contribution to the development of City Comedy is as crucial as his influence on the wider stream of Jacobean drama.

In the case of Jonson, paradoxically, the best-known critical tribute is also in a sense a mistake, for in taking the world of *Volpone* for a convincing representation of life in London in 1605, critics only testify to Jonson's marvellous *art*. Jonson creates a world excluding everything but avarice, gluttony and lust; yet so convincingly is it realised that it comes irresistibly alive, cannot be denied, seems complete, inclusive. The artefact does indeed rival, not transcribe, the world.

To some extent Jonson will always suffer from his proximity to Shakespeare; but if the comparison must be made T. S. Eliot's essay of 1919 on Jonson probably does it best. Harry Levin's essay of 1938 began by appealing for recognition of Jonson as a great original artist, but could not resist a seemingly decisive, yet predictably profitless comparison with Shakespeare. Levin wrote that Jonson 'presupposes that life is fundamentally a compact, rational affair, needlessly complicated by impulse and artifice. To Shakespeare all experience, however variegated is of the same baseless fabric ... we must criticise Shakespeare in terms of movement and warmth, Jonson in terms of pattern and colour.'[9] Yet it was Jonson who

---

[7] Knights, op. cit., p. 224.

[8] 'English Folly and Italian Vice' in *Jacobean Theatre*, and editions of *Antonio and Mellida* and *Antonio's Revenge* (London 1965).

[9] *Ben Jonson: Twentieth Century Views* (New Jersey 1963), p. 53.

celebrated Penshurst by evoking it in the image of an ever-flowing
fountain of food and drink and open friendliness, in verse easily
and naturally moving, the diction and tone large, warm, and
generous:

> whose liberall boord doth flow,
> With all, that hospitalitie doth know!
> Where comes no guest, but is allow'd to eate,
> Without his feare, and of thy lords owne meate:
> Where the same beere, and bread, and selfe-same wine,
> That is his Lordships, shall be also mine.

It was Jonson in *Bartholomew Fair* who celebrated the vital, instinctive
and anarchic energies of man, the source of new life, growth, and
fruition. An appetite for roast pig and a joy in the greasy, gargantuan
figure of Ursula are organically related to a joy in the puppet play,
itself a ribald celebration in elemental terms of sexual instinct and
carnal appetites. The sources of life are identified with the sources
of art; to love life with the people of the fair is to love art; to hate
one, with Zeal-of-the-land Busy, is to hate both. It is wisdom to
rejoice in earth and flesh and new creation; and the creation of a
new work of art springs naturally out of the abundance and rich
sources of life itself, as the *Ode to Penshurst* stems out of Jonson's
enjoyment of Sir Robert Sidney's generous way of living.

In *The Alchemist* a perpetually intense intelligence, lucid, subtle yet
powerful, shapes and disciplines a creative energy and a magnanimity
reminiscent of Chaucer. In *Bartholomew Fair* these essential Jonsonian
elements fuse in a celebration of creative richness in life and art:
so, as Yeats declared,

> Homer had not sung
> Had he not found it certain beyond dreams
> That out of life's own self-delight had sprung
> The abounding glittering jet.

I would like, lastly, to offer the suggestion that Jonson's closeness
to Nashe is important. Both writers had a love of artifice: they
revelled in great feasts of languages. Nashe is forever carrying the
reader off into wild flights of fantasy, suddenly flagging, then seizing
on some word and careering away on a new, vivid adventure where
every turn brings new-minted comic ideas. He has a marvellous
capacity to render the surface of life, but his essential genius is in the

invention of his own supremely lively, artificial world of unin-
hibited absurdity and comic gusto. Jonson, like Nashe, could not
deny the primacy of invention, his joy in art: even in such purposeful
plays as *Volpone* or *The Devil Is An Ass* it is the creation, not the criticism,
which is paramount. Jonson may censure, satirise and punish his
villains, rogues and fools: but he rejoiced in bringing them alive.
He told Drummond how

> he heth consumed a whole night in lying looking to his great toe,
> about which he hath seen tartars & turks, Romans and Carthaginions
> feight in his imagination.

Appendix A

A Minor Genre: the Coney-Catching Pamphlet

THE QUALITIES OF liveliness, vigour, flexibility, and strongly Anglo-Saxon vocabulary, characterise good Elizabethan low prose. These qualities manifest themselves in the drama, but they also account for much of the attractiveness of non-dramatic writing about low life. It is no coincidence that the term 'non-dramatic' indicates what it also denies — a link between the two kinds. For though a pamphlet is not so overtly shaped by the requirements of artistic convention as is a play, it must be shaped carefully, especially when the writer seeks to appear the mere reporter of directly observed event. There was, of course, no Elizabethan Henry Mayhew, no deliberate attempt at sociological study in the modern sense. Many of the writers under discussion here were also repertory playwrights who made a living — rarely a good one — from their pens. It is certain that the boom in low life pamphlets in the late fifteen-nineties attracted such writers because of the financial rewards. As a consequence it seems reasonable to examine their work in literary terms: if they wrote to entertain and attract readers, they should be judged accordingly. In any case, at least enough emphasis has been placed on the documentary value of their work, and not enough on its relation to dramatic comedy.

John Awdelay and Gilbert Walker wrote the first important narratives of low life printed in sixteenth century England. Neither

208

work is a straightforward account of direct observation; yet Awdelay's *Fraternitie of Vagabonds* was perhaps the most influential work of all. It follows the German *Liber Vagatorum* of 1510, which was partly based on manuscript accounts of criminal trials at Basle. Awdelay follows the tripartite form of the pamphlet and reproduces the classes of vagabond and many of their tricks. This attempt to add an official air to the work with formal classifications also involved a restriction on the intensity of moral indignation that could be expressed: as a result, the prose style itself is hamstrung. Moreover, Awdelay lacks a sense of narrative timing, fails to point up his key line and dissipates the interest in his material, for example in the anecdote[1] of the Patriarke Co. A more basic failure is his inability to visualise a scene and indicate its dramatic development:

> They thus ticklyng the young man in the eare, willeth him to make as much money as he can, and they wil make as much as they can, and consent as though they wil play booty against him. But in the ende they so use the matter, that both the young man leeseth his part, and, as it seemeth to him, they leesing theirs also, and so maketh as though they would fal together by the eares with this fingerer, which by one wyle or other at last conveyeth himselfe away, & they as it were raging lyke mad bedlams, one runneth one way, an other an other way, leaving the loser indeede all alone. (op. cit., p. 9).

It is valid to analyse Awdelay's work in these terms because the anecdotal nature of his material demands compression, a sense of timing, apt vocabulary, perhaps the dialogue form if it is to be effective. It is these qualities we find in the best anecdotes of the early jestbooks, e.g.

> 'I hope better' quoth Bolton, when his wife cried 'come in, cuckold.'

Walker's *Manifest Detection of Dice Play* is by contrast a sophisticated piece, fusing explanation of tricks with jestbook anecdote within a frame of moral comment. Walker's pamphlet is in the dialogue form, the victim of trickery standing for the reader in the following manner:

---

[1] Awdelay, *The Fraternitie of Vagabonds* ed. F. J. Furnivall E.E.T.S. (London 1869), p. 6.

O

M.   Thus give they their own conveyance the name of cheating law;
      so do they other terms, as sacking law, high law, figging law, and
      suchlike.
R.   What mean ye hereby? Have ye spoken broad English all this while
      and now begin to choke me with mysteries and quaint terms?[2]

The experienced M. has a firm attitude to vagabonds, but the freshness of expression gives some vitality to his rehearsal of a 'nowadays'
lament:

> Now, such is the misery of our time, or such is the licentious outrage
> of idle misgoverned persons, that of only dicers a man might have half
> an army, the greatest number so gaily beseen and so full of money,
>
> (*ibid.*, p. 34)

Walker's pamphlet form gives coherence to the material, and discussion of moral and social themes emerges naturally from the conversation of the two characters M. and R. He takes care with detail, his
prose rhythms imitate those of speech and his narrative control
gives clarity to the subject matter.

M.   So long as a pair of barred cater-treys be walking on the board, so long
      can ye cast neither 5 nor 9, unless it be, by a great mischance, that the
      roughness of the board, or some other stay, force them to stay and run
      against their kind; for without cater-trey ye wot that 5 nor 9 can never
      fall.
R.   By this reason, he that hath the first dice is like always to strip and rob
      all the table about!

> (*ibid.*, p. 39)

The clarity of this didacticism may be the explanation for its choice
as a model by the authors of *A Notable Discovery of Coosnage* and of
Mihil Mumchance, both of whom plundered it extensively.

The rational clarity of Walker is not characteristic of prose writing
designed for quick sales, however; and in Harman's *Caveat for Common
Cursetors* the sensationalism starts the mainstream of development in
low life narrative.

The *Caveat* is an expansion of the *Fraternitie*. The expansion takes the
form of anecdote, comment and emotional colouring; much of the
latter is effected by a clumsy scattering of adjectives, word pairs and
crude alliterative fustian:

[2] Walker, 'A Manifest Detection of Dice Play' ed. A. V. Judges, in *The
Elizabethan Underworld* (London 1930), p. 35.

their drowsey demener and unlawfull language, pylfring pycking, wily wandering.[3]

and against this tale of evil is set the familiar positive symbol always seized by the popular dramatist at a loss for a sentimental conclusion for a sequence:

> the Queenes most excelent maiestye, whom god of his infinyte goodnes, to his great glory, long and many yeares make most prosperously to raygne over us.
>
> (*Harman*, pp. 21–22)

Harman is nothing if not effusive. But the crude style conceals some surprisingly shrewd modifications which point towards a successful formula for popular pamphlet writing.

To each of the terse and ineptly phrased 'characters' in Awdelay Harman adds illustrative material, usually jestbook style anecdotes; and though many of these may be traditional some seem freshly conceived. Thus in the episode of Genyngs we find

> The boye that so folowed hym by Water, had no money to pay for his Bote hyre, but layde his Penner and his Ynkhorne to gage for a penny
>
> (ibid., p. 54)

and even a sociologist could scarce forbear to cheer when he reads

> he relented and plucked out another pursse, where in was eyght shyllings and od money; so had they in the hole that he had begged that day xiij shillings iii pens halfepeny.

The earnest moral approach of Harman — or, to look at it another way, his emphasis on the sensational wickedness of his subjects — leads him to tedious tumidity in style. Superlatives are used too generously, as, typically, here:

> most subtyll people: the most part of these are Walch men, and wyll never speake, unlesse they have extreme punishment, but wyll gape, and with a marvelous force wyll hold downe their toungs doubled.
>
> (ibid., p. 57)

It is characteristic of such narratives to insist on the amazing villainy which is being unmasked: popular writers do not ignore religious opinion. It is, however, also in the interest of these writers to make

[3] Harman, *The Caveat for Common Cursetors* ed. F. J. Furnivall (op. cit. of E.E.T.S.).

trickery attractive and crime glamorous; if there is comedy to be
found they do not ignore it. In the following example Harman
invites his readers to enjoy, vicariously, the pleasures of knavery,
and then to enjoy the pleasure of self-righteous condemnation
of it, of escape from the consequences. Here a parson, robbed by
rogues who make him promise to spend twelve pence at the inn,
arrives at the inn and asks after them:

> 'Which two men?' quoth this good wife. 'The straungers that came in
> when I was at your house wyth my neighbores yesterday.' 'What!
> your nevewes?' quoth she. 'My nevewes?' quoth this parson; 'I trowe
> thou art mad.' 'Nay, by god!' quoth this good wife, 'as sober as you;
> for they tolde me faithfully that you were their uncle . . . I never saw
> them before.' 'O out upon them!' quoth the parson; 'they be false
> theves.'

(ibid., p. 40)

The main body of Elizabethan narratives of low life is of interest
primarily for technical and stylistic developments, for although a
large number of narratives have survived, the writers are strikingly
economical in their use of material, and the coat made by Awdelay
is turned and turned again. The first famous Coney-Catching
Pamphlet, for example, *A Notable Discovery of Coosnage* (1591), owes
heavy debts to Awdelay, Walker and Harman, and actually para-
phrases Harman in the following passage:

> Yet, Gentlemen, am I sore threatened by the hacksters of that filthy
> faculty that if I set their practises in print, they will cut off that hand
> that writes.[4]

The *Notable Discovery* is no less interesting in technique for this, for
here is coined the phrase 'coney-catching', a most useful device for
unifying somewhat diverse material and a brand name easily
remembered by the public. The style is lively, the dialogue has
point, speed and verisimilitude in rhythm and vocabulary:

> So they shuffle and cut, but the verser wins. 'Well,' saith the setter,
> 'no butter will cleave on my bread. What! not one draught among
> five. Drawer, a fresh pint. I'll have another bout with you.'

(ibid., p. 127)

---

[4] ?Anon, 'A Notable Discovery of Coosnage' in *The Elizabethan Underworld*,
p. 122.

By this date of course developments in dramatic writing were occurring with mounting speed: it is no coincidence that the best effects here are gained in dialogue.

The Second Part of Coney-Catching, registered in the same month, assumes knowledge of the first and refers to it several times, particularly the self-dramatisation.

> [they will] cut off my right hand for penning down their abominable practices . . . But . . . I live still, and I live to display their villainies.[5]

The reader is addressed as an old friend, a valued, right thinking citizen: he is courted as the spectator is courted by the Prologue speaker in the theatres. Greene was a repertory playwright and one of the great talents of such writers was in the adaptation of diverse material to the conventional structure of Popular plays. Situation comedy and sequences of melodrama are the basis of low life narrative episode, and it would have been natural for Greene to handle such material with the same skill and freedom he used as a dramatist. The Coney-Catching Pamphlets, seen in this light, appear not as reprehensible attempts to deceive a gullible public or gullible historians, but as narratives written within a convention analogous to the conventions of stage comedy. The second pamphlet shows Greene establishing conventions, for example in the manner of introducing episodes

> a gentleman, a friend of mine, reported unto me this pleasant tale of a foist. (p. 167)

and providing familiar and specifically located settings:

> their (nips' and foists') chief walks is Pauls, Westminster, the Exchange. (p. 162)

This latter convention is particularly significant, for it seems likely that it directly influenced the location, in contemporary London, of sequences in City Comedy and before that in Shakespeares later Histories *Henry IV* and *Henry V* (though there the date is ostensibly over a century earlier).

What Greene does is to appear personally knowledgeable, expanding the briefer remarks of Walker with dramatic imagination, adding details of geographical setting and physical appearance of

---

[5] Greene, 'The Second Part of Coney-Catching' in *The Elizabethan Underworld*, p. 151.

the characters, occasionally using jestbook anecdote, and enriching the whole with racy and fastmoving dialogue.

In *The Third Part of Coney-Catching* the material is thin, and Greene's interest seems taken up by technique; thus an obvious and crude Merry Tale is dressed up in obligatory criminal robes:

> the carders receive their charge, the dicers theirs, the hangers-about-the-Court theirs[6]

and the action is set in 'St Laurence Lane' or 'the conduit in Aldermanbury'. Yet an episode he would have related in five hundred words in the *Notable Discovery* is here spun out to nearly two thousand, and the writing lacks edge. Greene does explore the convention of erecting pseudo-classifications of criminals, as the quotation (above) indicates, but with little conviction: he is 'cashing in' on earlier success. This is no less true of the *Disputation*[7] published also in 1592, full of rogue slang and classifications which may be traced back to Awdelay in most cases. Here Greene adds a fictional criminal biography, the latest fashion in low life narrative, probably resulting from the translation of the Picaresque novel *Lazarillo de Tormes* in 1586.[8] Greene's biography of the whore Nan is little more than crude anti-Woman Complaint, while his *Black Book's Messenger* is really a jestbook given continuity by the presence of the hero Ned Browne in each episode, as in the anonymous collections *Scoggins Jests* and *Tarltons Jests*. Greene at any rate shows his versatility in incorporating such techniques under the 'Coney-Catching' label, in order to attract as many readers as possible. In no sense is he a writer of picaresque fiction as it is defined in a recent thesis.[9]

It is not to the point here to establish how far Nashe's loose biography of Jack Wilton, or the *Unfortunate Traveller*, diverges from the strict picaresque novel; but it is to the purpose to note that as a fictional biography of a rogue it appeared two years after Greene's.

---

[6] Greene, 'The Third Part of Coney-Catching' in *The Elizabethan Underworld*, p. 182.

[7] Greene, 'A Disputation &c.' *The Elizabethan Underworld*, pp. 206–247.

[8] This fashion and its possible connection with *Lazarillo de Tormes* is discussed by F. W. Chandler in *The Literature of Roguery* (London 1909), Vol. I.

[9] A. Blackburn, *The Picaresque Novel*, PhD thesis in the University of Cambridge (unpublished, 1963), pp. 9–18.

The disparity between Greene's failure and Nashe's success in the form marks the difference in talent between the two writers; but it also marks the difference between the markets for which they were written: *Jack Wilton* is a long work, and written with care as well as boisterous energy.

The life of the rogue *Jack Wilton* has usually been discussed as an example of early experiment in the novel form — a somewhat double-edged compliment to say the least. In the present group of prose narratives, on the other hand, Nashe's work is so dazzling a triumph it almost stifles discussion, drawing all the oxygen to feed its own vigour. Nashe has a sophistication which derives partly from Martin Marprelate, but is far beyond the grasp of Robert Greene. Here is the tapster, for example:

> he was an old servitor, a cavelier of an ancient house, as might appeare by the armes of his ancestors, drawen verie amiably in chalke on the in side of his tent dore.[10]

More centrally important in this discussion is Nashe's marvellous facility in rendering, through choice of detail and appeal to the visual imagination, actuality of setting:

> for comming to him on a day, as he was counting his barels and setting the price in chalke on the head of them, I . . . tolde his *alie* honor I had matters of some secrecy to impart unto him, if it pleased him to grant me private audience. With me, yong *Wilton*, qd. he, mary, and shalt: bring us a pint of syder of a fresh tap into the three cups here, wash the pot: so into a backe roome hee lead me, where after he had spitte on his finger, and pickt of two or three moats of his olde moth eaten velvet cap, and spunged and wrong all the rumatike drivell fro his ill favored goats beard, he bad me declare my minde, and thereupon hee dranke to mee on the same.

Nashe gets his effects through specific attention to detail — 'wash the pot' 'a fresh tap'. His careful physical geography and his dramatist's eye for telling gesture only emphasise his fertile visual imagination and superb skill in verbal artifice. But joined to these is the admirably sustained pose of youthful humorous contempt —

> if it pleased him to grant me private audience.

---

[10] *The Works of Thomas Nashe* ed. R. B. McKerrow corr. F. P. Wilson (Oxford 1958), Vol. II, p. 211.

— and finally the extraordinary sensitivity to rhythm and to vocabulary ('rumatike drivell').

Nashe's imagination is fecund, and his flexible syntax suits his perpetual alertness to the possibilities of absurdity in what he writes as he writes it. His satiric attitude to his surroundings and his fellows fixes his work in physical detail only to make highly sophisticated patterns, striking out new combinations in witty incongruity. Thus a piece of dialogue may be based on indecorous mixture of literary and social styles:

> Not to make manie words, (since you will needs knowe,) the King saies flatly, you are a myser and a snudge, and he never hoped better of you. Nay, then (quoth he) questionles some Planet that loves not Syder hath conspired against me.
>
> (*ibid.*, p. 215)

But immediately Nashe substantiates the broad outline with physically visualised detail in which he follows the train of absurd thought to its conclusion:

> the King hath vowed to give Turwin one hot breakfast onely with the bungs that he will plucke out of your barrells.

In fact even when he carries an idea to completely fantastic lengths the sheer accuracy of detailed observation makes the reader reluctant to dismiss the fantastic artifice. Here description of a heatwave brings us closer to the physical stuff of Elizabethan London than all Greene's pamphlets put together: his pose of confident assertion and flat statement ('I have seen') are more convincing than the less absurd and certainly more credible fictions of lesser pamphleteers:

> Felt makers and Furriers, what the one with the hot steame of their wooll new taken out of the pan, and the other with the contagious heat of their slaughter budge and connieskinnes, died more thicke than of the pestelence: I have seene an old woman at that season, having three chins, wipe them all away one after another, as they melted to water, and left hir selfe nothing of a mouth but an upper chap . . . Masons paid nothing for haire to mixe their lyme, . . . it dropped off mens heads and beards faster than anie Barber could shave it.
>
> (*ibid.*, p. 229)

To examine the extant narratives which follow those discussed here is to learn nothing significant about the development of low life narrative — it had been absorbed into the drama. The same conventions are followed, the same incidents recur, reproduced from the narratives of Greene, Walker, Harman, Awdelay: they even recur in Richard Head's *English Rogue* of 1665. One exception to this is the justly famous *Gull's Horn Book* in which Dekker shows the beneficial influence of Jonson and the early Jacobean vogue for dramatic satire, though his characteristic yeomanlike distaste for bitter satire preserves the tone of Nashe in what is in fact a parody of the pseudo-didactic low life pamphlet. Plainly the parody indicates that the material, if not in dramatic form, is *vieux jeu* now:

> Short let thy sleepe at noone be,
> Or rather let it none be.

Sweete candied councell, but theres rats-bane under it: trust never a Bachiler of Art of them all, for he speakes your health faire, but to steale away the maidenhead of it: *Salerne* stands in the luxurious country of *Naples*, and who knowes not that the *Neapolitan*, will (like *Derick* the hangman) embrace you with one arme, and rip your guts with the other?[11]

Only an Elizabethan pamphleteer like Dekker could so deftly parody its essential style.

[11] Thomas Dekker, 'The Gull's Hornbook' ed. G. Saintsbury in *Elizabethan and Jacobean Pamphlets* (London 1892), pp. 226–227.

1597	PEMBROKE'S MEN The Isle of Dogs (L)	ADMIRAL'S MEN *An Humorous Day's Mirth*
1598	CHAMBERLAIN'S MEN Henry IV I & II Much Ado About Nothing *Every Man In His Humour*	
1599	*Every Man Out Of His Humour* As You Like It Henry V	The Shoemakers' Holiday Old Fortunatus Cox of Collumpton (L)
1600	Twelfth Night The Merry Wives of Windsor	The Four Prentices of London The Blind Beggar of Bethnal Green
1601	Hamlet *Satiromastix*	
1602	All's Well That Ends Well Troilus and Cressida The Merry Devil of Edmonton	The Tragedy of Hoffman The Family of Love
1603–4	KING'S MEN Sejanus	PRINCE HENRY'S The Honest Whore I
1604–5	*The Malcontent* Measure for Measure Othello The London Prodigal	The Honest Whore II
1605–6	King Lear *Volpone*	
1606	The Revenger's Tragedy Macbeth (Timon of Athens)	
1607	Anthony and Cleopatra	QUEEN ANNE'S The Travels of the Three English Brothers
1608	Coriolanus Pericles	A Shoemaker a Gentleman

1599	CLARE COLL. Club Law ST JOHN'S COLL. The Pilgrimage to Parnassus	PAUL'S (BOYS) *Antonio and Mellida* Histriomastix
1600		Antonio's Revenge *Jack Drum*
1601	BLACKFRIARS (BOYS) *Cynthia's Revels* Poetaster Liberality and Prodigality	*Satiromastix* *What You Will*
1602	The Gentleman Usher *May Day*	*The Phoenix*
1603–4	*The Malcontent*	The Old Joiner of Aldgate (L)
1604–5	*The Fawn* *The Dutch Courtesan*	*Westward Ho* Bussy d'Ambois
1605–6	*Eastward Ho* The Widow's Tears	*Northward Ho* *A Mad World My Masters* *Your Five Gallants* *Michaelmas Term*
1606	The Isle of Gulls *The Fleer*	*A Trick to Catch the Old One* *The Puritan Widow*
1607	The Knight of the Burning Pestle	WHITEFRIARS (BOYS) Every Woman In Her Humour The Turk
1608	The Faithful Shepherdess	Two Maids of Moorclack *Ram Alley* Humour's Out of Breath

1609	Cymbeline	Fortune by Land or Sea
	Philaster	
	The Atheist's Tragedy	
1610	*The Alchemist*	The Fair Maid of the West
	The Winter's Tale	The Golden Age
	The Maid's Tragedy	
1611	A King and No King	Match Me In London
	The Tempest	Tu Quoque, or the City Gallant
	Catiline	
1612		The White Devil
1614	The Duchess of Malfi	
1616	*The Devil Is An Ass*	
1617	The Mad Lover	The Devil's Law Case
	The Queen of Corinth	
1621	Women Beware Women (?1615)	
	The Wild Goose Chase	
1622		
1624	A Game at Chess	

1609	The Coxcomb *Wit at Several Weapons* *Epicoene*
1610	The Insatiate Countess
1611	LADY ELIZABETH'S *A Chaste Maid in Cheapside*
1614	Bartholomew Fair
1622	The Changeling

Theatres 1597-1624

From *Annals of English Drama*, A. Harbage and S. Schoenbaum (London 1964).

Select Bibliography

Jonas Barish, Ben Jonson and the Language of Prose Comedy (Cambridge, Mass. 1960).

Jonas Barish ed., Ben Jonson: Twentieth Century Views (Englewood Cliffs, N.J. 1963).

Eric Bentley, The Playwright as Thinker (New York 1946).

M. C. Bradbrook, Themes and Conventions of Elizabethan Tragedy (Cambridge 1935).

M. C. Bradbrook, The Growth and Structure of Elizabethan Comedy (London 1955).

O. J. Campbell, Comicall Satyre and Shakespeare's Troilus and Cressida (San Marino 1938).

T. W. Craik, The Tudor Interlude (Leicester 1962).

Patrick Cruttwell, The Shakespearean Moment (London 1954).

J. F. Danby, Shakespeare's Doctrine of Nature (London 1949).

T. S. Eliot, 'Christopher Marlowe' and 'Ben Jonson' in Selected Essays (London 1932).

Alfred Harbage, Shakespeare and the Rival Traditions (New York 1952).

Bernard Harris, 'Men Like Satyrs' in Elizabethan Poetry Stratford-upon-Avon Studies II. (London 1961).

Bernard Harris (ed.), Marston, The Malcontent (London 1967).

G. K. Hunter, 'English Folly and Italian Vice' in Jacobean Theatre Stratford-upon-Avon Studies I. (London 1960).

G. K. Hunter (ed.), Marston, Antonio and Mellida, Antonio's Revenge (London 1965).

A. Kernan, The Cankered Muse (New Haven 1959).

L. C. Knights, Drama and Society in the Age of Jonson (London 1936).

J. R. Mulryne, 'The White Devil and The Duchess of Malfi' in Jacobean Theatre. Stratford-upon-Avon Studies I. (London 1960).

J. Peter, Complaint and Satire in Early English Literature (Oxford 1956).

Bernard Spivack, Shakespeare and the Allegory of Evil (New York 1958).

F. P. Wilson, Elizabethan and Jacobean (Oxford 1960).